praise for
Wicca for Beginners by Thea Sabin

★ "In her first book-length work, Sabin presents a first-rate, fresh, and thorough addition to the burgeoning field of earth-based spiritual practice volumes … written in a light, informative style that magically mines depth, breadth, and brevity."

—*Publishers Weekly*, starred review

"Sabin offers a practical and cohesive look at the earth-centered religion of Wicca, offering crisp definitions of what the elements of Wicca practice are. … Highly recommended."

—*Library Journal*

"Practicality and common sense are the keys to Ms. Sabin's approach. … Her presentation is fair and balanced, showing both sides of issues. … This book is one that I am proud to recommend to the new seekers out there. Overall, this is an excellent book; one of the best in recent memory."

—Mike Gleason, eCauldron.net

Teaching is leaving a vestige of oneself in the development of another. And surely the student is a bank where you can deposit your most precious treasures.

EUGENE BERTIN

About the Author

Thea Sabin is an editor and writer whose professional work currently focuses on web content management, curriculum development, and instructional design. She holds a master's degree in education and has taught a variety of subjects—including writing, editing, high school English and theater, gardening, cooking, crafts, Wicca, and astrology—off and on for more than two decades. A practicing Wiccan since her teens, she first started teaching Wicca—very, very badly and long before she was ready—in college. She wrote this book in the hope that it would help other teachers find the confidence to teach Paganism and get a better start than she did. Her first book was *Wicca for Beginners*. In the little spare time she has, she likes to do anything related to art, play with her megalomaniacal parrot, watch very bad foreign movies, and travel whenever possible.

A
TEACHING
HANDBOOK
FOR
WICCANS
&
PAGANS

Practical Guidance
for Sharing
Your Path

THEA SABIN
Author of *Wicca for Beginners*

Llewellyn Publications
WOODBURY, MINNESOTA

FIRST EDITION
First Printing, 2012

Book design by Rebecca Zins
Cover design by Lisa Novak
Cover image of Japanese maple © Jonathan Cohen / Vetta / PunchStock
Cover illustration from *1100 Designs and Motifs from Historic Places*
by John Leighton (Dover Publications, 1995)

Llewellyn is a registered trademark of Llewellyn Worldwide Ltd.

Library of Congress Cataloging-in-Publication Data
Sabin, Thea, 1967–
A teaching handbook for Wiccans & Pagans : practical guidance for sharing your
path / Thea Sabin.—1st ed.
     p. cm.
Includes bibliographical references and index.
ISBN 978-0-7387-2710-3
1. Wicca. 2. Neopaganism. I. Title. II. Title: Teaching handbook for Wiccans and
Pagans.
BP605.W53S23 2012
299'.94—dc23

2011051066

Llewellyn Publications
A Division of Llewellyn Worldwide Ltd.
2143 Wooddale Drive
Woodbury, MN 55125-2989
www.llewellyn.com
Printed in the United States of America

CONTENTS

Life is amazing, and the teacher had better prepare himself to be a medium for that amazement.

EDWARD BLISHEN

ACKNOWLEDGMENTS

I would like to acknowledge the Pagan teachers who took time out from their often-crazy schedules to allow me to interview them for this book: Anne Marie, Brian, Christopher, Ellen, Holli, Melanie, Oberon, Patrick, Pete, Sarah, Stephanie, Sylva, and Thorn. It was very important to me that this book reflect the experiences of many teachers, not just mine. Thank you for generously sharing your stories and wisdom.

Every teacher is the product of the hard work of many other teachers. It's impossible to list all my teachers, but I especially want to acknowledge Shekinah, Otto, Dot, Adam D., Abuela M., Eran, Akasha, and my extraordinary grandmother. This book is as much the result of your hard work as it is my own.

I'd also like to thank my students, who have taught me far more than I have ever taught them and who have been incredibly patient while I neglected them to finish this book. All of you inspire me every day, and I am proud to know you.

Thanks also to the people closest to me, who have put up with me during this not-so-pretty writing process. Thanks to Alicia and Pam for understanding the therapeutic properties of bad monster movies and road trips involving coconut cake and drag queens. Thanks to Susan, my patient and serene sister-friend, who helped keep me (reasonably) sane and who I want to be like when I grow up. And thanks to Ken, who made me laugh throughout this process and who stubbornly refuses to understand how incredibly important that was. I love you, goofy boy.

And extra-special thanks to my mad scientist-Zen-ninja-MacGyver-caveman-ubergeek husband, who did extra chores, taught extra classes, transcribed endless interviews, took care of my beloved pets, put up with my crankiness, and never let me give up. You are my partner in crime, my rock, my love, and a kick-butt high priest to boot. Go make fire, baby. But not in the living room this time, okay?

Whatever you can
do, or dream
you can do, begin it.
Boldness has genius,
power, and magic in it!

GOETHE

INTRODUCTION

Teaching Our Teachers

I was inspired to write this book because I frequently get letters, email, and Facebook messages from people looking for teachers. All the time, I hear things like "There aren't any teachers in my area," "I don't know where to start," "I know there are online classes, but I don't know which ones are best for me," "I want to find out if this path is for me," "I really want to learn the [name of tradition here] tradition," and "I want to study with others."

Most of these people are aware that there is a ton of information on the Internet, lots of books available, and mentorship and even community online. But many people yearn for more. They want a personal connection in their spiritual growth. They want someone to see their magic and feel their energy and tell them that they're "doing it right." They want the experience of communing with deity in the presence of like-minded others—whether that be in person or online—or at least with the guidance of like-minded others.

As more and more seekers explore Paganism, there just aren't enough teachers to go around. Although having a teacher is not necessary for being Pagan—self-training is perfectly valid, many Pagans never have a teacher, and some prefer to be self-taught—the demand for teachers is still far greater than the supply. The upshot is that Pagans who have never taught are stepping up to fill the gap, which not only educates one person or group but ultimately strengthens the whole community.

1

Druid and author Ellen Evert Hopman considers service to the community—including teaching—an essential part of being a Druid:

> In ancient times, Druids were advisors to the kings. The Druid was the teacher, the genealogist, and the historian for the tribe. In other words, they were serving the tribe.... You performed a function for the tribe. There is no such thing as a solitary Druid. So in order to really be a Druid, as far as I'm concerned, you need to be serving somebody.

And Stephanie Raymond, cofounder of Our Lady of the Earth and Sky in Seattle, which provides classes and rituals, marvels about the effect the organization has had on the teachers and the community:

> We get so much good feedback from people, and it certainly is something that keeps us going. Because there have been moments when we all kind of look at each other and we're all like, "Really? What are we doing this for?" But then something else will turn around, and you're just in tears at how amazing this thing that we've created can be for us and for everybody who's involved. I've just seen such amazing things happen in the community. It takes my breath away.

Teaching others is one of the most powerful and important things we can do as Pagans—or as people, for that matter. Good teachers are the "glue" and continuity in a community, and they enrich the lives of the people in it. Pagan teachers are facilitators, providing others with ideas, tools, support, mentoring, or practice in allowing people to find, explore, and work with the Divine, both within and outside of themselves. Teaching Pagans is life-affirming, transformative, joyous, satisfying, difficult, terrifying, and frustrating work. But I can tell you from personal experience that helping students find that "aha!" moment—when they glimpse their own connection to the sacred—is worth whatever it took to get them (and you) there.

Although this work is absolutely vital to our community, we don't seem to spend much time teaching others how to do it. I know a lot of Pagan teachers from diverse traditions and paths, and almost none of them received any real teacher training. Their teachers—if they had any—made sure they had a thorough knowledge of the material they would teach, but in most cases they didn't or were unable to give them the tools for passing it on to others.

Being great at doing something or knowing a topic well doesn't mean you can teach it, though, as anyone knows who has had a teacher who was a genius in his or her subject matter but couldn't communicate with mere mortals. Teaching is a very different skill from drawing a magic circle, using divination, meditating, or whatever else a Pagan teacher might teach. As Pagan teachers, we owe it to our students not just to learn the material we might pass on but also to learn ways of communicating it well to others.

The good news is that with a little effort, most people can learn and use basic teaching techniques. For many Pagans who want to pass along their knowledge, learning how to teach feels like it completes the circle of their own learning or like it is the next step, or evolution, of their own spiritual development. You have all this great stuff inside of you that you're bursting to share, and suddenly you have a way not only to share it, but to share it well. Learning to teach can be a very empowering and energizing experience.

You Have to Start Somewhere

Learning a little about teaching before you actually take on students can help ensure that both you and your students have a better experience, and that, in turn, is better for the Pagan community as a whole. There is some feeling in the Pagan community that inexperienced teachers can be damaging, because classes and groups led by inexperienced teachers have the potential to fall apart (sometimes dramatically), and inexperienced teachers sometimes pass on bad or incorrect information and set a less-than-admirable example for others.

People who are wary of the effects inexperienced teachers can have on the community aren't completely wrong in feeling that way. Bad teaching can be misleading for students at its best and downright destructive at its worst. But the problem is that you can't become an experienced teacher without having been an inexperienced one. You have to learn somewhere, sometime, on somebody—there's no way around the fact that your first students will be human guinea pigs. Experienced teachers don't pop up fully formed, like Athena springing from Zeus's head. Their abilities are honed over time, often through making some very big mistakes.

So—in my view, anyway—it's unrealistic to expect new teachers to be great the first time they try. If I had been held to that standard, I would not be teaching now. It is realistic, however, to expect new teachers to be patient, prepared, responsive to their students, and willing to learn from their mistakes. And it's crucial for them to go into their first teaching experience with the understanding that teaching is a sacred trust—that they are carrying on a cherished and indispensable tradition—and approach the role of teacher with the respect it deserves. A crucial part of approaching the role with respect is learning some of the teaching methods that generally have been accepted as effective through trial and error, and in some cases through scientific study. (These are called "best practices" in teacher-speak.)

THE GOAL OF THIS BOOK

All teachers start out inexperienced, but that doesn't mean they have to start out inadequate. There are people who seem to be born teachers, and then there are the rest of us, who have to learn the hard way. I'm definitely in that second category. With this book, I set out to write the Pagan teacher training manual I wish I'd had when I began teaching. In my professional career I have worked for two educational foundations and taught all sorts of things, from writing and editing to crafts, gardening, and astrology, and even high school. It's been an amazing journey of successes and challenges, and I've rolled all of those experiences into this book, along with twenty years' worth of teaching Paganism off and on. I'm hoping that this book can give new Pagan teachers a foundation they can build on through experience to become great teachers—whether they're "naturals" or not—and help them find some courage and inspiration too.

There is no one way to teach Paganism, just as there is no one true Pagan tradition or path. But there are techniques and best practices for finding appropriate students; creating a structure, curriculum, or lesson; teaching to adult learning styles; handling group dynamics; and troubleshooting problems that can help any Pagan teacher, even if it's just an informal, one-on-one situation. My goal in writing this book is not to tell you exactly how and what you should teach but to give you tools to help you contribute to our community as a teacher, in whatever way you are called to do so.

Wicca and Paganism in This Book

Some people use the word *Pagan* to describe their religion or spirituality in much the same way that a Christian uses the word *Christian*. Others see the term *Pagan* as referring to a group of spiritual paths that includes—among others—Wiccans; Druids; Asatru; Feri; Celtic, Greek, and other Reconstructionists; and anyone else who follows a "Pagan" path and/or considers him- or herself Pagan. And some people who previously identified as Pagan are walking away from the word *Pagan* entirely. For the sake of simplicity and for the purposes of this book, when I refer to Pagans, I mean the "umbrella group" that includes Wiccans, Druids, etc.

In some cases I will be mentioning Wiccans specifically, rather than talking about all Pagans. I am not doing this to exclude other Pagans.

Rather, my personal experience is more "Wicca-centric," so many of my examples and anecdotes will be about experiences with Wicca, and I don't want to assume that they necessarily apply to all Pagans. They might, or they might not. Wicca and Paganism aren't the same thing, but the techniques in this book will work for both groups. Non-Wiccan Pagans might need to do a little extrapolating from my examples in some cases, however.

A Word about Children and Teens

This book is about teaching adults. I have never taught children Paganism, and I don't have children of my own, so I will leave teaching children to people who have them. There are some good books, websites, and email lists specifically on that subject, and about raising Pagan children, for people who are interested.

And although this book isn't geared toward teenagers, it could still be very useful for teens who end up teaching each other. Some teens step up and teach their peers simply because they can't get any adult help. Many adult Wiccan and Pagan groups don't accept teens, either because they feel that teens aren't old enough or they are worried that the teens' families might not want their children learning Wicca or Paganism, and they don't want to deal with the backlash from angry parents. These concerns are understandable, especially in an environment where Wicca and Paganism aren't seen as valid spiritual paths and can even be viewed as evil or satanic. But since so many adult groups won't accept teens, there are a lot of teens out there struggling to learn Paganism without any adult guidance. I don't have a solution to that problem, but teenagers teaching their peers should find that much of the information in this book can be applied to teens and adults alike.

You Are Not Alone

As with many experiences in life, when you start to teach, it helps to know that there are other people out there in the same situation. It helps so much, in fact, that I've included quotations from other Pagan teachers of various paths and traditions—some famous, some not—so you can learn from their experiences as well as mine. For example, my friend Anne Marie Forrester, a Wiccan high priestess and artist, has a story about being thrown immediately into the deep end of teaching:

> I got my initiation, and at the end of the evening they dumped me off at home and said, "Good luck." I said, "What do you mean, 'good luck'? What do I do now?" And they said, "Well, now you start teaching other people." And I went, "What do you mean I start teaching other people? I don't know anything yet!" And they said, "Sure you do. You're initiated. You're a witch!" I knew I wasn't ready to teach yet, so I redid the year-and-a-day training as something in between a student and a teacher in order to feel more prepared. There's nothing quite like teaching to make you learn, so that just threw me right in, but I still didn't really feel ready to teach on my own for many, many years afterward.

I didn't want to limit my interviewees to teachers with years of teaching under their belts. To make sure I captured the "newbie" experience, I interviewed Brian Rowe and Sarah Davies, who are just starting out as Wiccan teachers:

> Sarah: It's kind of by the seat of your pants. I mean, that's sort of how you learn the tradition anyway. It was just, "Here's some hot water; we're gonna throw you in it." And that's where we are, and it's kind of fun. We feel like we fail a lot. Once, our only student left, and we thought, "Oh my god, we look like complete idiots."

7

Brian: That happens occasionally. I would like to see us failing forward.

Sarah: Failing forward into the future.

When you're reading the interviewees' stories, remember this: as smooth and accomplished as they are now, all of these teachers were new once, and they made mistakes—some of which you'll read about in this book. Here is a quick list of my interviewees (you can read their full bios on page 289):

- T. Thorn Coyle, author and teacher
- Sarah Davies and Brian Rowe, first-time Wiccan teachers
- Pete "Pathfinder" Davis, archpriest of the Aquarian Tabernacle Church
- Holli Emore, executive director of Cherry Hill Seminary
- Anne Marie Forrester, artist, author, and high priestess
- Melanie Henry, high priestess and editor of a Pagan newspaper
- Ellen Evert Hopman, Druid, master herbalist, and author
- Sylva Markson, high priestess and author
- Patrick McCollum, Wiccan chaplain in the California Department of Corrections and coordinator for the Lady Liberty League
- Christopher Penczak, author, teacher, and healing practitioner
- Stephanie Raymond, co-founder of Our Lady of the Earth and Sky (OLOTEAS), a Pagan organization
- Oberon Zell-Ravenheart, Pagan elder, author, and founder of the online Grey School of Wizardry

I hope that the information in this book will make it easier for Pagan teachers to get started or deepen their practice if they've already begun, and maybe even help them avoid making some of the mistakes I did. I actually thought about titling it *Learn from My Mistakes So You Don't Repeat Them: Go Out and Make Glorious Mistakes of Your Own Instead*, but that doesn't do much to inspire confidence, and it won't fit very well on a book spine. I can't tell you that you won't make glorious mistakes of your own—you absolutely will—but I can tell you that the risk is worth taking. There are few things in the world more rewarding than teaching, especially if you love your path or tradition and want to see it grow and its members thrive. As a Pagan teacher, you can change the world. I hope this book will help you take your first step.

The dream begins with a teacher who believes in you, who tugs and pushes and leads you to the next plateau, sometimes poking you with a sharp stick called "truth."

DAN RATHER

CHAPTER 1

Benefits and Challenges of Teaching

Maybe you have always known you want to teach. Maybe you want to teach, but you're not sure you're ready. Maybe you're so excited to teach that you can barely contain yourself. Whatever your situation, it's a very good idea to have a clear vision of what you want to get out of teaching, what your motivations for doing it are, and what it will require of you before you begin. Knowing these things can help you start your Pagan teaching path on sure footing and with your eyes open to possibilities and challenges.

THE BENEFITS OF TEACHING PAGANISM

We all know that teaching is passing along knowledge or skills to other people. But teaching—especially spiritual teaching—is much, much greater and richer than just the transfer of information. Here are some benefits of teaching that go beyond the satisfaction of increasing others' knowledge.

Teaching Is a Devotional Act

Teaching Paganism is one of the most important ways we can acknowledge, honor, and worship our gods. One of the things I like most about Paganism is that many of us have a reciprocal relationship with our gods. It's not like they live on some lofty plane somewhere and we're groveling here on earth. We interact. They benefit from our relationship, as do we. I can't think of a better way to give back or show appreciation than to pass along what we've learned from these interactions to others.

Author and lecturer Christopher Penczak talks about teaching as an act of devotion:

> Divine guidance is my plan. I make ritual before, after, and during a must, even if no one else knows I'm doing it. I feel that I can be a vessel for something greater, though by no means is it mediumship or channeling. Maxine Sanders told me it's "sitting on Solomon's chair," and that's as good of a name for it as anything. I believe each class is a ritual of service.

Stephanie Raymond agrees:

> Every aspect of it is about service. Service to the earth, to the community, to my gods. So, for me, doing the rituals is really a way to express that need and that calling that I have.

And Patrick McCollum is also following a divine calling:

> I had this near-death experience, and in that experience the Goddess asked me to serve her. And that's what I'm doing. So I just basically do what feels right; I open myself up to what I should be doing, and the message I get is I should be continually sharing what it is that I'm sharing.

Teaching Makes You Learn and Can Strengthen Your Connection to Your Path

Teaching others can engage or re-engage your mind. You have to know and love your subject matter to be an effective teacher, and you will learn even more from your students as you explore their perspectives and answer their questions. Each time my group does a sabbat with a new student, I learn something from listening to the new student's experience of it. In addition, teaching can help you discover new aspects of your path that you hadn't considered before, or find new things to love about the aspects you were already well familiar with. It can give you a fresh perspective.

Melanie Henry, priestess of Green Star Grove in Washington, told me:

> I have learned more since I've hived off with my own coven—not just about how to run a coven but about my own connection to the Craft. It's like having my third degree sort of released me to draw to myself people that I learned incredible amounts from.... It actually hones my own abilities a huge amount.

Sylva Markson, high priestess of a coven in the Midwest, expressed similar feelings:

> I will often learn more from them than they learn from me, and I will get a great deal of insight from their different perspective of the same things that I've been studying for years, but looking at them in a way that I would never have thought to look at them.

And author, teacher, and lecturer T. Thorn Coyle talked not only about learning from one's students, but also being inspired by them:

> This sounds like a cliché, but I learn a great deal when I teach. My view is always expanded by the process and by what people bring to the work. People's bravery inspires me, as does their wisdom. Over and over, people show up to practice, to face fear, to have deep communication with the Gods, and all of this has a profound effect on me.

Teaching Is Great for Your Own Personal Growth
Teaching can give you a sense of purpose, a feeling of accomplishment, and a boost of self-esteem. It can reveal strengths you never knew you had and give you the satisfaction of helping others. Christopher Penczak says:

I teach because it's my true will at this time. I was guided to teach by the Goddess, and I've become very fulfilled by it.... I feel like my job now is to teach teachers, and I get quite a bit of satisfaction from it, to see our community grow in healthy and meaningful ways. Students inspire my own personal practice and force me to think and feel deeply, which serves to enrich my own experience.

Patrick McCollum adds:

It fulfills you. It fulfills your spirit. There is not a time when I go out and teach somebody that I don't come back feeling really good about having done that. It isn't that you first think, "Wow, I'm really great because I went out and taught somebody and they thought I was really great." It isn't that at all. It's rather you come back and you feel that you did something that is appreciated and you see something come out of it. That's good, and you can take that to the bank.

And Melanie Henry credits teaching with changing her whole worldview:

I think teaching is one of the things that's changed the center of gravity of my worldview. I've always loved the Craft, but watching what happens in classes is some of the stuff that has changed my center of gravity from being basically a rationalist to being, well, frankly not a rationalist. And I think I accelerated that process by teaching. Nothing will make you grow up faster—if you're willing to grow up—than teaching.

Teaching Will Bring New People into Your Life

Whether they're your students or other teachers, teaching can expand your horizons by connecting you with like-minded people whom you might not have met any other way. It will also bring people into your life who are not like you at all, but whom you will learn a great deal from.

I'm pretty sure my current crop of students—with their wildly diver-gent histories, jobs, family situations, and needs—would never have crossed paths if it weren't for our class. Yet they come together to learn Paganism. They don't always agree—actually, they usually don't, and it can get pretty emotional at times—but the members of the group are nevertheless richer for knowing each other and having the opportunity to see the world through each other's eyes. Together they make a vibrant—if occasionally volatile—little community.

Brian Rowe, a Wiccan new to teaching, talked about teaching to create and experience a sense of community:

> One reason I teach is a connection with a small-group com-munity. And when you get a group of people together, there is such potential to work together—and to take the best aspects of one another and build off of those—that it's very differ-ent from doing solo practice or individual work. I'm some-what driven by that small sense of trustworthy, intimate community.

Teaching Can Expand Your Tradition and Practice

Want to find others who practice your particular flavor of Paganism? One of the best ways to do that is to teach them yourself! I speak from experience here; when my husband and I moved to our current city, there was nobody here who was practicing our tradition. Ours is a path that works better with more people, so our best option was to teach others and have them join us. Sylva Markson had a similar experience:

> I want a group of people to work with who are as excited and engaged in the Craft as I am. And I feel that I have not been able to find that. I want to do it within my tradition. I mean, there are people who are engaged and excited about what they are doing in every tradition, and that's great, but I want

to do it in *my* tradition, and I'm at a point where I need to make it in order to have it.

Melanie Henry talks about finding others who share her love of ritual:

Teaching brings me new ritual partners, which is huge. There's just nothing like doing really beautiful ritual with people who really know what they're doing on an energetic level…. Teaching is my doorway to doing that.

Teaching Is Being a Steward of Pagan Knowledge and Traditions

Many of the people I interviewed for this book told me that one of their prime motivations for being a teacher was not just to educate others about Paganism but also to preserve and transmit Pagan traditions.

Patrick McCollum commented:

One of my big motivations is to make sure that we don't lose the knowledge we already have, because we're expanding so rapidly as a community. It is far easier to lose the knowledge than it was in the past, even in the very ancient past, because we move forward at a rate like fifty or a hundred times faster than everybody else. Modern society teaches you to skip and make shortcuts to get from point A to point B as quickly as you can, and so we have a tendency to cut through stuff…. Ours is not a tradition that works well under that model, and so I just want to help preserve the knowledge.

Ellen Evert Hopman had a similar take that is focused on our rich Pagan history:

I think it's really important that Pagans have a sense of how old these traditions are. My concern is that if we are going to be considered a great world religion, then we all need to know our heritage, and know that our heritage is as old and older than what the Christians have, what the Muslims have, and perhaps even what the Jews have. So we are one of the great world religions, but we don't always act like it.

Anne Marie Forrester spoke about stewardship of the Craft, not only to preserve our past but also to ensure its survival:

> Teaching helps preserve the Craft, and I get a great deal of satisfaction knowing that the Craft is going to grow and thrive and continue.

Teachers Experience "The Light Bulb"

Once in a while when you're teaching and everything is going smoothly—or even somewhat smoothly—there comes a magic moment when your student or students have a breakthrough. They make an important connection, they have a personal epiphany, they have a paradigm-shifting insight, and the light bulb goes on over their heads like in a Bugs Bunny cartoon. It's an incredible rush for them, but it's even better for the teacher, knowing that you helped facilitate this discovery. Many teachers I know, including Sylva Markson, say that the light-bulb moments are what keeps them inspired and doing the work.

Markson comments:

> I find great satisfaction when people come to great realizations on their own. And if I've had some small part in guiding them or giving them the opportunity, then I feel great reward in that. I feel very strongly that each individual has his or her own path, so it's not like I'm taking credit for it. I don't feel like, "I've done such a great job, look at how spiritual this person is!" But at the same time, as an initiator you are offering them an opportunity to explore a certain path, and to go along with them on that path—to walk alongside them—is really exciting.

When I asked Patrick McCollum what inspired him to teach, he had a similar answer:

> The excitement of people learning something they didn't know and seeing that mental connection go on. The light in their eyes when they connect something that they know and something else that they know, but they were missing a link between those two things, and all of a sudden the things connected, and then they realize that they have a wealth of knowledge already that they couldn't tap into because they didn't know the connections.

Stephanie Raymond talked to me about wanting to create ritual that could be a catalyst for participants to have spiritual discoveries:

> I know when I came to my very first Pagan event, it just made my head spin how in those four or five hours that I was there, so many of my preconceived notions of how the world was— that this is just how things are, and how people act, how they have to be—were just completely tossed out the window, but in a way that wasn't confrontational.... That still stays with me, and I think about that with what I'm trying to create with my rituals. It's like, "How can I make that happen for people—take something that everybody assumes 'this is how it is' and turn it on its side?"

And T. Thorn Coyle talked to me about helping each student make one important discovery:

> In each class, I hope someone will get one thing they feel they can work deeply with. Overall, my hope is that people will become more themselves, commit to their lives, walk further and further toward integration and wholeness, and become more effective in their work on this planet. But that all begins

with making a deep commitment to that one practice, that one insight, that first step.

Teachers Have a Reason to Be Proud

Almost everyone I interviewed for this book mentioned the joy and pride they took in seeing their students succeed, both while they were teaching the students and afterward. When I asked him what inspired him to teach, Oberon Zell-Ravenheart—author, teacher, and Pagan elder—answered:

> Seeing my students go forth into the world and put into practice the things I've taught them. Seeing them become effective and beloved leaders and teachers in their turn, with students of their own. Seeing the legacy of my life's work and studies becoming manifest in succeeding generations. (I've now taught three generations!) And having my students come back to me decades later and tell me how grateful they were to have learned from me.

Anne Marie Forrester had a similar point of view:

> I feel so proud when I see former students casting a circle, invoking the gods, or stepping up to take leadership roles in the community. They do such a good job, I just burst with pride. I love it when they become my equal (or better), because then the relationship changes from "master and pupil" to simply good friends who share a common bond. It's been a real privilege to have these quality people in my life.

SOME POSSIBLE CHALLENGES

As you can see, teaching can be a profound, life-changing experience. However, like most things that are really worth our time and energy, it can present some challenges too. You might not encounter any of the following challenges, but it can be very helpful to be aware of them as you begin to teach and think about ways you might avoid or handle them if they pop up.

Teaching Is a Big Responsibility

To be a Pagan teacher is to stand up as a representative of your path and community. You are representing Paganism to the next generation and to the outside world. Your choices will have an effect both on the community and interpersonal levels. What you say and do as a teacher is likely to have a bigger effect on the community or on an individual than if you said it or did it as a non-teacher.

Helping people make spiritual decisions is not something to be taken lightly. Your choices and those of your students can have long-term effects. If you are teaching a specific tradition, you have the responsibility to transmit that tradition accurately. If it is an initiatory tradition and students aren't privy to the whole tradition until after initiation, you also have the responsibility of deciding if your path is right for them and if they are right for your path. Even if you are teaching strangers online, you have an obligation to take it seriously and do it responsibly.

Teaching Can Be Time-Consuming and Expensive

Preparing for classes, finding students and a space to teach in, and teaching the classes themselves requires time and effort, often for little or no money. If you are teaching a class with several sessions or running a standing group, you might also need to work with students individually between classes. For example, I run a coven, and we teach regular classes, but our coven also has a list of requirements—things like reading books, writing papers, performing energy work, and doing community service—and my husband and I need to work individually with each of our students as they go through the list by reading their papers, discussing books with them, and more.

If you teach out of your home, you will spend a fair amount of time getting your space ready for students to be in it and cleaning up afterward. (If you're lucky, they'll help.) We run full moon and sabbat circles in our home as well as classes, so we have people in our living room several times a month. Preparation time for that adds up.

If you are teaching in a more intimate setting or in one where you get to know your students reasonably well, you will also spend a lot of time dealing with students' personal and interpersonal problems. This can take up more time than anything else if the people in your class are going through tough times.

And unless you have a large family, you'll never know how many supplies a group can use in the course of a class until you hold one in your home. I have said that if you teach Paganism, you should automatically be given a magical Costco card so you can stock up on pens, printer cartridges, cleaning supplies, food, and myriad paper products—plates, toilet paper, printer paper—you'll need. And a little wine, too, for ritual or therapeutic use, or both.

Teaching Can Be Hard on the Ego

It's important to remember that teaching has at least as much effect on the teacher as it does on the students. Teaching demonstrates and reinforces what you know, but it can also show you in glaring neon light what you don't. Students can act as mirrors, and they will reflect every great and every dumb thing you say back at you, either inadvertently or on purpose. Are you ready/confident enough to look in the mirror and roll with whatever you see? I can almost guarantee that if you teach for any length of time, you'll have students pointing out blind spots you didn't know you had. Teaching can be very vulnerable experience—a giant serving of humble pie.

Teaching Can Make You a Target

Teaching puts you in the public spotlight and makes you more visible in the community, which can attract negative as well as positive attention. As wonderful as the Pagan community can be, Pagans can also be very catty, and as a teacher—as someone who claims to know something worth teaching—the sad truth is that you might be more exposed to that kind of treatment. In some areas the Pagan teachers band together and help each other, and in others they view each other as competition. We'd all like to think that people who purport to be spiritual teachers would have well-developed ethics, but the truth is that teachers are people—with all of the good and bad qualities of anyone else—and some of them are very threatened by other teachers.

When I first moved to my current city, some of the Pagans I met urged me to stay away from a particular teacher. They gave me all sorts of reasons, from generic things like "She's not ethical" to the more extreme "She forces her students into prostitution!" The idea that someone might possibly be misusing her power that way—taking advantage of people who were vulnerable and coming to her for help—was horrifying to me, so at first I gave this teacher a wide berth. But as fate or chance or the gods would have it, I eventually had an opportunity to meet and get to know this teacher personally through some volunteer work (volunteer work, I might point out, that her accusers were not doing). Once I'd known her for a while, I told her about what I'd heard. When I got to the prostitution part, I expected her to be angry, but instead she laughed so hard she could barely breathe. "How on earth do they think I could get my students to do that, even if I wanted to?" she said, once she'd caught her breath. "I can't even get them to show up to ritual on time!"

The accusations against this particular teacher were over the top, but I tell this story to make a point: You will garner attention from the community when you put yourself forth as a teacher. And in some cases you will be held accountable for the actions of your students too. Even if your reputation in the community is generally positive, a mistake by someone you taught can reflect badly on you, even if the incident was an accident and you had nothing to do with it. A few years ago one of my students unintentionally offended a local elder at a public Pagan event without realizing it. I wasn't at the event, but believe me, I heard about it—in no uncertain terms and from multiple sources. The "put a leash on your student" message came through loud and clear. The student's mistake was definitely seen as my responsibility.

Teaching Can Be Emotionally and Energetically Draining

Don't underestimate the emotional impact that getting involved with people's lives can have on the teacher. If you are teaching a one-off class or online and not interacting too much with students individually, this might not be such a large factor. But if you end up teaching in an intimate setting, you will get to know your students and all of their issues very, very well.

Melanie Henry told me:

> No matter how mellow they might seem, or how young and full of beans, or whatever, every student brings you new problems that you have to learn to solve, and if you're going to teach something like the Craft, some of those problems will be very big.

An example from my own experience is the emotional impact teaching high school initially had on me. I taught tenth-grade English in a tough school in a low-income neighborhood in a large city. The school had metal detectors, a police officer, and a clinic and daycare for students' children on-site. My students were from a wide variety of backgrounds, many of them lived below the poverty line, and fourteen languages were spoken in my first-hour class alone. Since I taught English and writing essays was part of the curriculum, my students would often write about their own life experiences, and some of the things they would disclose were so awful—rape; sexual, physical, and emotional abuse; gang violence; drug abuse; time spent in refugee camps literally being tortured— that I'd feel angry, devastated, sad, and helpless. Most of all, I wanted to fix everything, which I obviously couldn't even begin to do. If I hadn't eventually learned to shield a lot of my students' energy and not take their pain home with me, I would have been a complete wreck.

The energetic impact on the teacher is a consideration too. Some students are very needy and naturally latch on to a teacher, and, in worst-case scenarios, they might inadvertently drain your energy unless you learn how to shield. Even if that doesn't happen, it takes a fair amount of energy to be a teacher—to stand in front of a class or devise a curriculum or mentor someone. It's important to ask yourself if you have the energy and shielding skills necessary to teach.

QUESTIONS BEFORE YOU BEGIN

Whether you feel great, excited, terrified, enthusiastic, nervous, angry, or nauseated at the idea of teaching—and believe me, you might feel all of those emotions—it's a good idea to ask yourself the following questions before you begin.

Why Do You Want to Teach, and What Do You Want to Get Out of It?

Knowing why you're teaching is vitally important. More specifically, having your expectations somewhat in line with what you might actually get out of teaching is vitally important, so you're realistic and not disappointed. If you are interested in serving your gods and the community, helping others grow spiritually, and/or passing on your path, you are more likely to be happy teaching than if you are interested in making money, becoming the Pagan High Muckety-Muck of your community, having disciples, or becoming a nationally known BNP (Big-Name Pagan). One thing is for certain: the more ego-centered your reasons for teaching are, the less likely you are to be happy teaching.

Are You Hesitating? Why?

If you are hesitating about beginning to teach because of the time, energy, or financial commitment, then you probably have a pretty good sense of what you can and can't offer the community at this time. This is good. If you are reluctant to teach because teaching doesn't speak to you, it's good to acknowledge that too.

Do You Know Your Stuff?

Good Pagan teachers don't have to be omnipotent geniuses, but they should have a firm grounding in their material.

Patrick McCollum told me:

> If you're going to be a Pagan teacher, you have to know your stuff. So you can't just go get a book on Wicca and decide that you're a teacher. You really need to be around for a while and experience and be interacting with other teachers and other groups and other forms of Paganism and such to have a bigger picture of what's going on before you can really take on the role of teaching in a bigger way. Obviously, if you're in your own little circle and you've got five or ten people in it and no one knows anything and you've read four books, then you're the best there is for that group. There isn't anyone in the group who knows more than you, and so you share what you know. So continue to try to learn, but you do need to make sure you know what you're talking about.

If you feel you need to learn more before you're comfortable teaching, your gut instinct is probably correct. Although they should be firmly grounded in their subject matter before they teach, many Pagan teachers are called to take on students before they have finished their own training.

T. Thorn Coyle told me about beginning to teach perhaps a little too early:

> I began teaching in my late twenties via the Reclaiming Tradition, which at the time had the theory "take a class, student-teach a class, co-teach a class." On one hand, this was refreshing and liberating; on the other hand, I likely began teaching a bit too soon.

Brian Rowe is currently teaching Wiccan students while he is still a Wiccan student himself. About that experience, he says:

> For me, the place where I am as a student also incorporates a lot of learning how to teach and getting feedback on things that I create as teaching tools, so it's actually been pretty valuable for me to teach as a student. I would definitely even encourage students who are in a similar place to teach at that time. It's difficult. It's challenging. It's a lot of work, because you're doing that teaching and you're learning, so you're doing double. But what you can gain from seeing that second side, that reflection, is worth it.

As you're considering whether you know enough and whether you are ready, bear in mind that your perception of your own abilities might be skewed. After all, most of us have a hard time looking at ourselves completely objectively. I have a close friend who wants to teach but has been waffling about it because she "doesn't know enough yet." The truth is that she knows more than just about any other Pagan I've ever met—far more than I do, and I've been teaching for years. So if you think you don't know enough yet, you might want to ask others for their opinion. Maybe you do know enough, but you don't realize it. I have found that teaching is like skydiving or anything else that you know is worthwhile but you're worried about doing: if you wait until you're completely ready and confident, you'll never do it. Brian Rowe essentially agreed: "Don't wait until you are prepared and understand everything, because you will never get to that point."

What Are Your Priorities and Goals as a Potential Teacher?

Are you interested in teaching a particular path or tradition? A particular subject? A particular age group or demographic? Do you want to teach to please someone else? Do you want to find and practice with like-minded people? Do you want to teach as a steppingstone to becoming a high priest, priestess, or coven leader? Are you willing to bend or change your goals if the situation doesn't unfold the way you want it to? Taking the time to write out your goals can help you make the decision about whether you're ready and give you a place to start if you are.

What Are Your Strengths as a Potential Teacher?

Are you very knowledgeable about a subject or subjects? Do you have previous teaching experience? Are you a good public speaker? Do you have good people skills? Are you patient and flexible? Are you good in a crisis? Do you have a well-developed sense of humor? Are you confident and grounded? Do you have a mentor or mentors? You don't have to have every single one of these traits to be a teacher, but you should have many of them. You will need every possible resource at your disposal.

What Are Your Weaknesses as a Potential Teacher? How Can You Turn These Around?

Are you shy? Unsure of your knowledge? Do you feel like you don't have very good people skills? Do you have problems speaking in front of groups? Are you impatient? Do you get sensory overload when you have to deal with too many people at once?

Is there a way you can work on any of these weak areas to improve them before you teach? Is there a chance that the act of teaching itself will improve them?

Do You Have the Time and Energy to Teach Right Now?

Teaching time commitments vary, but in general, if you are going through a big life change (marriage, divorce, having a child, going back to school, moving, transitioning jobs), this might not be a good time for you to begin teaching. These life events require energy, time, and emotional resources. If you have a family with young children, elderly parents to care for, or a job that takes up a lot of your time, you might want to wait as well. Some chronic illnesses make it difficult to teach, while others require that you take very good care of yourself so you'll have the energy to teach. Carefully weigh your desire to teach against your other obligations. Don't forget to allow time for a social life, either. It's easy to get so wrapped up in the needs of your students that you forget to see to your own. You can't—and shouldn't—expect your students to meet all your social needs.

Do You Have Support for Teaching from Friends or the Community?

Having the support of friends, mentors, or elders can make all the difference in the world to new, inexperienced teachers. It's important to have people with whom you can vent, brainstorm solutions to problems, and get advice. Oberon Zell-Ravenheart commented, "It's best by far if you have had really great teachers you admire, as they can serve as your inspirations and models."

If you're teaching a tradition, you might be able to rely on the elders in your tradition, or the people who taught you. You might even have been taught how to teach within your tradition. If not, you might wish to find mentors outside of your tradition, either in person or online. Even if you can't find people to learn teaching from directly, there's a lot to be learned about teaching by simply hanging out with teachers. As T. Thorn Coyle points out:

> I wasn't taught much about this in any formal sense, though student teaching in Reclaiming was helpful, as was my experience teaching at Witch Camps, which made it possible to watch various teachers and experience success and failure going hand in hand. Mostly, though, I learned by osmosis, just by being around teachers. Luckily, I learn pretty well this way, though I've certainly had to struggle at times to fill in the gaps.

It's also helpful to have the support of your local Pagan community. Members of the community can refer students to you, get the word out about your classes, and sometimes provide advice or feedback. They can also give you a window into how the community perceives you as a teacher.

What Concerns Do You Have, and How Can You Get Them Addressed?

What are you most afraid of or worried about? It's good to take some time and really think about what scares you most about teaching. It's possible that whatever it is isn't likely to happen or could be avoided. What can you do before you start teaching to minimize the chances of those things happening?

WHAT DOES IT TAKE TO BE A PAGAN TEACHER?

When I was doing the interviews for this book, I tailored my questions to each interviewee, based on his or her areas of expertise, but I asked all of them what qualities they thought a Pagan teacher needs to have. I got a lot of different answers to that question, but despite the variety of responses, several common themes bubbled up across most or all of the interviews. All of these qualities are very helpful—even essential—for Pagan teachers.

Deep Knowledge of and Love for Your Tradition or Path

Perhaps the most often mentioned trait of a good Pagan teacher in my interviews was knowledge of and love for your particular spiritual path, or for Paganism or Wicca in general. Anne Marie Forrester commented:

> Teaching should never be undertaken for selfish or ego-driven reasons. It has to be about having a deep love of the Craft and wanting to see it continue and prosper. More than that, it's about having so much love for the God and Goddess that you are driven by a burning need to help others find it too.

And Oberon Zell-Ravenheart said:

> Well, first off, a good teacher has to know their subject intimately and really love it with a burning passion. They have to be constantly and obsessively researching and learning more all the time. Intense curiosity is essential!

He also gave some advice for potential teachers who want to feel well-grounded in their subject matter and ready to teach:

> Before you even begin to try and teach, take the time to study as many different paths and traditions as you can. Undergo initiations into the Mysteries. Study with different teachers, read many books, attend Pagan festivals, and go to lots of presentations and workshops. Hang out around the campfire or the conference party rooms and ask questions of the more experienced elders, teachers, and leaders who'll be there.

Humility

Humility was also mentioned frequently. It's easy to let teaching go to your head, especially if you have a bunch of attentive students hanging on your every word. But there are some potential pitfalls for teachers who are too arrogant or proud (more on those in chapter 10).

Patrick McCollum described it this way:

> I would say the first thing teaching requires is humility. Because when we think that as Pagan teachers or leaders we know it all, that's when we really lose the ability to fully gain the respect of the people who want to learn from us. And it's also when we cut off our own ability to expand and move forward from where we are....
>
> Over the last forty or fifty years, I've observed a number of teachers and leaders and such. Many of them are now not with us anymore, not in the sense that they're dead but rather

no one listens to them—they sort of faded into the woodwork. And those were the people who came forward and said, "I'm the Grand Poobah of whatever, and I know everything, and you all have to take everything I say and believe with no questions." Our community does not respond to that well.

So we really have to be humble and have the people who we're teaching know that we're open and willing to learn more, and that we don't know everything, but that we do know something. You can't have been around experiencing what we've been experiencing without having something to share.

Pete "Pathfinder" Davis, archpriest of the Aquarian Tabernacle Church, had a similar take:

It takes somebody who has a handle on their ego and recognizes when they start to slip into that sort of a mode. Because it's way too easy to start to strut around like a rooster, and then you're not conveying anything.... You have to recognize that what you're doing is sharing information that you learned—probably the hard way—with people who might or might not learn it from you.

And Sylva Markson drew a connection between love of your path and humility:

Ultimately, I think, to be a good and effective teacher, you need first and foremost to love the Craft and be thinking of what is best for the Craft rather than what is best for you.... Because we have no higher authority or human authority that says "This is the way it has to be"—we don't have a council or a senate or any of that stuff—since each priest or priestess is basically doing it their own way, it's very easy for it to become all about me and self-aggrandizement. And that, I think, is the downfall of a lot of groups and a lot of coven leaders. So, to me, I think you have to have a level of Craft that is bigger than your desire for personal glory.... It should be about what is best for the tradition and what is best for my students. And if you're thinking about that, then I don't think you can go too far wrong.

Patience

Another often mentioned quality of a good Pagan teacher was patience. You can't expect everyone to understand and absorb the information you give them immediately or on the first try. You also need the patience to deal with people's questions, issues, and imperfections—and to work on mastering your own.

Ability to Communicate

Communication is an essential skill for any teacher. Teachers need to be able to convey information in multiple ways, clearly and concisely, and preferably without putting anyone to sleep. Christopher Penczak said, "Generally I think good teachers are prepared and have good communication skills and a sense of humor." Oberon Zell-Ravenheart commented:

> They have to be able to explain things creatively in such a manner that their students can not only understand but really get it. And they need to have the charisma to inspire their students to want to learn more from them and to feel fortunate and blessed to have such a great teacher.

Ellen Evert Hopman talked to me about keeping students engaged:

> Well, in order to be a really outstanding Druid teacher—which I don't think I am yet—you have to have a fantastic sense of humor. I think you have to be a showman.

Integrity and Honesty

Many of my interviewees spoke about good teachers having integrity and honesty. After all, if we as teachers are passing along sacred knowledge, we need to act accordingly.

Christopher Penczak commented:

> I think one has to walk the talk. You must be practicing what you teach. Not doing so is the downfall of most teachers. You must integrate the teaching into your own life as you teach others.

People mentioned honesty in various contexts, not just in telling the truth. Anne Marie Forrester talked about being up-front with students about their progress:

> I think honesty is a big part of it. You have to be willing to tell people when they're doing good and when they're not doing good, and not shy away from confronting them about that.

Similarly, Brian Rowe talked about being honest with students about expectations: "Don't be afraid to set high expectations, but be clear in trying to put those forward to students." And Melanie Henry mentioned being honest enough to admit when you don't have an answer:

> You've got to know what you don't know, and know when to say, "I can't help you with this"—and, when you yourself need some help, it's really good if you can accept help. You're going to need it!

. . . .

Take some time to reflect on your goals, what you want to get out of teaching, and your strengths and possible weaknesses in terms of teaching. Talk to friends and other teachers, and meditate or ask your guides or deities for insight. Once you feel you have a handle on the benefits and challenges you might encounter and are aware of your strengths and areas for growth, your teaching journey has begun.

I never teach my pupils. I only attempt to provide the conditions in which they can learn.

ALBERT EINSTEIN

CHAPTER 2

Space, Time, Energy, Money, and Legalities

If you have been thinking about teaching for a while, chances are you have envisioned yourself doing it in a certain way. Perhaps you saw yourself at the head of a class, or leading an open circle, or in a coffee shop working with a small group. But before you make a decision about how you would like to begin teaching, there are several factors you should consider. And some of those factors might be large enough that you'll need to consider a different option from the one that you have envisioned.

The format in which you choose to teach will probably be influenced heavily by things like the space you can find to teach in, money, time, your personal energy level, other resources, and the number and type of interested and available students. It's kind of a chicken-and-egg thing: do you decide how you want to teach and then work out the logistical details accordingly, or do you look at what you have at your disposal in terms of space, money, time, energy, and resources and decide how you want to teach based on that? And of course you need to consider the availability and type of students you have access to, which takes your decision out of the chicken-and-egg category and escalates it to something more like a game of Twister.

In the interest of avoiding a Twister situation, I've separated the student element from the equation and dedicated the next chapter to discussing just students. In the meantime, this chapter focuses on the non-student elements you need to consider before you start teaching.

CHAPTER 2

Space

Unless someone hands you a teaching opportunity on a silver platter—
and, in some cases, even if they do—finding space for teaching, especially
cheap space, can be a challenge. Unfortunately, not everyone who rents
out space or allows people to use it for free will welcome a Pagan group
with open arms, and some organizations are not allowed to rent space for
teaching any kind of spirituality, Pagan or not. Of course, you can always
sidestep the whole space issue and hold classes online or via email. But if
you want to teach in person, you're going to have to find a place to do it.
Here are some options.

Your Home

Unless they are thinking of holding a formal classes with media equipment and chairs or tables, many Pagans start out teaching from their own
homes. They might do this because they prefer it, but often they do it
because they feel it's their only option.

There are some real advantages to holding class or rituals in your
home. You don't have to cart your stuff somewhere, you're probably
more comfortable on your home turf, you can pass out in your own bed
immediately after everyone leaves, and you have already paid the rent
(hopefully). There are disadvantages, too, though. You have to clean the
house or apartment, have enough parking and places for people to sit,
and make sure you have plenty of the essentials, such as candles and toilet paper.

Before you plan on inviting a student or students over, there are some
questions you should ask yourself about your space. Perhaps the first is
whether or not your home is in a good location for teaching. This can
mean all sorts of things, depending on where you live. Here in the foothills of the Cascades, it often means "Do you live on a hill, and is it ever
plowed?" or "Do you live out in the woods somewhere?" But it can also
mean the following:

- Are you close to a highway?

- Is your home on a bus/train/subway line?

- Are there places to park?

- Are you likely to annoy your neighbors by having a bunch of parked cars out in front of your house regularly?

- Is there any way you can minimize the impact of your class on your neighbors?

As for your home itself, there are questions like:

- Do you have enough room to have a class in your home?

- Do you have enough tables and chairs, or at least pillows so people can sit on the floor?

- Is your home accessible to people with disabilities?

- Do you have pets that might make it difficult for some people to be in your space, either because they're frightened of the animal (some people are very afraid of large dogs) or allergic?

If your space is suitable for holding a class, it's good to think about the issues around having people you might not know that well in your personal space, or having people in your space on a regular basis. Most people who are seeking Pagan teaching are honest, normal folks, but there are a few crazy and unethical people out there too.

I know a Wiccan couple who for many years held open public full moon rituals in their basement. This was an extraordinary community service. It gave solitaries a chance to practice with others, everyone could network and socialize, and teachers and students could find each other. But not everyone was courteous and respectful of their space, and more than once the guests left the house in a shambles or the couple had personal items stolen. Of course, if you do decide to teach in your home, you don't have to hold open classes or circles, and you can screen your potential students (see chapter 3) to avoid some of these problems. But even if the people in your living room are nice, normal, ethical people, they can leave their stuff behind and make a mess.

Our coven meets in our home, and although it can be a lot of work hosting circle or class—furniture has to be moved, supplies purchased, bathrooms made respectable, cats corralled and banished from the circle room—I have found that I like the camaraderie and sense of closeness that holding events at home seems to foster. It's worth the inconvenience, and, over time, my students have gotten a lot better about picking up after themselves. Sometimes when they leave, the only evidence that they were there is the heavy scent of incense in the air.

Most Pagan teachers I know, regardless of their path, believe that if you teach out of your home, it's okay to ask students to help shoulder the burden of supply costs by occasionally contributing things like candles, paper plates, potluck dishes, wine, a ream of paper, or incense. At our house, we call these "in-kind toilet paper donations," whether they consist of toilet paper or not.

I grew up in the upper Midwest, where gracious, uncomplaining hospitality to the point of self-sacrifice is built into our DNA, but continually providing supplies and not asking regular students to pitch in can reduce your resources to the point where at best it's a hardship, and at worst you can't offer classes anymore because you can't afford it. In-kind toilet paper donations make it much easier to run a class, and they also help students feel more involved and invested in the class, and like they are contributing.

Your Students' Homes

It's perfectly acceptable to ask your students to host classes and rotate between houses to minimize the amount of prep work and cleanup that any one person has to do. If you have students whose homes aren't appropriate for holding a class, these students can volunteer to help set up or clean up when a class is held at someone else's home.

Outside

Pagan paths are nature-oriented—or at least use nature symbolism—and teaching outside is a great way to help students connect with the natural world. Although not all Pagans like the great outdoors, and it's not always easy to teach outside—carting teaching materials into the woods, being heard above the wind, weather issues, and the dreaded mosquito can all cause problems—teaching this way can be very rewarding and very inexpensive. Some Pagans would even say it's essential or required.

Patrick McCollum explained to me some of the reasons why he prefers to teach outside and gave the example of teaching people about making wands:

> The first thing I do is take people into the wilderness, and we sit outside someplace where you're in nature and look at all of the stuff around you, and then I say, "Who knows the origin of the wand?" And then I...start talking about some of the early Pagan creation stories and bring the students to understand that the first spiritual practices ever done in any of our traditions, and for that matter any religious traditions, took place in association with the sacred wells throughout the Middle East and Europe.... And at those wells grew particular trees whose roots went right into the well, and as people moved and became more nomadic, they cut branches from those trees connected to the sacred well. They carried the sacredness of that initial spirit or whatever that initiated all creation....
>
> And on Imbolc, something very unique happens to the trees at the sacred wells...they are dead for all visual purposes, and at an exact moment...they come back to life, and that's because the sap returns to the trees.... That is the moment that our ancestors waited for to cut the branch: to capture the magic of the renewal of creation. So that's what a wand really originally is, that piece of branch from the sacred tree that

went into the sacred well that captures the magic that created everything, and it became a symbol or thing to carry around that energy with them to utilize for different things.

I like to take people into the wilderness, and I walk them—not to a sacred well in Ireland or the Middle East or something— just to a simple well or spring here in the U.S. in some state I'm in. I show them the same trees grow right there, and I take them there at Imbolc, and we watch the tree come alive, and I teach each of them how to cut the tree and what the rituals have been that have been passed down, and share the stories and such, and they walk away with a whole different connection about their own spirituality and faith that they didn't know before.

I think it's very hard to convey that through some other means. You could convey it in the same way I'm telling you, but when you are holding a branch in your hand, and you actually see a dead tree come back to life before your eyes, it shifts you and adds something. We are a faith and spirituality based on nature and on the whole concept that there is something bigger and more than just words.

Outdoor teaching spaces do have some logistical considerations that indoor teaching spaces are less likely to have. Stephanie Raymond explains:

Sometimes there are theatrical challenges, especially at the site we're using now, which is an outdoor site, which on the one hand lends tremendous opportunity…. Running electricity to that stone circle involves three extension cords. And what time we're doing the ritual—what's the natural lighting going to be like? What if it's raining? You always have to consider if people can meditate when there's a million mosquitoes buzzing around their heads.

40

If you're interested in teaching outside, your three best options are your own yard, private land, and public parks. If you teach in your yard or on your own property, you might want to take some precautions to make sure you're not seen (if that's important to you) and that you don't make so much noise that your neighbors call the cops on you. The last thing you want to do is explain to the police why a bunch of your friends are jumping naked over the hibachi in your back yard.

If you want to teach or lead ritual on private land that's not yours, be sure you get permission from the owners. Be respectful of their land, and leave everything as you found it when you go. Don't start a fire without permission, and if the landowners have neighbors, don't do anything obnoxious to annoy the neighbors and thus make life more difficult for the landowners who were kind enough to let you use their property.

In a public park in a city or town, you can gather and walk through the woods or teach in a circle on the grass, but if you're interested in holding a bigger class or event, you might need to reserve facilities in advance and pay a fee. When teaching in a public park, be aware of the rules; parks and park systems often have websites where you can find them. Many municipal parks will not allow alcohol or let people use the park after dark.

City parks are great, but holding a class in a large, wild state park can be an amazing experience too. If you choose to do this, check out the site you'd like to teach in beforehand so you know exactly how to get there and back and are familiar enough with the area that you can tell students exactly what to expect and what kind of gear (if any) to bring. Also follow these commonsense rules:

- Comply with any ranger requests and all the rules posted at the ranger station, including checking in with the rangers if that is required and paying any parking fees.

- If you're going to make a fire, make sure it's in a spot designated for fire, and put it out completely when you're done.

- Clean up after yourself, and pack out any garbage you bring in, unless there are trash receptacles provided.

- Don't remove anything from the park, including sticks, stones, shells, and animals. Respect the space so others—Pagan and non-Pagan—can continue to enjoy it.

It's quite possible that the municipal and state parks in your area won't allow weapons, including knives and swords. And yes, your athame is considered a weapon, even if it's not sharp. The park's weapons policy should be posted online with the other park rules, although the weapons rules might not specifically mention swords or knives. You're more apt to get busted for having a sharp, pointy object if the people busting you don't recognize or understand what you're doing or if they perceive you as dangerous. Your best bet is to leave the pointy objects at home.

Festivals, Conferences, and Events

You might want to try presenting at a Pagan event, such as an outdoor festival, a conference, or your local Pagan Pride day. The advantages in doing this are:

- You can do just one session.

- The event organizers are responsible for getting people to come, so you don't have to find students.

- You can get feedback from other presenters.

- You can try out new material on a "captive," Pagan-friendly audience.

- Event organizers might provide equipment, such as projectors and screens, so you don't have to.

- You can opt to be a member of a panel, so you're not the only person up front speaking.

- Presenting at an event can get your name out in your community.

Indoor Public Spaces

There are a lot of options for teaching in indoor public spaces—many cheap, some free—but you might have to think creatively to find them. Creative space-finding reminds me a little of those old Judy Garland–Mickey Rooney "let's put on a show" movies from the late '30s. Mickey says something like, "Hey kids, let's put on a show!" and Judy says, "We can use my dad's barn!" You might have to explore a lot of options—some of them seemingly crazy—until you find one that works for you. I've seen classes or rituals held in such diverse places as a parking lot, a garage, the back of a VW bus, a tent, a fake Irish cottage on the grounds of a renaissance festival, a literary convention in a hotel, an abandoned grocery store, and, yes, an old barn. I hope you won't have to be quite that creative, but you've got to do what you've got to do, right? Just don't trespass! Here are some of the better places I've seen used to teach Paganism.

Pagan or Pagan-friendly bookstore. Pagan bookstores are an obvious choice because they are "friendly space." I have also seen classes taught in (non-Pagan) used bookstores, and I've taught a few myself, even in the Bible belt. In my experience, people who truly love books and learning tend to be fairly open-minded.

Coffee shop or pub. You might be able to run an informal class, study group, or Pagan meet-up in a coffee shop or pub, as long as you keep your meeting low-key, don't disturb other customers, and buy some coffee or beer. Being good, courteous customers is the key.

Public libraries. Many public libraries rent meeting rooms, which can range from small rooms with a table and a few chairs to large spaces with audio-visual equipment. Some libraries will let you use their space for free, and others will charge.

College campuses. It is often possible to rent or borrow space on a college campus, especially if the person teaching or the students go to the college. Contact the student union on campus or the community education program office.

Unitarian Universalist churches. Unitarian churches are sometimes willing to allow Pagans to use their meeting spaces.

Masonic halls. I know of more than one Pagan group that has held events in a Masonic hall. Some halls might allow you to use their space for free or with a small fee. Others will charge more. If you know a Mason, you should get a better rate.

Retreat centers. Retreat centers can be very expensive, but don't rule them out. Not all retreat centers are huge facilities with lots of buildings and lodgings on-site. Some are much smaller and less posh. If the owners are at all Pagan-sympathetic, or if you're willing to schedule an event at an off-peak time, they might cut you a break.

As you read this list, you might be saying to yourself, "This is all well and good, but I can't use any of those ideas because the people running those places won't rent to Pagans / allow Pagans to use their space." But you'll never know until you ask. Taking risks and putting yourself out there for possible rejection can be scary, especially if you're not out of the broom closet. There is no way to teach Paganism without risk. But sometimes people are more open-minded and open-hearted than we give them credit for, and you (and they themselves) might never know how open they are until they're given a chance to prove it. As for the rest of the people, they might be willing to put aside their biases to make a few bucks. The point is, don't rule out a perfectly good potential teaching space before you ask if you can use it.

TIME

One big mistake that I see many beginning teachers make—and that I have made myself, more than once—is underestimating how much time it will take to teach or overestimating how much free time they have in their schedules to devote to teaching. Even seemingly small commitments—teaching a one-off class, creating a single podcast, or mentoring someone over coffee—take time, and sometimes it's not obvious how much until you're in the middle of it. I know that when I'm thinking about making a teaching commitment, my immediate response is usually, "Oh, sure, it'll only be a two-hour class; I can do that!" and I completely forget or ignore the time it will take to get to the class and back, research, prepare, and acquire any materials I might need—and do any follow-up, such as answering student questions after the class or even making notes for myself about what worked and what didn't. All of that other stuff adds up. A two-hour class is not a two-hour commitment.

Remember to take all the prep and follow-up tasks into account before you decide you have the time. If you haven't taught before—or haven't taught the kind of class you're thinking about teaching before—and aren't used to estimating the time it will take to do all the tasks required for a class, ask someone who has taught to help you. When I'm considering teaching a class, I've found it helpful to actually put all of my commitments on a paper or electronic calendar (Google Calendar is great for this), with different colors for different commitments. The places where I'm overcommitted and the holes where I might be able to squeeze something else in become very apparent.

ENERGY

Although many of us act as though this isn't so, the sad truth is that like our space, our money, and our time, the amount of energy we have to devote to anything in our lives is finite. The energy we have for teaching at any given time is affected by a lot of factors, including the energy required by our other commitments, our health and age, our stamina, and—perhaps most important—our attitude and morale.

Obviously, if you teach, you will need to have enough energy left over after your other responsibilities are met to create an effective learning experience. But this requires more than just the substantial amount of energy it can take to put together and lead a class.

In addition to all your prep work, you will also need energy to engage your students and keep them interested. Students aren't going to listen to you if you're drooping in front of their eyes, and if you don't have much natural charisma, it really helps if you can fake it. (Trust me: I'm speaking as one of the introverted charisma-challenged here; we need our own support group.) You can do this with good presentation skills, eye contact, and a big smile, but it also requires quite a bit of energy output. (There is more information about presentation skills in chapter 8.)

You will also need to be strong enough to have healthy shields and boundaries. Sometimes when Pagans talk about using shields, they're thinking about protecting themselves from malevolent energy or all-out attack. Usually you won't have to deal with anything that extreme when you teach; however, some students can project a lot of disruptive energy, and others can inadvertently leech energy off of you, so knowing how to deflect or defuse with shields and good boundaries is very helpful.

It's true that you can actually derive energy from teaching—that interacting with your students can be motivating and energizing. This is where morale and attitude come in; you're more likely to be energized by teaching if you go in with a great attitude. But you probably shouldn't expect that the energy you get from teaching is going to immediately replace the energy you put into it, as if it were an energy paycheck being direct-deposited to replenish the investment you made. It's better to learn how to manage and preserve your own energy than to rely on your teaching to energize you. Then any energizing effects you get from teaching are gravy.

MONEY

Money is a touchy subject in the Pagan community. It's kind of silly, really, although there's also a certain sense to it. We all need money to pay the rent, eat, and get transportation. Most of us also want money, but there seems to be some sort of stigma attached to admitting it, as if you're not a spiritual person or you're not being true to your spiritual path if you are concerned with money. It's a little ironic that many Pagan paths seek to find the sacred in the mundane, but lots of people in our communities can't reconcile the "baser" things in life, like money, with their spiritual goals. The topic of money rears its ugly head in two ways for teachers: the money it might cost you to teach, and the money you might charge for your teaching. You'll have to make some decisions about money if you are going to teach. Let the uncomfortable squirming begin.

Teaching Costs Money

Teaching can cost very little money in the right circumstances, but it is almost never free to teach. Even if you're simply mentoring someone at a coffee house, you should at least buy a cup of coffee there. In other cases, you might have to rent space or equipment, cover transportation or lodging costs, and provide supplies and handouts. Even if you teach out of your home there are costs, from coffee to printer cartridges. And don't think you'll escape without cost if you're teaching online. You will definitely be paying for Internet access, and—depending on what tools you use—you could very well be paying for server space, software, technical support, and a computer, along with other equipment such as speakers, a digital video recorder, or a microphone.

So one of the big questions you'll need to ask yourself is whether or not you can afford to teach in the manner and setting that you'd like to. Before you start teaching, I recommend taking a hard look at your budget and determining how much you can afford to spend on teaching and how much you're willing to spend. Of course, you can recoup some of your costs and maybe even turn a profit by charging for teaching. But that isn't necessarily as simple as it sounds.

Charging for Teaching

Some people charge for certain types of teaching or for teaching in certain circumstances, but not for others. Some people charge only enough to cover the cost of their space and supplies. Some Pagan traditions flatout state that accepting money for teaching is against the rules. Some people feel that teaching Paganism is a gift to the community that they shouldn't charge for. And some people are happily making a living (or part of a living) teaching Paganism.

Whether or not you charge can depend on your costs, but there are social factors to consider as well. Many people in our community are perfectly fine with a teacher charging, as long as the fee is reasonable, and are happy to support a Pagan teacher if they can afford to. But other Pagans feel that in sacred settings money truly is the root of all evil—that it corrupts and has no place there. And some people have very unrealistic expectations of teachers when it comes to things like money. They put their teachers on a pedestal and think of them as somehow more connected to the sacred than the rest of us. As paragons of Pagan-ness, their teachers (and elders and leaders too) should be unsullied by (or unconcerned with) such vulgar things as money, and they should be willing to give their time and share their knowledge for free for the good of the community. These people forget that we're Pagans, not religious ascetics. And we all need to eat.

Spiritual communities do not always value their teachers enough to pay or support them. A Hopi friend of mine told me once that "the priestess is the lowest one on the mesa." What she meant was that the priestess supports the community through thick and thin, but the people only support the priestess when they feel they can. If they fall on hard times, feeding their families becomes a higher priority than feeding the priestess. The priestess doesn't have a "day job," so in lean times she suffers. I have seen this theme echoed in the Pagan community. There are a lot of Pagan elders who have given a great deal of time and energy to the community but who are not helped or paid by those they serve.

My tradition strictly forbids charging for teaching. I have never charged my students and coven members, and I am perfectly fine with that. Teaching can be, and is for me, an act of love and community service, and I'm fortunate enough to have a regular job that pays the mortgage, so I don't need to look at teaching as a source of income. But in my opinion, Pagan teachers have every right to charge for their time. In fact, unless their traditions say otherwise, there are several good arguments why they *should* charge for their time:

Time is money. When you spend time teaching, you give up the option to spend that time doing something else—including something else that could make you some money.

Student investment. It has been the experience of many teachers I know, both Pagan and non-Pagan, that if students pay for a class, they're more likely to show up, pay attention, do the work, and get something out of it.

Perceived value. A related point is that although many people would welcome free teaching, some people—especially here in the United States—only value what they pay for. If your teaching is free, some people will be grateful—and some will assume it's not worth charging for, and therefore not worth their time.

Boundaries. Charging can help create positive boundaries. Not the kind of boundary that makes a teacher seem unapproachable, distant, or holier-than-thou; it's more like the kind you have in a respectful professional relationship. In a professional relationship there is a different set of expectations, which can make it easier for the teacher to teach and for the student to believe he or she is going to get something out of the class. (There's more information on boundaries in chapter 8.)

Legitimacy. Having paid teachers in a spiritual community increases that community's perceived legitimacy among people both outside and inside the community.

"Follow your bliss." This isn't exactly what the late Dr. Joseph Campbell meant by that phrase, but you can argue that you have a right to try to make a living doing something that is meaningful to you. Aligning your source of income and your spiritual work—as long as you do it ethically—can be extremely fulfilling.

Breaking even. Even if you don't want to go all-out and embark on teaching as a spiritual career or income booster, you can at least recoup the costs of teaching the class. Most students are able to pay small fees to help cover these costs, and you can always offer a sliding scale if you're concerned that some people are in difficult financial situations.

Not Charging for Teaching

Although you can justify charging for teaching in many cases, there are definitely some circumstances in which charging might not be practical or feel appropriate, or it might be beneficial *not* to charge. Here are some examples:

- Offering some free classes as a community service
- Teaching a free class to get the word out about your teaching, which can lead to paid teaching opportunities
- Teaching people you want to form a coven with, in which case teaching might be shared among multiple members for mutual benefit and charging might not be appropriate
- Helping another teacher by being a "guest teacher" in his or her class
- Casual one-on-one mentoring
- Doing a dry run of a class for a small group in order to practice for delivering it to a larger group

- Circumstances in which it's more important to pass along certain crucial teachings than it is to make money for teaching them

How Much to Charge for Teaching

If you've decided to charge for your teaching and you're trying to figure out how much, here are some guiding questions:

Are you teaching in person or online? It shouldn't make that much of a difference, but it does. You might find it harder to charge more for online classes than in-person ones because of the (mis)perception that in-person classes take more work on your part. But online courses can often take even more time to set up, depending on the technological requirements, and there can be a lot of follow-up and individual assessment of students' work too. There's also the lingering issue that people still expect stuff on the web to be free. There's been a lot of discussion about "monetizing," or making money off of things you offer on the web. The best ways to do that are still emerging.

How much work and time will you need to put in? It seems reasonable to charge more for a class that takes more time to put together and teach.

How much will it cost you to teach this class? This formula is completely arbitrary, but it can be useful for getting an idea of what your class costs you. Estimate (or measure) how long it will take you to set up and teach a class, and then multiply the number of hours by a reasonable hourly rate that you'd like to be paid. The resulting number is an estimate of the value of the time you will put into the class. Add it to the cost of rental space, supplies, handouts, and anything else you'll use in the class, then add any travel expenses. The final number is a rough estimate of what you need to make to break even. If you're not going to charge for your time but want to recoup your other expenses, just add up the other items.

What are others charging? See if you can find out what others are charging for teaching services similar to the ones you are offering. You can also try writing up a syllabus and sending it out, either in person or online, and asking people what they think the class is worth.

What do you feel comfortable charging? You need to feel good and satisfied about the amount you charge. You don't want to feel like you're selling yourself short, and you don't want feel like you're taking advantage of your students.

Making a Living Teaching Paganism

Once you start teaching, you might decide you like it so much or find you are so good at it that you'd like to do it as a career. Certainly it is a wonderful way to bring your spiritual and material worlds together. I have never taught Paganism professionally, so I asked Christopher Penczak and T. Thorn Coyle how they decided to make the transition from teaching once in a while to doing it more or less full-time. Christopher responded:

> On a Friday, in meditation, the goddess Macha appeared to me. She had done this so many times before, asking me to "teach more." I refused many times, and my personal practice was falling apart as I could progress no further in meditations and journeys. That Friday I said okay—but listed all the things in my life that took up my time that I didn't want to lose. I guess I thought the job was a no-brainer, but on Monday, I was laid off.

> I think it was decided for me. Being directed by the Goddess to do something and having all your other job prospects close down in an otherwise prosperous economy is a good sign. After eight temp jobs to make ends meet, the last one burned down the day before I started, so I stopped looking for a real job and actually started teaching meditation classes first, and found I could make some money, enough to survive.

I was technically on unemployment for seven months, which helped me start a professional practice of healing and reading for clients, establish a class schedule, and I wrote my first two books.

T. Thorn Coyle's story of her transition was more about an evolution than a calling:

I didn't decide to teach Paganism professionally. Many years ago, after I'd been studying magick for around a decade, a mentor must have seen something in me and asked me to assist her with a class before she moved across country. This was eye opening—all of a sudden I saw that teaching could be a revolutionary act. So I started teaching like most people in Paganism, with small groups in living rooms. I also was on teams, helping to lead ritual. Teaching and leadership was an organic process unfolding over many, many years' time. It was never my thought or plan to make a living teaching magick or spirituality.

After several years, there came a point when I decided to say yes to whoever asked me to teach, wherever their group was in the country. A floodgate opened, much to my surprise. This was even before my first published book came out. After about a year of this, I realized I could no longer hold a day job and teach as much as people wanted me to. There still wasn't quite enough income at this point, but I was able to "fill in" in various ways. There have been many points since then when I considered taking on another job, but something has always shifted—whether in my attitude and approach or in the cosmos in general—and I've been fortunate enough to be able to pay my bills this way.

This whole process—from beginning to teach to making a decent living without a lot of financial stress—took twenty years. Would this have been different if I had set out to teach professionally? It is difficult to say. The thing I appreciate about my career, as it stands, is that the whole process felt very organic to me. I was working on my practice and my skills, started out sharing some things, people responded, I kept up my work, more people responded… and over time the transition happened to full-time. It doesn't feel like something I could have or should have planned, and I am therefore loath to give "business advice" to people who want to do this as their primary occupation.

Both Thorn and Christopher pointed out that it's very difficult to make a living solely teaching Paganism. Thorn was hesitant to provide any sort of a "formula" for others to follow to make teaching Paganism a successful career:

Most Pagans have deep distrust of professional clergy, and I don't see this changing anytime soon. Most people I have encountered who have set out to try to make a living teaching magic or spirituality full-time in a Pagan context have not been successful. I live in amazement and gratitude that I'm able to make a living this way. It feels like a fluke or a confluence of so many factors that it would be difficult to even tease out the components necessary to making it work.

Christopher's advice was about diversification:

If you want to do it as a full-time vocation, have multiple streams of income. Don't think you can make a living just teaching Paganism. If you are going to teach, branch out into other topics that have an audience with a little wider range and more disposable income—tarot, crystals, mediumship,

Reiki, etc. Classes just on Paganism don't have enough of a draw for a large-enough income to live on.

Along those lines, one thing that is very important if you are going to build a career for yourself as a Pagan teacher is to diversify and market. In addition to branching out into other topics, as Christopher suggests, it's a good idea to supplement your teaching and build your reputation as a teacher by doing teaching-related things that can get you noticed, such as blogging, creating a website, doing free workshops and "guest teaching" in others' classes, having a strong presence on social media sites (especially Facebook, Twitter, and Google+), and posting podcasts and videos online. All of these things will help you become better known in the Pagan community and give potential students a taste of what your teaching is like. You are basically building a brand around yourself and your offerings.

Although Thorn was hesitant to mark out any sort of pathway others could take to make teaching Paganism a career, she did offer these words of advice:

> There are five things I can share: Do your work. Maintain integrity at all costs. Stay clean. Don't get into public personality battles. Know your worth. Other than that, all I can say is good luck, because I don't think this is an easy way to make a living. I really should say "good fortune" because success requires a combination of us showing up at our best, with all of our talents and effort, but there is also chance—the roll of the dice cup—that will either meet our efforts or not. I'm more interested in people following the course of their soul's work, knowing that the current might shift in a direction that is different than what we first thought. That certainly happened to me. If you asked me fifteen or twenty years ago what career I was working toward, I would have said "novelist." But here I am, because I kept following the energy as it opened in front of me.

LEGALITIES

It's certainly not the most scintillating aspect of teaching, but Pagans who are considering teaching professionally need to consider legalities, such as insurance and taxes. The information here is meant to give you a starting place for examining these issues, but it's not comprehensive, and different rules apply in different cities and states.

Insurance and Waivers

If you're teaching out of your home, it doesn't hurt to check your homeowner's or renter's policy to make sure you're covered if someone has an accident on your property or tips over a candle and sets the place on fire. If you're teaching in a building or on land you don't own, whoever owns the space should have insurance. Ask the person you're renting/borrowing from about the insurance policy and safety procedures for the building or area. Some buildings won't allow you to have open flames or might have other restrictions to meet the terms of their insurance policies.

If you are teaching anything physical where people might get hurt, you might want to have participants sign a waiver. Waivers are enforceable only to a point, and even if you have one you might still be sued if something goes horribly wrong, but making participants sign a waiver signals to them that what they're doing might injure them, and that they need to be careful and take what you're doing seriously.

Another instance in which you might want to get waivers or permission letters is if you are teaching children or teens. As we all know, not all parents are happy about having their children run off to learn Paganism. Waivers or permission letters help you keep parents fully informed of what their children are getting into and what to expect. If an underage student's parents or caregivers won't sign your waiver or permission letter, don't take on that student.

Taxes and Licenses

If you are charging for teaching, in many cases you will need to report your income and pay taxes on it. The government doesn't recognize the spiritual meaning teaching might hold for you—it just sees a revenue source. As T. Thorn Coyle put it: "No matter how we look at it emotionally or mentally, the government requires that we treat anything we take money for as a business." The government isn't going to hunt you down if you teach one or two classes and charge $10 for materials, but if you are thinking of teaching regularly or even sort of regularly, taxes are part of the picture.

In some cases you can declare your teaching income on your personal taxes, and in others you will need to get a business license of some kind. Another option is to start a small nonprofit and derive an income through that. Whether or not you need the license or to file for nonprofit status will depend on how much you teach, how you market yourself, what percentage of your annual income comes from teaching, and the laws of your state and city.

As I mentioned, I have never charged for teaching Paganism, but I have charged for teaching other things. Originally when I charged for teaching, it was related to a small sole-proprietor business I owned, so I reported the income as part of the business. More recently my teaching income has been very small, and I've been able to declare it on my "regular" taxes as consulting fees using an additional schedule.

If you have an accountant, ask him or her if you can get away with not having a business license. If you don't have an accountant, check out the government website for your state for the requirements and/or for information on forming a nonprofit. In my state, the information about business licenses and sole proprietorships (the kind of business where you are the only employee, and the most commonly used type of business license for people teaching by themselves and not as part of an organization) is in the Business License Service section of the Department of Revenue. In your state, it might be somewhere else. If you get lost in your state government website (most of them are such a mess that you'll need a compass and a canteen to get out alive), just Google "business license" and the name of your state. You might also want to check out any requirements that your city has on top of the state ones. The city I live in requires business licenses in some situations that are not required by the state.

For a couple of different perspectives, I asked Christopher Penczak and T. Thorn Coyle how they handled taxes and licensure. Christopher draws income from more than one source, and he told me about his situation (a DBA allows you to do business under a name other than your legal one; it means "Doing Business As"):

> I am a sole proprietor for my main business of teaching and writing and private sessions. I run a 501(c)3e temple that pays me a percentage of the income I bring in, as if I were doing a split with a local store or center, and I pay taxes on that income. I have a publishing company that is established as a LLC. I don't have a DBA, as Christopher Penczak is my legal name. I do have insurance at my office, more liability if some-one falls, but I do have protection if someone wants to sue me in general. But most of what I do falls under my ministerial work—spiritual healing and counsel. I don't set myself up as a medical professional.

Thorn's situation is somewhat different:

> I taught as a self-employed person for many years, paying my own social security and all the other required taxes, filing quarterly, and everything else required to run a business in this way.... Currently, I am the one paid minister of Solar Cross Temple, which is a nonprofit religious organization founded by myself and two others.... Any income that used to go to me from teaching classes, writing books, and one-on-one spiritual direction now goes to the temple organization, which pays me a small salary.

If you can manage it, I highly recommend that you get an accountant if you are going to get a business license. It sounds expensive, but it doesn't have to be that bad, and the grief the accountant will save you is well worth the money. When I ran my sole proprietorship, I used an accountant only to do my taxes—I handled the books myself. She specialized in taxes for sole proprietorships, worked out of her home, was reasonably priced, and sometimes would do trades for certain services. It didn't cost me that much, and I had the peace of mind of knowing that my paperwork was done correctly.

There are three things to remember when teaching: know your stuff, know whom you are stuffing, and then stuff them elegantly.

LOLA MAY

CHAPTER 3

Finding and Screening Students

In his answers to my interview questions, Oberon Zell-Ravenheart offered his version of a saying you've probably heard: "When the teacher is ready, the students will appear!" It's true that if you are ready—if your will is aligned to teaching—then you're more likely to attract people into your life who want to be taught. But, like most things, it's not as simple as it seems. Obviously you can't camp out in meditation on your couch like a guru at the top of a mountain and hope your chanting and positive vibes draw people to you. A big part of finding students is marketing. And although many Pagan teachers find that idea dismaying or distasteful—even me, and I work in marketing—it doesn't make it any less true.

In any marketing campaign, you need to know who your desired audience is so you can pinpoint your marketing plan. If you know something about the kind of person you would (ideally) like to teach, you can tailor your class to that kind of person, or focus on your particular strengths and skill set and market them to attract the kind of person who would benefit most from it.

If you're teaching a one-off class, doing a podcast, or making a presentation somewhere, this might not seem very important, since chances are you won't be developing any long-term personal relationships with your students. And, of course, in certain teaching situations you have no control whatsoever over whom you will be teaching. But even in those cases when you have limited interaction or no say about whom you are teaching, it's good to think about what kind of student would benefit most from your teaching style, if only so that you can buffer up your less-developed skills in order to meet the needs of a wider range of people. Students are more successful if they're learning in the right place, at the right time, in the right format, and with the right teacher. Even if you have little control over some or all of those factors, thinking about them will help you craft a better class. Here are some areas to explore.

POTENTIAL STUDENT DEMOGRAPHIC

Younger or Older Students?

Would you be more effective with younger or older students, or a mixed group? If the average age of your group skews higher, the class is likely to have different needs and a different feel than if it skews lower. There's more information about age and learning styles in chapter 4. And think about a related question: are you willing to teach minors? How would that change how you teach?

Beginners or More Experienced Students?

Beginners are often very eager learners, which can make teaching them seem easier and more fun. Their enthusiasm can be infectious, which can inspire you to be more enthusiastic too, especially if you've been studying the material you're teaching for a long time and it's not fresh for you. Their enthusiasm can also make them very willing to meet an inexperienced teacher halfway by overlooking nervousness and being more forgiving of mistakes. In addition, beginning students are also more likely to be "clean slates," with fewer preconceived notions about the material than someone who has studied it before from a different teacher or a different angle.

Some teachers like beginners because they feel less threatened by them; if you always teach beginners, chances are you always know more about your subject matter than your students. (I wouldn't encourage this mindset because I don't think it's healthy in the long term, but it's fairly common and very human.)

Teaching beginners might not be for you if you get frustrated by questions and repetition. Beginners will have a thousand questions, which can be invigorating at best but can also be frustrating and put you on the spot if they come up with a question you didn't anticipate. (It will happen, trust me!) They also need repetition to retain skills and concepts, so if you teach them, you'll be saying the same things over and over again in different ways. And if you add new beginners to an established group, you will find yourself explaining the same concepts even more often.

Working with beginners might not be appropriate for you if you are more interested in engaging intellectually with peers than in building someone's skills. By "peers" I mean people who know the same or a similar amount about the same things as you do. Some teachers teach because they are looking for others to discuss and debate Pagan topics with, to further the knowledge of both student and teacher. This is a legitimate way to teach, but it's not a great way to teach beginners.

Teaching more experienced students also has its pluses and minuses. On the plus side, you are more likely to be able to have in-depth discussions and debates. All students teach their teachers, but experienced students can enhance your knowledge in ways beginners can't. Experienced students often have a better idea of what they want or need from a teacher, too, and can ask more specific and detailed questions and narrow down the ways in which they need your help. And if you have a mixed class of beginners and experienced students, the beginners can learn a lot from the others.

Of course, experienced students tend to come to your class with higher expectations. If they had great teachers in the past, they will hold you to those standards. If they had terrible teachers, they will be worried that you will be terrible, too, and they might withhold their trust until you prove that you're not.

Experienced students can also be a little more set in their ideas and less flexible, although this is hardly universal. They might also make assumptions that you need to work around or through. Sylva Markson told me about being in this position:

There was a guy who came to us looking for training who had been practicing a tradition that he thought was very similar to ours for quite a number of years, and he came to me express-ing, "Well, I feel since I've kind of been doing this all these years anyway, I might as well be official and get the title and the whole shebang." And I'm like, "Oh, dear; here is a guy who thinks he knows everything about our tradition already." So the question to me is, "Is this someone who is teachable or not? Is this someone who is going to be able to shed some of those preconceptions?" So I threw out to him a couple of examples of things that are very common misconceptions about our tradition, and his reaction was, "Well, maybe I don't know as much as I think I do." And then I thought, "Okay, this is someone I can probably work with, then, if he is willing to set aside what he thinks—what he knows in his mind for all of these years."

And obviously, if you're going to teach more experienced students, you need to know your material thoroughly—not just at the beginner level—so you have something to offer them.

Your Biases as a Teacher

The word *bias* often has negative connotations attached to it, but let's face it: we're human, and we're not objective. We all have preferences or leanings; we're predisposed toward certain things. And it helps to know what these are if you are going to teach. For example, my husband and I teach Wicca from a fairly shamanistic viewpoint. Therefore, we incorpo-rate a lot of shamanistic practices. People who aren't comfortable with or interested in shamanic practices would probably be less happy or suc-cessful in our group than those who are. Similarly, we're not as interested in magic, so although we try to give our students a solid foundation in the basics and practice in using the magical rites and spells our tradition provides, we don't go much beyond that unless someone asks. A person looking for in-depth magical training would be better off with different teachers.

Sarah Davies talked about understanding her own biases:

> I think that I require a lot more creation. I want people to write their own rituals and come up with their own meditations, as opposed to "here's a meditation; go home and do it." I also come more from an academic background, so I'm a little bit more structured about the curriculum, as opposed to "well, what do you want to know? I'm here, I'm your fountain of wisdom, ask me questions."

Your biases and inclinations can often be used in positive ways. Melanie Henry told us about making use of her particular leanings in working with students:

> I can deal with both dark and light energy, which is not unique by any means, but it is more rare than I first thought it was.... There are a lot of people who are more comfortable with one or the other, and there aren't that many people who kind of straddle the line, and I do that.

Your Communication Style

Are you assertive? Passive? Do you speak quietly or loudly? Do you rely on body language to get across the full meaning of what you're trying to say? Do you listen or interrupt, or both? What kind of student would benefit most from your teaching/communication style? Brian Rowe commented on trying to find students who could mesh with his and Sarah's teaching style:

> And we have looked at potential students that we've decided are not right for our particular communication style and our expectations, and in talking to them we try to be very clear that we're not saying that they're not necessarily right for

the path, but they wouldn't necessarily be a good fit with our group and our dynamic.

Your Material

Different people want and need different things from a Pagan class. What kind of student do you think could benefit most from the kind of material you teach?

Ellen Evert Hopman told me a story about what she teaches not meshing with what a particular student wanted:

> I had another person who was working with me; she asked me if I would foster her so she could go through her initiation. I said sure, but I don't know why she asked me, because I'm so into teaching the ancient ways. I want people to know the depths of what we do and the span of who we are and how our tradition goes back for thousands of years and the richness of it. All she wanted to do was her own thing. She wanted modern robes. She didn't want to wear anything that looked at all ancient. She wanted her tools to look modern. She said she wasn't interested in the ancient stuff, she was only interested in modern ritual. It finally got to a point where we just couldn't work together because we just didn't see eye to eye.

Your Tradition or Path

It sounds unfair, but the truth is that not every path is right for every person. Some people make, for example, better Druids than they do Alexandrian Wiccans because their natural skills, inclinations, interests, talents, energy, or whatever resonate more with the former than the latter. What kind of student would be most fulfilled on your path?

Some Ways to Meet or Find Students

Finding students is relatively easy for some Pagan teachers and much harder for others. For some it is a matter of logistics; there might not be many other Pagans where you live. As Sylva Markson commented, if you find yourself in this situation and you want to teach in person rather than online, you might have to adjust your expectations accordingly:

> I live in a small town—I don't live in a big metropolitan area—so there are not a lot of Pagans around here, let alone Pagans of like mind. And the consequence of that is that I have a very small group, and we're not able to meet as often as we would like because we don't all live right next door to each other, but you make of it what it is.

Pagan students and teachers who are isolated can now at least find like-minded others on the Internet. Online teaching and learning aren't for everyone, but at least it's an option, and one that I think Pagans in the 1970s and 1980s would have given their athames for. But whether you're teaching entirely in person, entirely online, or somewhere in between, the better connected you are—both in person and on the Internet—the more chances you have to meet students. Networking and advertising—two more evil, soulless marketing terms—really are the keys.

Networking and "Advertising"

Chances are, you will need to use multiple networking techniques to find students, not just one. Here are some of the networking and "advertising" (I use the quotes because they're not necessarily advertising that you pay for) techniques that have been most successful for me and many other teachers I know.

Use Witchvox/The Witches' Voice. It's hard to overstate the impact the Witches' Voice (or Witchvox) website has had in both education and networking in the Pagan community. In fact, every single one of my current students met my husband and me through a posting we had on Witchvox.

If you post a listing for a class or group on Witchvox, describe what you're offering clearly, and don't give out too much personal information—even a great site like Witchvox can attract some creeps. Provide an email address so people can contact you.

Put the word out on email lists. Email lists can be good forums for you to get the word out about your teaching services, and you can also learn about other events going on in your community and possibly network with other teachers and event organizers. If you don't have a local list, check out the Pagan email lists in Yahoo Groups and other list services. When you join a list, be sure to follow list rules; some list owners do not want people promoting goods or services on their lists. Ask the list owner what the policies are if you can't find the information easily on the list website.

Use word of mouth, in person and online. Tell your friends and anyone else who will listen about your class. Word of mouth works pretty well in the Pagan community. Every Pagan you know probably knows others you don't know. Like I said, all of my current students came to me initially through Witchvox, but everyone in the coven I was a member of before that was there because of word of mouth. They knew someone who knew someone who knew someone.

Consider asking people who organize Pagan events in your area to mention your class or that you are looking for students. Some people will be more receptive to helping you than others, but it's worth a try. Be gracious, not pushy, and you might be surprised at who will help you.

If you are on good terms with any Pagan elders in your community, they might pass along the information for you. I have found other Pagan teachers to be one of my best resources not only for finding students, but also for getting information about troublesome people in the community whom I might not want to take on. And if you have connections with other teachers and you find a great student who isn't a good fit for your teaching style, you can refer him or her to another teacher you trust.

In addition to telling people in person, tell them on Google+, Facebook, Twitter, a blog, or whatever other social networking tools you use. Also see if you can get others with blogs or websites to mention your class. If you're not doing social networking, start now!

Go to public Pagan events, and don't be shy. Pagan events—classes, open rituals, Pagan Pride, camp outs, conventions—are some of your best bets for finding potential students. These events are often full of new or even experienced Pagans looking for teachers; in fact, that's the primary reason some people go. And sometimes these events include forums for teachers to meet students, and vice versa.

Whatever event you choose to attend, see if you can get on the docket and do a presentation or class for greater visibility. Remember, though, that it's not appropriate to shop for students at all events. Some groups frown on people "poaching" their attendees, and some groups hold events for the specific purpose of finding students or members themselves. Tactfully ask around beforehand if teacher-student networking is okay.

Make flyers. Yes, flyers are old school, but they work. Give flyers to friends to pass along, and ask the leaders of Pagan organizations in your area if they'll do the same. Also try distributing them at places like these (but ask permission first):

- Pagan-friendly stores or coffee shops
- Irish pubs
- Colleges and libraries
- Music or art festivals
- Comic book shops and science fiction events
- Renaissance festivals, Highland games, and historical reenactment events

- Craft shops (as in arts and crafts)
- Co-ops (or, as my Glenn Beck–loving dad would say, "Anyplace you nature-loving hippies hang out")

Build a website. Check out other Pagan teachers' sites to see what kinds of features they have. Create a basic site with an introductory page, a page about your class(es) or teaching, an "about" page describing yourself, and student testimonials. Post any articles or podcasts you've done, too, so people can get an idea of your background and philosophy. Link your site to your Facebook, Google+, and Twitter accounts, and ask owners of other sites, blogs, or email lists to link to your site. You can also offer to put a notice on your site about someone else's services or products in exchange for them doing the same for you.

Actually advertise. Consider placing an ad about your services, either in a free publication or website or in a paid one. There are still some great Pagan magazines, and some communities still have local Pagan newspapers and newsletters. You could also create a Facebook ad and limit how much money you want to spend on it (you pay according to the number of hits you get).

Screening and Choosing Students

Screening—systematically examining your potential students to see if they have or don't have certain qualities or abilities that would make them a good fit for your class—is completely unnecessary, impractical, and impossible for some teachers and absolutely essential for others. If you are teaching in a situation where you have no control over who shows up, you can't screen, and you have no need to. Some examples of these situations are:

- Online classes
- Presentation at a Pagan event
- Public class at a bookstore or other venue
- Guest-speaking engagement

However, the following situations can warrant screening:

- Holding classes in your home
- Long-term classes where you're likely to get to know your students well and/or where group cohesiveness is vital
- Teaching an initiatory tradition or a tradition with levels that people need to be mentored through
- Leading a teaching coven or grove
- Teaching material that is very specific or advanced

In these cases, you will want to know more about your potential students before you take them on because they need to fit in well with a group, have previous experience, or you might work with them over a long period of time or become very involved in their lives.

Screening can be as simple as making sure students meet some basic prerequisite requirements so they'll understand what you're planning to teach (for example, understanding basic energy work before you teach them more advanced magic) and as complicated as interviewing people in depth to determine if they're a fit for your class or teaching group in terms of their skill level, temperament, preferences, and overall personality. Unless you are unbelievably psychic, can foresee every possible problem you might have with anyone and screen for these problems accordingly, or have your own polygraph machine, no system for screening that you come up with will be perfect, and you will not be able to truly tell with absolute certainty how your students are going to work out before you really get to know them. Anne Marie Forrester talked to me about this:

> I've also found—much to my dismay—that you can't always predict when you first meet them. There've been people I thought were going to be awesome who turned out to be full of B.S., and then there was a student of ours who we were initially not sure about, but the longer she's been with us, the

more awesome she becomes. So it's a hard thing to predict who's going to work out.

That said, screening can help you make a solid, educated guess as to whether or not someone is a good fit. It's certainly better than taking on strangers you met online just because they express interest or going solely with your gut (although your gut reaction is important too). Screening can help you determine if a potential student:

- Has enough previous experience to understand your material
- Is otherwise ready (maturity, has finished any prerequisites, etc.) for whatever you're teaching
- Appears to have needs and goals in sync with what you're offering
- Might benefit from your teaching style
- Might fit in well with your existing group, if you have one
- Is someone you're willing to allow into your home, if you're teaching at home
- Is someone you're willing to spend time with and you think you can get along with
- Appears to be ethical
- Is noticeably insane

One thing I'd like to point out here: you *do* have the right to choose *not* to teach people you don't want to, or who you don't think would work out in your situation. There are some people in the Pagan community who seem to believe that you must take on any poor soul who crosses your path, and some who seem very critical of teachers who don't teach everyone who asks. But we are educators, mentors, guides, and leaders— not saints. Taking on the wrong person for the wrong reason can be a waste of their time and yours if your teaching and learning styles don't mesh or if you clash personality-wise. It can be disruptive to your other students too.

Some Things to Screen For

So, when you screen, what are you looking for? Since every teacher's strengths, interests, situation, personality traits, and material will be different, different teachers screen for different things.

Here are some of the main things teachers screen for:

History and Previous Teachers

Knowing what Pagan subjects or traditions your potential students have studied in the past can help you tailor your teaching to build on the foundation they already have and fill in any gaps. And knowing who taught your potential students before can give you further insight into the students' background and mindset, particularly if you know their former teachers personally or by reputation.

Another benefit of finding out about a student's past teachers is that, if it's appropriate, you might be able to contact them and find out where the student left off, so you can pick up from there. You can also contact their former teachers for references. This can give you valuable insight and also help you avoid taking on a student who has caused trouble for another teacher in the past.

Commitment and Willingness to Do the Work

If you as a teacher are going to put in all the work to create, teach, and follow up on a class or lead a group, then you want to know that the people you're teaching are committed to the degree you need them to be. Melanie Henry's group is a tight-knit family, and commitment is very important:

> To enter the inner grove, they have to be known to us for a year and a day and have to be accepted by everybody else in the inner grove. It's a big commitment because it means that you'll be doing ritual on new moons, full moons, and sabbats potentially for the rest of your life. You can go on leave of

absence, but the assumption is that you are committing to doing this indefinitely. There's a little bit of a problem in that people want to join up without fully understanding what that commitment means in practice. Although that's one of the reasons it's good to have people stay in the outer grove longer—until they're sure—because if you're in the outer grove, it's like you're dating us, whereas if you're in the inner grove, it's like you're married to us.

Not every class or group requires that kind of dedication, but it is important to find out if your potential students are willing to make the level of commitment necessary for your particular situation. Nothing will take the wind out of a class's sails more quickly than a group of students who are not willing to do the spiritual and intellectual work you set out for them.

Brains and Competence

Your students don't need to be rocket scientists, but it helps if they have intellectual curiosity and are competent enough to grasp the information you're going to present. Sylva Markson commented:

> I don't think that you necessarily have to be a genius to be a Witch, but I think, for myself, in the kind of Craft I practice and want to practice, there has to be a level of experiential exploration as well as intellectual exploration.

Goals

In long-term or intimate teaching settings, it's vital to know what a student's goals are in studying with you so you can determine if your teaching might meet their needs, and you can help them meet those goals. It's also important to find out if a potential student's goals are completely out of line with what you're offering or if they have goals you don't approve of.

One example of this is "initiation hunters"—people who study with a teacher only long enough to acquire a title or degree, just so they can say they have it, and then move on to another. These people aren't worth your time and energy. Anne Marie Forrester told me a story about one pre-initiate student (a student studying toward initiation) she worked with briefly who was more interested in the title of "Witch" than in actually being one:

> A couple of years ago at a large community event, one of our pre-initiates came in with a gaggle of her friends, and our coven was sitting at a table in the big main hall…. From across the room she points at us, and I could clearly hear her say, "That's my high priestess, and I'm in her coven." And she puffed up with pride, and everybody appreciatively ogled us from across the room, and then she sort of shushed them into the dealers' room, which was out another door, and she never came over and said hi to us, and she never came over and spent any time with us.
>
> Later, in private, we asked her, "Why didn't you come over and say hello to us?" And she got all embarrassed and upset. So we talked it through and mutually agreed that she needed a month off to reevaluate her commitment to her studies and our group. But after that evening she never came back; that's the last we saw of her. I think she wanted the title and the pride of title more than she wanted to actually be part of our coven or do the work.

Why They Want to Study with You

Asking a student why they want to study whatever you're teaching, and also why they want to study with you in particular, can give you a lot of insight. Asking them why they want to learn the content of your class can be very helpful in tailoring the class to their needs. It can also help you determine if you are the right person to teach that particular topic to them; there might be a better teacher for them out there. For example, my husband and I had a woman approach us about teaching, and we asked her what kind of group she was looking for and what she hoped to learn. She was interested in a lot of things, but she kept coming around to magic; she had a deep interest in it and a lot of previous experience. Our group, however, is not magically focused; we're a teaching coven. Magic isn't high on our agenda. So I sent the woman to some other people in town I knew who offered a more magically oriented study group.

Speaking of magic, it can also be helpful to ask potential students how they plan to apply what they've learned. Do they want to learn about magic to create positive change in their lives or to hex their ex-lovers? If you don't agree with the way they are going to use the information you give them, you might not want to teach them.

It's also good to know why they want to study with you in particular. Is it to work with you, or do they just want to hang out with their friends, who happen to be in your class? It's helpful to know what they've heard about you or what they think you can offer them so you can determine if you really have the qualities they think you do. If you don't, it's good to get that information out on the table right away.

It could be that you're the only teacher in their area, or that you're the only person teaching your particular tradition or topic. This can make you very popular by default. My husband and I were the only people of our tradition teaching in our city for a long time, and it felt like every seeker in town who was even a little bit interested in our trad talked to us at one point or another.

It might also be because you have a good reputation or they feel comfortable with you. These are good reasons for students to want to study with you. But if they suck up to you or try to butter you up while you are discussing what they think you can offer them, take that as a red flag. They might only be trying to show you how interested they are in learning from you, but people who suck up to you—who are disingenuous about what they think of you or what they're after—usually make poor students at best, and can have ulterior motives at worst. It's also good to be careful with people who are sucking up to you because you might never live up to their expectations. They need to know up front that you are human, you will make mistakes, and you don't expect them to put you on a pedestal or pander to you.

What's really sad are potential students who prostrate themselves in front of you not because they're trying to manipulate you or get something out of you, but because they think that's what they're supposed to do. It's an unfortunate fact that there have been some Pagan teachers who have acted like they walk on water and like they are superior to their students and deserve accolades and adulation. This is a good opportunity to show your potential student that you are not one of those. (Because you're not, right?)

Compatibility

Screening to find out if a potential student's personality is compatible with yours and those of your other students is very important in any longer-term teaching situation. Sylva Markson explains:

> I look for basic compatibility of personality—I mean, they have to be someone we like, because ultimately a coven is in a lot of ways an adult family. We throw around the term "family of choice" a lot, but ultimately it's really true in that these are people you're working with on a deep level. You have to be able to let your guard down with them. You have to be able to trust them. You're going to have a level of intimacy just by virtue of the fact that you're dealing with your spirituality with these people. So they have to be people that you like, that you are willing to work with on that level.

And, as Melanie Henry points out, if you are doing any sort of energy work, it really helps if the student can gel with your energy and/or that of your group:

We're very flexible and have very few hard and fast rules, but you have to get the energy right to work with us. That might sound like sort of a loosey-goosey boundary, but it's not really. What I find is that people who do not hang with the energy kind of get ejected. That can be painful for everybody, unfortunately, which is not something I would desire, but it's an interesting process.

Brian Rowe also talked about the importance of new members being compatible with an existing group because of the impact that group members can have on each other:

When we're dealing with a small-group coven, each personality and each communication style has the ability to magnify other traits in people in the coven. If somebody brings something forward, it can ripple through the group.

This is not to say that everyone has to be a perfect fit. Flexibility in dealing with others' personalities and quirks can be a very important trait in potential students, and willingness to meet others in the group halfway can make up for some inherent differences in preferences or opinions. Sylva Markson commented:

Open-mindedness. I've talked about how you have to allow each individual to be an individual, but they have to allow the other people in the group to be individuals too. They can't come in with such firm ideas about what everybody has to believe or what everybody has to do, because if they do, they're going to wind up having lots of conflicts with other people in the group who don't fit in their mold.

Again, it's impossible to tell for certain during a screening process whether someone will be compatible with you and your group. You can try to ensure that people have the basic qualities you'd like up front, but the rest unfolds as people get to know each other.

And you can at least rule out people who have obvious compatibility issues with your group. For example, my husband and I once interviewed a potential student who had just moved to our city. During the course of our conversation, it became obvious that she wouldn't get along with our existing group for two reasons. First, she told us that she wanted a group that was "all business," with little socializing and chatting. However, our group is a coven, and socializing is critical to building bonds between covenmates. The real clincher, though, was when she told us that when she decided to move, she had simply *dumped* her dogs, because it was too much of a bother to pack them up and bring them along. She didn't try to find a home for them or even bring them to the Humane Society or another shelter. I was appalled and furious and practically in tears, and wanted to report her for animal cruelty. There was no way she'd ever get along with our pet-loving coven. This story also told me something about her ethics as well. It's often said that you can judge people by how they treat children, the elderly, and animals. This woman would not have passed the test.

You might not have the same ideas as I do about caring for animals, but if there are other issues that you really care about that you think will affect how you work with someone, it doesn't hurt to find out where your potential students stand before you take them on.

Stability and Commitments

Unless you're teaching a very informal class, during a screening process it's good to get a sense of what a potential student's other commitments are, where they are in their lives, and how stable things are for them. If their lives are in chaos or transition, it might not be a good time for them to be studying Paganism with you, depending on how intense or challenging your material is. On the other hand, if they are in crisis, your teaching might help provide them some stability to get them through it.

Ethics

Although you will never be able to ascertain without a doubt whether a person is ethical during a screening, asking questions about ethics is very important. The more intimate the setting of your class or group, the more you want to know that your potential students have a sense of right and wrong, and, preferably, a personal ethical code that is compatible with yours and with those of your other students. You don't have to pose ethical puzzles or grill your potential students about every little choice they have made or would make, but getting some idea of the students' sense of ethics can save you a lot of trouble in the long run. The closer-knit your group is, the more important it is to try to avoid taking on people who are either unethical or whose sense of ethics clashes with those of the rest of the group members. An unethical person in a situation like this—or in any teaching situation, really—can be a time bomb.

Red Flags and Obvious Nuttiness

"Red flags" are clues—usually odd behaviors or weird comments— that tip you off to the possibility of undesirable behaviors or traits in a potential student, or that the person is not in possession of a full set of marbles. Some of these can be fairly obvious, scary, funny, or all of those combined, like one that Melanie Henry mentioned in our interview: "The guy who told us he was a bounty hunter and that we had to have him in the class." Anne Marie Forrester also mentioned an obvious red flag she encountered:

> Not everybody who writes us are people we end up being willing to meet ... like one person who told us all about their Michigan vampire tradition and how they already knew everything there was to know and we could just initiate them via the mail.

And some of the red flags are more subtle, such as when people you're screening contradict themselves, repeat themselves a lot, or are generally twitchy. This can be an indicator that they are withholding information or even lying.

When we were talking about red flags in our interview, Melanie Henry commented, "It's not the obviously insane ones that'll get you. It's the subtly insane ones that'll get you." Although she said it half-jokingly, we laughed about it more because it's true than because it was funny. People who are obviously unbalanced aren't likely to make it past your screening, so they're less of a danger. People who are able to hide symptoms, or whose condition creeps up on them so even they don't know what's going on until it's too late, are much more problematic than the person claiming to be Elvis or an ambassador from Venus.

Unless you're a psychiatrist, chances are you aren't going to be able to tell if someone is "subtly crazy" during a screening. But one thing you can look for in advance that can be an important key to determining if someone's behavior is going to be a problem or not is empathy. If students display a lack of empathy—an inability or unwillingness to be aware of and sensitive to what another person is feeling or experiencing in a situation—chances are their ethics and behaviors aren't going to meet your standards. Lack of empathy can be an indicator of anything from an overinflated ego or selfish nature to full-blown narcissism. It can also be a sign of other mental health issues. In my experience, of all of the problems you can come across when working with people, lack of empathy—people who just don't give a damn about others—is probably one of the most subtly destructive and difficult to work with.

Remember, though, that sometimes people do weird things when you meet them for the first time not because they're nuts but because they're nervous, or, if you're meeting them in person, because they just don't interview well. So you need to take wacky behavior during a screening with a little bit of salt sometimes. And you need to think about your own behavior—how you might be coming across to the potential student—and how that might influence how he or she acts.

As Sarah Davies points out:

> As far as mainstream society is concerned, what we [Wiccans] do is freaking weird. You bring people into your home, and you're pointing knives everywhere and making geometric shapes. I can see where someone can go, "This is not what I signed up for."

We had one potential student who met us for coffee and attended one class. During both the coffee and the class, she repeatedly told us that her friends knew exactly where she was, what she was doing, and who she was with. It was obvious she wanted us to know that she'd be missed if we decided to kidnap her, indoctrinate her into a cult, and use her as a ritual sacrifice. After the first class she never came back, and she never called or emailed to let us know she wouldn't be returning. We can only assume we scared the hell out of her—not at all surprising, because she was already nervous and we're a loudmouthed, strong-willed group of people, and we were very vocal during the one class she attended. She probably wasn't a good match for our class, but even so, we knew she was nervous, and we should have toned down our discussion a notch. The point is, yes, she was acting a little weird, but our behavior didn't help.

This is one of those areas in which you really should rely on your gut. If you are uncomfortable with a behavior a potential student is exhibiting during screening, don't ignore that feeling, especially if you think they are being disingenuous or lying. They don't need to tell you every little detail about their lives before you take them on, but what they do tell you should be the truth.

Mental Health

Screening for mental health is tricky. On one hand, your students' medical situation is none of your business. But on the other hand, it *is* your business, because it can affect their behavior and ability to do well in your class, it can have an impact on your other students, and you as the teacher will need to deal with it directly if their illness causes problems. The phrase "mental health" spans a wide range of meanings, and most people don't like talking about their mental health status for fear of judgment or because they consider it private. But the more intimate your teaching setting is, the more important it is to at least know the basics of your students' mental health status.

Christopher Penczak told me:

> I have a questionnaire that I use for my long-term classes, and mental illness is not necessarily prohibitive to taking the class, as some of my most amazing students have had some serious clinical diagnoses, but the questions allow me to see if they are aware and are receiving support or will try to minimize or deny it. Some have been a problem in short-term public workshops and even a couple in long-term training. Usually when the person refuses outside aid or support from the mental health community it tends to end badly, and all you can do is bless them and hope they find a healing path.

There is more information about dealing with students' mental health issues in chapter 10.

Drug and Alcohol Use and Addictions

If you are going to be involved in students' lives in any more than a passing way, it's a good idea to ask students about their drug and alcohol use and whether or not they have any addiction issues. There is more information on dealing with students' drug and alcohol issues in chapter 10.

Arrest or Prison Record

It might seem extreme, but for your own safety and the safety of your other students, it's a good idea to ask potential students if they have an arrest or prison record. As with the mental health and addiction issues, you can decide on a case-by-case basis whether or not you're willing to take on someone with a prison record or rap sheet. In some cases, Pagan teachings can be very helpful to ex-cons and people who have committed crimes in the past who want to get their lives going on a better track. Just be aware of what you are taking on.

Screening Methods

So now that you know what you're looking for, how do you screen students? There are several useful techniques. Which one(s) you use will vary depending on what you're teaching and in what context you're teaching it.

Informative Emails

A high-level screening tool that many people use is a basic informative email that gives potential students background information on you—and your group, path, or tradition, if applicable—and details what you will be covering in class and what you expect from students. If students don't like something you talk about in your email, or if they don't think they'd fit in, they usually either ask clarifying questions or break off the conversation and start looking elsewhere, thus screening themselves.

The informative email that my husband and I send to people who contact us about possibly joining our group started out simply as a description of our group, tradition, and teaching style, but as people asked questions, we added more and more information to avoid answering the same question over and over again, and now the email has gotten quite long. We jokingly refer to it as "the scare-off email" because it has helped more than one person decide that our group was not for them. For example, it states up front that we practice skyclad after initiation (the training leading up to initiation is done clothed so people can get to know each other before they get naked together), and that there are no exceptions. This makes a lot of people uncomfortable; it certainly made me feel that way when I was new. Some stop talking to us right there, while others ask questions, and still others come to class even though they're nervous about it (and invariably get over it once they know everyone and are comfortable). Disclosing things like this up front gives students who might be bothered by it or who simply don't want to do it a chance to bow out before they've invested too much time.

References and Google

You can—and should—check out your potential students by word of mouth and online. Talk to their past teachers, if any, and ask around in the community to see if anyone knows them and would give them a reference. You can also ask potential students to provide references themselves. Don't go as far as cyber-stalking them, poring over their Facebook pages and tweets, but at least Google them and see if any red flags come up, and encourage them to do the same to find out more about you. (Remember, though, that several people might have the same name as your potential student, so it's possible that the information you turn up when you Google someone's name is about someone else.)

Weeder Classes

If you've got the time and resources, it can be very helpful to run a beginning "weeder" class or seminar to find students who might be good candidates for longer-term or more in-depth study with you. I think of it like Journalism 101 at my university, which was an entry-level class designed to be difficult. The class gave students a chance to show their stuff, and people who couldn't pass it didn't move on to more in-depth study or major in the subject. Melanie Henry's group has a fairly in-depth thirteen-week beginner class from which they draw new students for their coven. However, a weeder class doesn't have to be difficult or run as long as thirteen weeks, and it can be much less formal. My husband and I ran a Pagan arts and crafts class at the local bookstore for a few months both as a community service and as a way to meet and work with potential students.

Questionnaires

Questionnaires can be used alone or as a preliminary technique in conjunction with personal interviews. You can use them to whittle down a large group of potential students to just the ones you want to invite to your class or spend time interviewing. Questionnaires can be designed to give you very in-depth and personal information or simple, high-level information. They can also be less nerve-wracking for a potential student than an in-person interview, and of course they're much easier to administer online. Melanie Henry's group uses a questionnaire as a warm-up for personal interviews. "[Potential students] fill out a very long form, in which they tell us all their deepest secrets," she told me, laughing. "We ask them a lot of questions in the interview because we would rather ask a bunch and not be surprised."

Interviews

As you might have gathered, my husband and I—and a lot of the teachers and group leaders I know—use in-person interviews to screen students. In-person meetings are harder to organize and they take time, but you can get a lot more information than just using a questionnaire. You can ask follow-up questions in the moment and read body language—both very valuable when you're trying to find out if someone is a fit for you, and you for them. It's best to meet for interviews in a neutral public place rather than your own home, in case your interviewees turn out to be people you don't trust. Try to make your interviewees as comfortable as you can so you get answers that are less tainted by nervousness or the desire to impress you.

Like questionnaires, interviews can be fairly superficial or very comprehensive. Melanie Henry described the interview process her group uses:

> We have a rather intensive interview process. We do our best
> to weed out the really difficult ones before they even get in
> the class. We've had some real wackos come to our class inter-

views. By the time you've gotten through an interview, if you are a difficult person, at least we know what kind of difficult person you are, by and large.

There are some sample questions in appendix A that can be used in questionnaires or interviews or as a starting point for creating your questions.

The mediocre teacher tells. The good teacher explains. The superior teacher demonstrates. The great teacher inspires.

WILLIAM ARTHUR WARD

CHAPTER 4
Adult Learning Styles

Good teachers create a plan before they begin to teach, even if it's just a simple outline in their heads. But before you can plan what you're going to teach, whether it be for an informal session or something more structured, it's very helpful to have a basic understanding of how people learn, and specifically how adults learn. Knowing a little bit about how adults absorb information will help you plan a better, more effective learning experience, because you'll be able to work in activities that meet multiple learning goals and needs.

LEARNING STYLES

There are several different theories about learning styles, or about how people get and assimilate information. Each one has its fans and its detractors. I am not going to make an argument about the scientific validity of any of them; there always seems to be controversy—or at least disagreement—about theories such as these. The important thing to me is that using the theories I'm going to describe below has worked for me in teaching Pagans, so I have found them very valuable. There are other valuable theories, too, and I encourage you to do a little research on your own to find the ones that resonate with you. I also encourage you to dig deeper into the theories I'm discussing here since this is just a very basic overview.

Learning Modes

Some adult-learning theories state that learners absorb information in three ways: visual, auditory, or kinesthetic. Learners use all three modes but are not equally strong in all three. They tend to have one that is especially useful for them.

> **Visual learners** need to see what they're learning. They like graphics, diagrams, and pictures. They tend to be good readers and remember what they see or read better than what they hear.
>
> **Auditory learners** need to hear what they are learning. They tend to be good speakers and like group discussion.
>
> **Kinesthetic learners** are physically oriented and hands-on. They learn best by doing.

If you take this into account when you are creating your class, you will make sure that your presentation includes a variety of visual, spoken, and hands-on elements. This might sound obvious, but think for a minute: have you ever been to a long lecture that had no interactive portions? In the West, this is the "default" way to teach. One person in the room might enjoy it immensely, but you can bet that others are bored to tears or, worse yet, confused. Or did you ever have a teacher plop a project down in front of you and expect you to figure it out by doing it, with no auditory or visual instruction? For auditory and possibly visual learners, this is just as bad as a lecture-only class. If you balance your teaching between visual, auditory, and kinesthetic experiences, you have a better chance of your students absorbing and retaining what you teach them.

David Kolb

David Kolb divided learners into four types, based on a four-stage model of how he believed people learn. Each of the four stages in the model forms the basis for the one following it. First is concrete experience (CE), which is any learning experience; followed by reflective observation (RO), which means reflecting on the concrete experience; followed by abstract conceptualization (AC), creating a theory or model of what happened in the concrete experience; followed by active experimentation (AE), when you test the new theory. Active experimentation then leads back to concrete experience.

Each of Kolb's learning styles combines traits from two of the phases of the learning model:

> **Divergers (CE/RO):** Divergers learn best by intuition and observation.
>
> **Assimilators (AC/RO):** Assimilators learn best when focusing on sound theories and ideas.
>
> **Convergers (AC/AE):** Convergers learn best when focusing on practical uses for what they're learning.
>
> **Accommodators (CE/AE):** Accommodators learn best by trial and error and hands-on experience.

Following Kolb's model, you might create a learning experience that allows for all four of the phases in order to reach multiple learners, and/or you might take all four of the learning styles into account. For example, instead of just talking about how a person might call the quarters, you might provide some basic information about the quarters (CE), break the students into groups to discuss what you told them (RO), have each group come up with its own system for calling the quarters (AC), and then have them try out their system to see if it works (AE). This could appeal to all four of Kolb's types of learners, but another option is to plan the class from the point of view of the learner; that is, make sure that your class meets the needs of each group by including elements of observation where students can make intuitive leaps (divergers), theory (assimilators), practical application (convergers), and hands-on experience (accommodators).

Bloom's Taxonomy

Benjamin Bloom's initial work identified three areas of learning: knowledge (also called the cognitive domain), skills (the psychomotor domain), and attitude (the affective domain). These are often referred to as "the KSAs" (for knowledge, skills, and attitude). Bloom took this work further and divided the knowledge and skills areas into six sub-areas of learning. These sub-areas, taken together, are called Bloom's Taxonomy. They are:

Knowledge: The ability to recall, repeat, and define information

Comprehension: The ability to describe and explain information

Application: The ability to demonstrate or use knowledge, and transfer it to new situations

Analysis: The ability to question or analyze knowledge

Synthesis: The ability to make something new from different pieces of knowledge

Evaluation: The ability to assess information

As with Kolb's model, if you are taking Bloom's Taxonomy into account when creating your teaching plan, you'll make sure to include experiences that cover all six learning areas. It will be important not only to present information but give your students opportunities to use the knowledge in several of the taxonomy areas. For example, let's say you're teaching a class on using the sign of the moon in magic. You might present some basic information and ask questions to ensure that students are understanding you (knowledge); have students explain their own experience using the moon's sign (comprehension and synthesis); have them write a spell using the moon's sign (application and synthesis); and have them determine if their spell worked, and why or why not (analysis and evaluation).

Note that the example I've given covers some of the same areas as the example for Kolb's model, and both include experiences that are visual, auditory, or kinesthetic.

Teaching Adults vs. Teaching Children

Its important to understand how people learn, but as teachers of Paganism it's also important to know specifically how *adults* learn. If teachers don't understand how adults learn, or if they try to teach adults like they would teach children, teachers risk turning off, boring, talking down to, confusing, or alienating their students—or all of the above. Worse yet, lacking knowledge about how adults learn, first-time teachers of adults sometimes fall back on teaching examples or experiences from their own pasts. But whatever technique your middle-school English teacher used to teach you to diagram sentences is not going to help you teach adults how to use an athame. (Trust me; I used to be a middle-school English teacher.) Neither will imitating your college history professor's lecture style to teach about tarot trumps, even though your professor was teaching adults (more or less).

So how *do* you teach adults, then, and how do adults learn best? Many educators of adults have found the work of Malcolm Knowles to be invaluable in differentiating between teaching adults and teaching children.

Malcolm Knowles and His Six Assumptions

Malcolm Knowles is the granddaddy of andragogy (the art of teaching adults, as opposed to pedagogy, the art of teaching children), and his work is used widely by people who teach or train adults. Knowles puts forth six "assumptions" about how adults learn, or how they want to learn. All of them can be applied to teaching Paganism. This is my extremely simplified synopsis of Knowles's assumptions. There is much more in-depth information available than what I'm presenting here in Knowles's publications, including his book *The Adult Learner: A Neglected Species*.

Need to know. Adults feel the need to know *why* they are learning something. Although children will accept that what they're learning is the basis for learning something else, like learning their letters is the basis of learning to read, adults want to fully understand why learning something is worth their time.

Self-concept. Unlike children, who look to adults for direction, adults perceive themselves as self-directed and want to be treated accordingly.

Foundation, or the learner's experience. Adults come to learning with a lifetime of experiences, unlike children, who haven't built up as many experiences yet. Adults see new information through the filter of these experiences, which means each student in a group will perceive and think about a topic differently. This experience can be very useful for the teacher to mine when trying to find the best way to communicate with a student, but it also presents challenges because it means that no two students are alike, and a one-size-fits-all teaching format isn't likely to work.

Readiness to learn. Whereas children are taught information when the adults around them think they are ready to learn it, adults seek out new information for themselves when they are ready for it or need it. Therefore it's important when teaching adults to make sure the information presented is relevant to their lives and useful to them immediately.

Orientation. Children are often taught in a way that is "content centered," meaning that the information being taught is the focal point of the lesson. Adults, on the other hand, are problem-, task-, or life-centered and want to learn things that will help them perform everyday tasks or can be applied to solve problems.

Motivation. Children often learn in order to please their teachers or families; they are externally motivated by rewards, like good grades. Adults, however, are more internally motivated learners. They are influenced to learn by things like self-esteem and personal satisfaction more than they are by rewards.

Other Factors in Teaching Adults

Age. Many of us—especially those of us who are over thirty-five—would like to think that age isn't a factor in teaching adults, but it is. Generally speaking, older students can be less flexible than younger students in learning situations, in part because of their longer life experience. They've "been there," and they know—or think they know—what they want and need. They also know what has worked for them in the past and what hasn't, so they tend to be more inclined to go with what they know. Younger students tend to have fewer preconceived notions, and they can be more willing to "go with the flow." This does not mean that one group is better than the other! The important thing to remember is that people at different ages will have different expectations and needs, and you might need to ensure that the material you are teaching meets the goals of people in several different phases of their lives. And although it might be generally true that age makes a difference, there are many exceptions to the rule, so the trick is to take age/life phase into account without making prejudgments based on it.

Shared goals. When you are teaching children or teens, you can't necessarily assume that your students have the same goals that you have for the class you are teaching. This is largely because most children and teens have little say in what they are taught (and many of them would rather be anywhere but in class). Adults, however, as Knowles points out, usually self-select to take a class for specific reasons or to learn something to help them solve a specific problem. Their goals tend to be more in line with the teacher's goals. This factor, added to Knowles's assumptions about adult students being self-directed and internally motivated, indicates that it's important to treat adult learners as if they are on the "same side" as the teacher. You are more like peers working together to ensure learning than a guru speaking from on high to his or her acolytes or a professor lecturing a bunch of bored, hung-over freshmen.

. . . .

The main point to take away from Knowles's assumptions and the other factors is both simple and complicated: adults like to be treated like, well, *adults*. In my experience, all of Knowles's concepts are accurate portrayals of adult learners, but I've found the idea of the learner's experience to be most important—or at least it's the concept that I need to remind myself about most often when teaching Pagans. Ever been in a class or corporate training where, before beginning to teach, the trainer goes around the room to find out everyone's names and why they are taking the class? It might seem like a huge waste of time, but trainers do it for a good reason: so they can tailor the class to the life experience of the students.

Since Pagan paths are so experiential, with personal gnosis often a strong factor, I've found that the history, filters, prior knowledge, and set of assumptions that the learners bring into the class with them weigh more heavily on how the student perceives the class than they do when I teach something less personal, like proofreading. I once knew a teacher who said that to learn a particular Wiccan tradition, I had to "un-learn" what I had already learned about Wicca from other sources. The teacher wasn't taking into account that it was my prior eclectic learning and personal journey that had brought me to the tradition in the first place. What this teacher should have said was that I might need to shift what I had learned before to fit into the context of the new tradition. If I used to call the quarters starting in the east, maybe now I'd need to learn to do it in the north, but I'd still be calling the quarters. This approach would have incorporated my previous knowledge rather than discounted it.

Although the learner's experience is important, Knowles's other concepts definitely come into play in teaching Pagans. Their motivations are likely driven by their own personal journeys rather than by some outside factor. Pagans want to know why it's important to learn something, how the knowledge can be used, and how it relates to their own lives before they invest time and money; they are very self-directed—which, I believe, is part of the reason it's often said that working with Pagans is like herding cats.

I cannot teach anybody anything; I can only make them think.

SOCRATES

CHAPTER 5

Some Basic Teaching Techniques

After reading the section on learning styles, you probably figured out that providing a wide variety of experiences and opportunities for learning is a good way to make sure you address the various learning types of the students you are teaching. And communicating clearly about what you're teaching and why—and how it will help your students, while keeping in mind whatever you know about their personal viewpoints—will help you reach adult learners.

Some of these things might take you out of your comfort zone, but it's important to push your own boundaries a little in order to reach the most students. If, like me, you're not a fan of listening to yourself talk, you'll naturally want to focus more on doing activities or using media in your classes. But sometimes the teacher explaining is exactly what students need to grasp a concept. The point is, don't allow your own biases to keep you from trying a technique or a teaching strategy that might be very useful for your students.

Here is an introduction to some of the basic techniques you might want to use in planning your class. Some of the techniques and strategies will be familiar from classes you have taken, and some might be new to you. In chapter 6, we'll discuss how to incorporate these techniques into a class outline. For many of these activities/techniques, it is important to debrief afterward. For example, if you have groups brainstorm on a topic, have at least some of the groups report what they came up with afterward. Students are more likely to remember the activity and what they learned from it if you debrief, and they also get to hear other students' answers and ideas.

LECTURE

Whether you use any of the other tactics or not, a good portion of your class is likely to be lecture, or at least you talking in front of the student(s). In some cases, having the teacher stand up in front of a class and talk is still the best way to deliver information. To keep students interested, keep the lecture sections of your class relevant and only as long as they need to be to convey the information well. Ask students questions along the way, and/or allow them to ask you questions. And be sure to break up lecture segments with activities, discussion, or other techniques, such as think, pair, share (see page 106). Consider team-teaching or bringing in guest speakers, too! Having someone else to play off of helps alleviate any nervousness you have; it also can be energizing.

QUESTION-AND-ANSWER TECHNIQUES

Active Listening

One of the most important things teachers can do is listen carefully to their students. Sometimes teachers assume that because they're the ones delivering the information, they're the only ones who have anything useful to say. But, as I mentioned in the chapter on learning styles, teaching adults is a cooperative experience, and cooperation requires listening.

Active listening is a simple technique you can use to get valuable information from your students and show them that what they're saying is important to you. To listen actively:

- Look directly at the person speaking, and stop doing anything except listening.

- Listen to what the person is saying, but also listen for the feelings behind what is said.

- Show interest.

- Ask questions to make sure you understand, and repeat back what the person said in your own words to show that you understand.

- Don't let your own views shut down your listening before the person has finished speaking, and don't express your own views until the person is done speaking.

If you are having students work or discuss things in small groups or with a partner, encourage them to use active listening too.

What Do You Think?

In the coven I trained in, the teachers were wise enough to know that they could feed us answers to any question we asked, and we could learn them and parrot them back, but that it would be better if we came up with an answer for ourselves first. So if we asked them a question, rather than answer us right away, they would say, "What do you think?" and require us to give an answer before they'd provide one. This was often said jokingly, with the "you" drawn out to "yooooooooou" for extra drama and the rest of the coven chiming in, but it was a great technique for getting us to consider what we thought about a subject rather than just accepting whatever answer the teachers gave us. I use this technique with my own students all the time, and they hate it just as much as I did. I encourage you to carry on the tradition—not to torture your students, but because it helps them develop critical thinking skills they can apply to Pagan topics.

Along the same lines, it's important to ask students open-ended questions, not just yes-or-no ones. Open-ended questions require more critical thinking from the students, and, of course, "What do you think?" is an open-ended question.

Youngest Goes First

If you're working with a group that includes people at varying levels of experience, when you ask a question of the group, it's a good idea to start with the "youngest" member first. By "youngest" I mean the person who either has been in the group for the least amount of time or who has the least amount of experience. If you allow the "older" people to talk first, the "younger" ones often clam up because they think their answers aren't as good or they wouldn't state them as well. You are much more likely to get a lively conversation going if you make sure the newest members' voices are heard first.

Brian Rowe told me about the benefits of using this technique:

> Sarah and I work to ask the individuals who've been in the class the least amount of time what their perception of something is first, so that they don't feel like they need to parrot back or give an answer that an elder has already given, and so we have a better opportunity to bring forward new items or new ideas with regard to that topic.

Everyone Speaks

Since some students are naturally reticent to speak up in class, it's important to have a technique in your back pocket to get everyone to speak. It can be a talking stick or a sharing circle, or you can jot down the initials of students who have answered questions already and make sure to call on someone who hasn't. Whatever way you choose to do it, it's very important to include everyone. Oftentimes the person not speaking has some of the most profound things to say. Brian Rowe comments:

> Another teaching technique is going around and making sure everyone has an opportunity to talk. I've done some larger-group teaching and ended up running into individuals that, if not given the opportunity directly, they will not speak up and participate. Having a formal mechanism where everyone is given an opportunity is one of the things I strongly believe in.

Parking Lot

Oftentimes you will be working with a group of students and someone will raise a question that, although valuable, would pull the class off track if you stopped to answer it immediately. The parking lot is one technique for keeping the class moving along but still meeting the needs of people who ask off-topic questions. To do the parking lot:

- Have a sheet of chart paper posted on the wall, labeled "parking lot."

- Write the off-topic question(s) on the parking lot when they come up.

- Come back to the questions in the parking lot at a more appropriate time in your class, or save a few minutes at the end of class to answer them.

Socratic Circles

The Socratic Method is a method of questioning based on the work of Socrates (and Plato's accounts of it) that is used by teachers and trainers to encourage critical thinking. Using the Socratic Method to its fullest extent is beyond the scope of this book, but the principles behind it can be very useful to people teaching Paganism.

Socratic circles are a teaching technique based on the Socratic idea of encouraging critical thinking. To do Socratic circles:

- Give students a piece of text to read or a question to think over.

- Allow time in class for the students to make some notes and analyze the question, or assign this as homework.

- When you are ready to do the Socratic circles, divide the class into two concentric circles.

- Have the inner circle discuss the question or reading for ten minutes or so, while the outer circle listens.

- After ten minutes, have the outer circle give the inner circle feedback on their process, and then have students switch roles.

- Debrief. Ask students what they learned and how the experience worked for them.

This activity allows students to not only mull over a question together but to think about the way in which they approach the question.

LARGE-GROUP TECHNIQUES

Group Discussion

It's possible to have a group discussion off the cuff, but they tend to work a lot better if you plan ahead.

- Choose a topic that students already know something about, so they can speak spontaneously, or prepare students before a group discussion by giving them something to read or think about. You can even give them a list of questions to answer beforehand.

- Work with students to come up with an agreement about who speaks when and what to do when there is disagreement.

- Set up the room beforehand so students can see each other. Don't sit in the front of the room; join the group or sit off to one side.

- Try not to intervene unless there is an argument, the discussion has stalled, or it has gotten so circular that the students need to be nudged back on track.

These guidelines can also apply to small-group discussions.

Brainstorming

Write a question or a problem on the board or a flip chart and have students call out creative answers. Write all the answers on the board or flip chart. While you are brainstorming, don't do anything to shut down creativity: all answers are good answers! When you have finished generating answers, you can go through each one and assess whether it could really work. Brainstorming is a great way to get the creative flow going, and it also gives everyone a chance to contribute in a nonthreatening environment.

SMALL-GROUP TECHNIQUES

The Gallery Walk

The gallery walk is a cooperative learning strategy that employs brainstorming and gets people up and moving around. To do a gallery walk:

- Write several questions or problems on separate large sheets of paper, and hang them around the room.

- Have students form the same number of groups as there are questions.

- Assign each group one of the questions.

- Have the groups brainstorm answers and write them on the sheet of paper for a limited time (such as five minutes).

- After five minutes, have the groups rotate to the next question and add to what the previous group wrote.

- Continue rotating until all the groups have answered all the questions.

- Have each group summarize the last question they worked on for the class.

- Debrief. Ask students what they learned and how the experience worked for them.

The Jigsaw

The jigsaw is a great way to get students to teach each other. To do a jigsaw:

- Divide the class into several small groups.

- Give each group a different assignment to be completed in class (usually in twenty minutes or less).

- When the assignment is completed, remix the groups so that one member from each original group is in each new group.

- Have each person in the group teach the rest of the group what he or she learned from doing the assignment in the first group.

- Debrief. Ask students what they learned and how the experience worked for them.

Partner Techniques

Think, Pair, Share

Think, pair, share is often used with younger students, but it works well with adults too. It's useful for breaking up lectures and getting students actively engaged in the topic being discussed. To do think, pair, share:

- Have students pair up.

- Ask the group a question, and give students a few moments to think of an answer.

- Have students turn and tell their partners their answers.

- After both partners have had a chance to talk, ask if anyone would like to tell the whole class what they came up with.

Peer-Partner Learning and Skill Practice

In peer-partner learning, students work in pairs, with one answering questions or doing a task and the other providing feedback and/or helping. To do peer-partner learning:

- Have students pair up.

- Tell pairs to choose which partner will be the "doer" first and which will be the "helper."

- Assign students a task or give them questions to answer.

- Have the doer do the task, while the helper helps or gives feedback.

- Give students enough time to do the task (usually just a few minutes), then tell them to switch roles, so both get a chance to be the one doing and the one helping.

- Debrief. Ask students what they learned and how the experience worked for them.

Skill practices are very similar to peer-partner learning, but students practice doing a skill, such as calling the quarters, rather than completing a task or answering questions. Practicing or pretending to do a task is a great way to learn how to do it for real.

Whether you're doing peer-partner learning or a skill practice, circulate through the class and give assistance and feedback to pairs of students as necessary. At the end of the exercise, ask if any pairs would like to report back to the group about their experience.

Debates

Have students pair up and debate a given topic with each other, taking opposite sides. Whether students end up taking a viewpoint they agree with or whether they make an argument for a viewpoint that they don't hold, this exercise will help them sort out why they believe what they do, and it might challenge their basic assumptions about a topic.

AN INDIVIDUAL TECHNIQUE

Reflective Writing

Reflective writing is having students think back over something they have learned and respond to their learning in writing. Rather than just having students respond free-form, give them some questions to answer to help shape their writing and reinforce main points from the exercise. For example, if you had a class where you taught students to write and use invocations for the God and Goddess, you might ask questions like, "What words or ideas did you think it would be important to include in your invocations, and why?" "What did it feel like to invoke the God(dess)?" or "Having tried your invocations, what changes, if any, would you make to improve them?" You might also ask students to keep a journal of reflective writing assignments.

To teach is to learn twice.

JOSEPH JOUBERT

CHAPTER 6

Creating a Class Session

By now you have some idea of where you might do your actual teaching and what it might require from you in terms of time, energy, and money (chapter 2), and how you might find students (chapter 3). But what are you going to teach, and how are you going to organize the information?

This chapter is about how to build a single class session and how to expand those concepts into building an entire course. Knowing how to structure a class is very important. You might be saying to yourself that it doesn't matter how you structure your class because it's going to be an informal course taught in your living room, or you're only teaching one person, or spiritual things shouldn't be so structured, anyway. And you're right, in a sense. You might choose never to use the information in this chapter. And if you've taught before, whether it's Wicca or Paganism or middle-school math, you might just skip this information and move on to another part of the book. But the great thing about knowing how to structure a class is that once you get good at it, you will understand how a good class works. Then you can choose to use the structure, or you can toss the structure aside and work free-form—whichever you determine will be most useful in the moment for your students.

Good teachers know that there is freedom within structure. It's kind of like using a recipe. Once you know the basics of baking bread—once you understand what gives it its structure, flavor, and form—it's easy to experiment by removing or adding ingredients. You know what you can remove or add to change the recipe but still have the result be some type of bread. In the same way, it's a lot easier to adjust a class mid-stream if you have a plan for it in the first place.

I like to structure classes in three parts. Part 1 is the introduction, where I set the stage for learning and tell the class what they're going to learn. Part 2 is the heart of the teaching, and part 3 is the wrap-up, where we summarize. It's sort of like writing an essay: you tell people what you're going to tell them about the topic, you actually tell them about the topic, and then you tell them what you told them about the topic. In this chapter I'm going to walk you through designing a class like this, but we're going to start in the middle, with part 2: the core. Although the techniques described in this chapter are geared toward teaching a formal class, the concepts can be used in informal settings as well.

STARTING IN THE MIDDLE: BUILDING PART 2, THE CORE

Step 1: Determining What to Teach

Sometimes it's hard just to figure out what you want to teach, never mind how to actually teach it. There are several approaches you can take to help you decide what the main content of your class will be. Using one of these approaches—or more than one—should help you narrow down what material you'd like to build a class or course around. Here are four:

Time-based approach. If you know exactly how much time you have to teach—let's say, for example, that you managed to get a room to teach in, but only for three hours, or that you're presenting at a Pagan conference and you've been given an hour-and-a-half time slot, or you're really nervous, so you only want to teach one one-hour class to get yourself started—you can choose what to teach by what will fit into your time frame.

Talent-based approach. You could decide to teach a class or series of classes about something that you are particularly good at or interested in, such as protective magic or using music in ritual. In this case, you would build your class and determine its length based on how much information you had to share on that specific subject.

Subject-based approach. You might have a body of information to teach, such as a particular Pagan path or Wiccan tradition. In this case, you'd structure your class and content developmentally, starting with the foundational ideas and/or skills of the path or tradition and building on those.

Experience-based approach. You might know who your students are going to be already. In this case, you could try to discover what they need or want to learn about Paganism, and design your class by identifying their relevant experiences and knowledge and building on them.

For first-time teachers, the time-based approach might be easiest, since planning material for a fixed period of time dictates how much you can and can't cover. The talent-based approach is good for beginners too, because you'd be presenting information that you know well, like, and are comfortable with. It's also a good approach if you are interested in starting with a one-off class instead of a series of classes. However, the subject-based approach can be good for first-time teachers as well. If you're passing on information that was taught to you—or if you had to teach it to yourself—you might already have some idea of how to teach it. The experience-based approach is possibly the most difficult for begin-ners—in part because it takes a little finesse to figure out what people need, how to give it to them, and whether or not you even can provide what they need—but it is also very rewarding. As we saw, adult learners like material that is immediately useful, and teaching to a group's experi-ences is a great way to ensure that the information is relevant.

For the next several steps in building part 2 of your class, let's assume we're building a class for a single session. Later in the chapter we'll talk about how to expand that to multiple sessions.

Step 2: Writing Learning Objectives

Once you have a general idea of what you'd like to cover, one of the most important things you can do is to write learning objectives for the class. Learning objectives are statements of what you want learners to know or be able to do when they have finished your class. Objectives are the basis around which your entire class is built. Why should you bother with this, especially if you're teaching an informal class? Writing objectives will help you determine:

How you want to teach the material. That is, what teaching techniques to use.

What kind of resources you'll need. Include teaching space; equipment, such as DVD players, flip charts, props, or projectors; and supplementary materials, such as handouts.

How many class sessions you might need. Or, if you're only teaching one session, how long that session needs to be. Or the other way around: if you know how much time you have to teach, you can write enough objectives to fill the time.

There is a formula that people who teach adults use to write learning objectives. It's called SMART. In the SMART model, learning objectives should be:

> **Specific:** The objective should be to the point but detailed enough to be clear. There should be no vague language.
>
> **Measurable:** The outcome of the objective should be measurable, or there should be another clear-cut way of determining whether it was achieved.
>
> **Achievable:** The objective should present a challenge, so it's worth achieving, but not be so challenging that it can't be met in the time you have allotted or by the students you are teaching.
>
> **Relevant:** The objective should relate directly to the experience of the students or the material you are teaching.

Timed: The objective should state when the students should have learned it—for example, by the end of the course or before the next class.

Let's say, for example, that I am planning to teach a three-hour class about the symbolism of the four quarters, or four directions. Some of my learning objectives might be:

- Not SMART: Students will learn about the symbolism of the quarters.
  SMART: Students will be able to demonstrate verbally or in writing a basic understanding of each of the four quarters, including the symbols associated with each, by the end of the class session.

- Not SMART: Students will learn about quarter calls.
  SMART: During the class session, students will work in groups to write simple quarter calls based on what they have learned in class and on their own experiences of the quarters.

- Not SMART: Students will learn to call the quarters.
  SMART: Students will practice calling and dismissing the quarters using X technique during the class session.

All of the SMART objectives give specifics about what students will learn, are "measurable" in that you'd be able to tell if the objectives were met by the students' performance, are achievable with a little work, are relevant to the topic (the quarters), and specify the time frame in which students will achieve the objective. The time frame is more important for classes with multiple sessions—it's pretty obvious in a one-session class that the objectives should be met in one session—but I included it here as an example.

Once you've written your objectives, look at them carefully again. Do any of them need to be broken down into smaller pieces? If so, take some time to do this. Breaking objectives down makes them easier to work with. Objectives often need to be broken down if you're trying to achieve more than one thing in them. For example, if I had an objective that said, "By the end of the class, students will be able to list five correspondences associated with prosperity and write a simple spell using these correspondences," I would probably separate the part about listing the correspondences from the part about writing the spell: "By the end of the class, students will be able to list five correspondences associated with prosperity," and "By the end of class, students will write a simple spell using their five correspondences." I would do this because the method I would use to teach the first half of the objective would be different from the method I'd use to teach the second. If you think you can teach both halves of a two-part objective together, then there's no need to separate them.

Step 3: Putting Objectives in Order— Creating the Core Framework

Breaking objectives into their smallest parts makes it easier to do the next step, which is to put them in a logical order. This might be very simple, because you might only have two or three of them, or it can be complicated if you are writing objectives for multiple class sessions.

Depending on what you're teaching, a "logical order" for your objectives might mean chronological order, categorical order, or listing them from the simplest to the most complex or the most general to the most detailed. The way you choose to order them will depend on their content. For example, if I were teaching a skills-based class like spellcasting, where one of the objectives might be dependent on another, I'd make sure the foundational objectives were listed first. I personally wouldn't teach students to do a spell until I had taught them how to feel and move energy, so I'd put objectives related to energy work before those related to spellcasting.

Once you have put them in a logical order, your list of objectives—and their "sub-objectives," if you broke some of them into smaller pieces—should form the beginnings of a basic outline. This is the core of your class.

Step 4: Fleshing Out the Core

Next, look at your objectives and think about what would be the best way to ensure that your students achieve each one. What will your students need to know or be able to do in order to meet the objectives? And what is the best way to teach that knowledge or skill?

Patrick McCollum told me that it's very important to choose activities or class components that will set up a situation in which students can't do anything but learn:

> Teaching is the art of placing a student in a situation they cannot get out of by any other means except learning. I've made that my motto, and so I look at the people who are around me and kind of judge who they are, what motivates them and such, and I then try to set up whatever it is that I'm going to share with them so that it's presented in a manner where they have no other alternative but to learn it....
>
> Each person has different skills for figuring out how to do that, but instead of just getting up and talking and figuring there is some kind of osmosis going on and everyone will get what you have to say, you have to spend a little time thinking about it, maybe doing some research about the audience you're actually going to be working with, but figure out the best way to present it to them so that they will get it for sure. That's an art.

Think about each tool at your disposal—activity, media, lecture, guest speaker, etc.—and try to determine which will not only help you meet your objectives but make it difficult for students *not* to absorb some or all of what you're trying to get across.

Are you teaching something where you'll need to impart chunks of information, like the history of Paganism? Then maybe you'll need to do some lecturing. Are you teaching something more hands-on, like energy raising? Then maybe you'll need to weave in some small-group or partner-practice sessions. Bear in mind that you might need to use more than one teaching technique to teach a single objective. For example, to teach my first SMART learning objective, "Students will be able to demonstrate verbally or in writing a basic understanding of each of the four quarters, including the symbols associated with each, by the end of the class session," I might break them up into groups and assign each group to discuss one quarter, then have them jigsaw (see page 105) to explain to the other groups what they came up with. I might present some information in lecture form. I might have them do timed reflective writing (see page 107) about each quarter. I might have them do a gallery walk (see page 105) to brainstorm correspondences for each quarter. I might combine one or more of these techniques, depending on how deeply we were going into the material and how much time I had.

Think about what you learned about learning styles, adult learning, and teaching techniques, and choose techniques for teaching each of your objectives. Write them down with your objectives. Remember to mix things up so you are meeting the needs of multiple learning styles. In other words, don't have a class entirely composed of group work, or one of lecture. Don't worry if you don't pick the exact "right" technique for each objective for your first try. Teachers don't always like to admit it, but much of what they know, they learn from trial and error. If you're a beginner, your first students are going to be guinea pigs, no matter how much inherent teaching talent you have.

Here are some things to consider when choosing an activity or exercise to teach an objective:

Can you explain the activity instructions well? If you're not sure you can do it clearly, either practice on some friends or choose a different activity.

Will the activity work with the number of people you have in your class? Some activities, such as the jigsaw, don't work very well in very small groups.

Does the activity clearly help meet the objective? Do you know for certain that doing the activity will help get the point across? Another way to look at this is, is the activity relevant to the group and the objective you're trying to teach?

Does everyone in the group have the right skills or background knowledge to do the activity? As you observe your students, if you think one or more of them might have trouble with an activity because of lack of previous experience, think about ways you could help. Having the less-experienced student work with student(s) with more experience is one way you might be able to solve this problem.

Do you have enough time to do the activity? Remember that you will need to explain the activity, do the activity, and then, in many cases, debrief.

Is the amount of time you will spend on the activity proportional to what students can learn from it? If you're planning a long activity to make a small point, you might wish to reallocate the time toward a more important objective.

This is also a good time to consider using media, if you can find it. Do you have access to a video demonstration of what you're trying to teach? Or is there a section of a film that you might want to show the class that pertains to your objective? For example, when we teach about mythology, we often use clips from the Joseph Campbell *Power of Myth* interview series. Media is a great way to add variety. It also appeals to and works for multiple learning styles. (There's more about media in chapter 7.)

Remember, too, that if you're teaching Paganism, there's a spiritual aspect to choosing your activities or teaching techniques too. It's not just a matter of using teaching techniques and activities to make your material accessible to people with multiple learning styles. There are spiritual learning styles as well. Christopher Penczak discusses balancing the intellectual with the spiritual:

> I like to make things participatory, and I find myself using more ecstatic techniques to balance out the intellect. I am using more specific herbs and incense, chant, and dance whenever possible.

Don't be afraid to work in more spiritual participatory activities, as long as you feel comfortable facilitating them. Some ideas are:

Drumming. Even if you don't see any way to incorporate drumming into the middle of your presentation, using it to open your session can help the group gel and set the tone for the class.

Dancing. It never hurts to get people moving, even if it's just to keep them awake. A basic spiral dance can be a great way to close a class too.

Arts and crafts. Depending on what you're teaching, it might be appropriate to have students draw something relevant to the class. Art can be great way to express things that are not easy to say in words, even for people who aren't particularly artistic. You might also want to have a craft project in your class, such as having students create a "tarot" card about the subject of the session or make a tool, such as a wand.

Meditation or guided journeys. Most students can benefit from doing a mediation—and it can certainly help quiet a rowdy group—but it's especially good for people who are intuitive and need time to process what you're saying during your class. A guided journey can help students access information on your topic from their own inner voice/guide/subconscious, rather than just listening to you. Both techniques are great ways to give students a chance to experiment with or explore the information you're giving them before they leave the class.

Once you have chosen and written down how you're going to teach each objective, think about and make some notes on how you'll transition from one section or objective to another. These transitions are the glue between the sections of your class. Together with the sections, they form the full core, or part 2, of your class.

Step 5: Adjusting the Scope

Look at what you've written down, and try assigning an amount of time to each item on your list. You'll need to guess, and yes, you might guess incorrectly. Remember that you as the teacher can and should decide how long an activity or lecture segment can take. But remember, too, that sometimes things take on a life of their own, such as a debriefing after a particularly useful activity. Students can become very engaged in what you're doing and unintentionally pull you off track. It is times like the latter when it really helps to have a plan. If you know how long everything should take—or if you have at least assigned every element a specific time, whether you know the amount of time is "right" or not—you can shorten some other part of your class to allow more time for a discussion or something else that the students are finding particularly helpful.

Some things to take into consideration when estimating how long it will take to do an activity or technique are:

- Generally speaking, the larger the class, the more time you need to allow for an activity.

- You should allow a little more time for activities that require moving around, especially if you have to rearrange any furniture.

- Remember to figure in the time it will take you to explain the activity, pass out any materials (such as markers for a gallery walk), and answer questions.

- Be sure to allow time to debrief after activities.

I highly recommend that you get friends to help you try out one or more of the teaching techniques you've chosen before you use them in an actual class. For example, if you think you might like to do a gallery walk (see page 105), see if you can get four friends to do it first. Give them a time allotment—ten minutes, perhaps—and see if they can finish the activity in the established time frame. Don't forget the debriefing!

Once you've assigned times to each segment and tried out an activity or two with friends, look at your list of objectives and activities again. If you were planning on teaching a single three-hour session, do you think you can fit all the material into one class? Remember that you'll be adding an introduction (part 1) and a closing (part 3) to what you've already got. This is the "cut or fluff" stage; cut a little if you have too much, or fluff up your content if you don't think you have enough.

There's a saying that writers use that is attributed to Ernest Hemingway: "Kill your darlings." Sometimes, in order to make a class cohesive or to get it to fit into a certain block of time, you have to cut, and that can mean cutting the parts you like best or are most proud of. But remember: if you cut something, you can always keep it in your back pocket in case the class goes more quickly than you thought and you find yourself with extra time. Along the same lines, if you don't feel you need to cut or fluff, it doesn't hurt to have an extra activity or discussion ready to go in case you overestimated how much time presenting your content would take. Personally, I prefer to have a little too much content than not enough. I keep an eye on the clock, and if I think things are going long, I shave a few minutes here and there until we're back on track. But many teachers feel the opposite way and would rather slow things down to fill time rather than cut. You'll need to think about this for yourself and decide which makes you feel more comfortable. Either way, you'll have to be "in the moment" with your students, monitoring what's going on and adjusting appropriately. This, to me, is the core of the art of teaching.

Once you've completed steps 1–5 and cut or fluffed, you might have something like this for a three-hour class on calling the quarters:

Objective	Activity/Techniques	Time
Students will be able to demonstrate verbally or in writing a basic understanding of each of the four quarters, including the symbols associated with each, by the end of the class session.	Divide students into four groups. Gallery walk: what symbols, colors, beings, etc., do you associate with each quarter? Debrief: go over what the groups came up with; fill in any traditional associations they might have left out.	30 minutes
During the class session, students will work in groups to write simple quarter calls based on what they have learned in class and on their own experiences of the quarters.	Brainstorm and debrief: what elements does a good quarter call contain? During debriefing, summarize what was brainstormed and fill in any holes.	15 minutes
	Short follow-up lecture: give students a formula for writing simple calls.	20 minutes
	Break	15 minutes
	Group work: writing quarter calls. Break group into four groups; have each group write one quarter call. Debrief; have groups read their calls to the rest of the class. Discuss what elements they included and why.	30 minutes
Students will practice calling and dismissing the quarters using X technique during the class session.	Bring group back together for short lecture: explain the basics of X technique for calling quarters.	20 minutes
	Have students pair up and do skill practice, where they practice using the quarter call they wrote. Circulate and answer questions. Make sure both partners get a chance to practice. Debrief.	20 minutes

Note that I've planned this class for three hours, with twelve beginner students, and I've left thirty minutes for the introduction and closing. I included debriefs and short transitions between segments where necessary. I also had to cut this down from my original plan; I chose to trim out a planned mini-lecture on the historical correspondences of the quarters in favor of having more time for hands-on practice. If I were planning the class for more advanced students, I might add more history and have fewer brainstorming sessions. We're still covering a lot of ground in this class—like I said, I like to have a little too much content rather than too little—and as I look at this schedule, I think I might need to watch the clock carefully, especially around the brainstorming sessions, to keep the class on track.

BUILDING A GREAT BEGINNING: PART 1, THE INTRODUCTION

The introduction to a class sets the tone for the entire session. The introductory segment can be used to do the following things:

1. Introduce yourself and your credentials
2. Tell students what they are going to learn in the class
3. Go over logistical stuff (Where's the bathroom? Did I park in a no-parking zone?)
4. Set up ground rules, if necessary
5. Do an icebreaker or lead a meditation or blessing
6. Do student introductions
7. Set the intent of the class

At the bare minimum, the introduction should cover items 1–3. But items 4–7 are important for a good class, too, especially if it's an all-day session or multi-session course.

Introducing Yourself

It's important to introduce yourself and your credentials to adult learners because they will want to know why you want to teach them and why you are qualified to teach them. As mentioned in chapter 4, adult learners are very self-directed, and they select classes that will teach them something they either want to know or need to know. Spending a couple of minutes introducing yourself and your credentials will help them feel more at ease, both because they will understand your background and because they will be getting to know you a little bit.

Telling Students What They Are Going to Learn

Adult learners like to know ahead of time what they're going to learn in a class and, if possible, a little about how they're going to learn it. They want reassurance that they're in the right place, that they've taken the right class, and that what you're going to give them will be worth their time. Letting them know up front what you're going to cover allows them to think about it and ask any questions before you dig in. Write your objectives on the board or a flip chart. Go through them with the class and explain each one.

Going Over Logistical Stuff

Whether you're teaching in your home or some rented or borrowed space, it's a good idea to explain to students where the bathrooms are, where they can park (if applicable), and where they can get water or coffee (also if applicable).

Setting Up Ground Rules

It can be very helpful to take some time at the beginning of the class to work with students to set up ground rules. It might sound silly, since you're supposedly working with grown-ups; however, ground rules can be very useful in keeping you from being the "bad guy" if things start to go wrong. If two students start arguing, or if someone is being disruptive, you can point to the ground rules and remind everyone that you all agreed to follow them. Students can do this too if they're having a hard time with another student. Creating ground rules can serve as an icebreaker and help you begin to learn students' names. They can be whatever the class needs them to be. They should always be created collaboratively and never imposed by you, although you can make suggestions and help shape others' suggestions. Here are some example rules:

- We will treat each other with respect.

- We will listen to each other's ideas with respect.

- We will return from breaks on time.

- There will be no cross-talking.

- There will be no interrupting.

- Only one person speaks at a time.

- We will limit critical comments to ideas, not people.

You might also want to set up a "misery is optional" rule and let students know that if they need to use the facilities or get some coffee, they're free to get up and do so without asking permission.

Doing an Icebreaker

Icebreakers are simple activities that help students get to know each other. The goal of an icebreaker might be to get the class to know each other a little bit, to get them moving, to get their brains working, or all of the above. There are probably thousands of icebreakers online. You can use games you find as they are, or modify them to reflect your class material. For example, a simple game is to have each person turn to a partner and learn the partner's name and three things about him or her. Then go around the class and have each person introduce the person they learned about. You can give guidelines for the things they should learn, such as, "Ask your partner what his or her three favorite tarot cards are" or "Ask your partner what his or her favorite sabbat is and why." You can use the information you glean to tailor your class to your students' needs, too: "Ask your partner what he or she would most like to learn in this class." If you can't think of or find a good content-related icebreaker, a brainstorming session might be a great substitute.

Doing Student Introductions

Going around the room and having students introduce themselves is a great way to find out what they hope to get from the class and what their skill level is. Both pieces of information can help you tailor the class as you go. It's also helpful for pairing less-experienced students with more-experienced students for partner and group work. Allow one minute or less for each student. It's likely you'll have one student who likes to talk a little too much, so it's important to politely but firmly keep things moving.

If you have a larger group, consider polling the class instead of having each person introduce him- or herself. Ask questions designed to give you information about your students' backgrounds and experience, like "How many of you are new to Paganism? How many of you have called the quarters in a Pagan ritual? How many of you have written quarter calls before?"

Setting the Intent of the Class

In addition to (or instead of) the icebreaker, you can take a couple of minutes to get everyone focused on the purpose of the class. Do a brief meditation where students leave the cares and concerns of the outside world behind and concentrate on what they want to get out of the class. Or simply have them ground and center, breathe deeply, and set their focus and intent on what they are about to learn.

For my theoretical three-hour quarters class, I would probably allow twenty minutes for part 1. Since I've included several interactive activities, I would reluctantly skip the icebreaker, but I would definitely do items 1–3 on page 122 and have students introduce themselves, so I could get an idea of what they knew about the quarters and what they wanted to learn.

PART 3: THE CLOSING

Part 3 of a class consists of one or more of the following elements:

1. Summary of what was learned

2. Answering any unanswered questions

3. Thanking students for attending

4. Evaluations

Summarize

Take a couple of minutes to go through your objectives again with the class and summarize how they were met.

Answer Questions

Students might have some leftover questions. Take a couple of minutes to address these. If you used the parking lot technique, go through the questions that were written down. Cross out the ones that you already answered as part of the class, and answer the rest.

Thank Students

Thank students for attending. If you feel moved to do so, describe or acknowledge what *you* learned from *them* during the session, or offer a group blessing or closing.

Evaluate

It's a good idea to evaluate how the class went. If you are open to taking the heat (and the compliments), you can do this verbally. But bear in mind that many students won't give you a bad review or bring up issues they had with the class in front of other students. A better way to get feedback is to create a short questionnaire and spend the last five minutes of class having students answer it. If you keep it anonymous, you'll get more honest feedback.

In the closing of my hypothetical class, I'd allow two minutes or so for summary and the rest for questions. If I wanted to do an evaluation, I'd trim a little time from the questions or possibly shave five minutes off of the mid-session break.

My final class outline might look like this:

Part 1		
OBJECTIVES	ACTIVITY/TECHNIQUES	TIME
Introduction	Introduce self; go over objectives; discuss logistics; student introductions.	20 minutes
Part 2		
Students will be able to demonstrate verbally or in writing a basic understanding of each of the four quarters, including the symbols associated with each, by the end of the class session.	Divide students into four groups. Gallery walk: what symbols, colors, beings, etc., do you associate with each quarter? Debrief: go over what the groups came up with; fill in any traditional associations they might have left out.	30 minutes
During the class session, students will work in groups to write simple quarter calls based on what they have learned in class and on their own experiences of the quarters.	Brainstorm and debrief: what elements does a good quarter call contain? During debriefing, summarize what was brainstormed and fill in any holes.	15 minutes
	Short follow-up lecture: give students a formula for writing simple calls.	20 minutes
	Break	15 minutes
	Group work: writing quarter calls. Break group into four groups; have each group write one quarter call. Debrief; have groups read their calls to the rest of the class. Discuss what elements they included and why.	30 minutes

Students will practice calling and dismissing the quarters using X technique during the class session.	Bring group back together for short lecture: explain the basics of X technique for calling quarters.	20 minutes
	Have students pair up and do skill practice, where they practice using the quarter call they wrote. Circulate and answer questions. Make sure both partners get a chance to practice. Debrief.	20 minutes
Part 3		
Closing	Summarize objectives; answer questions.	10 minutes

Extending One Class to Several

The same principles that apply to creating one class apply to creating several. First, write out the topics you would like to cover, then put them in order. For your first try at this, I'd recommend putting them in developmental order; that is, putting the foundational topics first—the ones you need to cover to lay the groundwork for the others—and then building on them with subsequent objectives. You could also put them in chronological order if it applies, or list them from easiest to hardest.

Once you have listed the topics and put them in order, break up the list in logical places. Each clump will become a single class. For example, if I were teaching an introductory Wicca class in six sessions, I might arrange and clump my topics this way:

Session 1: History and Background
Define Wicca
Define Witchcraft
History of Wicca

Session 2: Foundations of Practice
Grounding and centering
Creative visualization

Meditation
Ethics

Session 3: Deity
How Wiccans define deity
Pantheons
Honoring the gods
Invoking the gods

Session 4: Altars and Tools
Wiccan tools and their uses
Creating an altar

Session 5: The Wheel of the Year
Sabbats
Esbats

Session 6: Ritual Basics
Cleansing sacred space
Casting and taking down the circle
Calling and releasing the quarters

Once you have everything clumped, you can use the formula we discussed for single classes to create each individual session. First, write objectives for each topic on your list. You might have several objectives for one topic, or only one. You might also discover in doing this that you have way too much stuff crammed into one session, and you need to move it to another. For example, in my topic list above, session 6 covers a lot of ground. I might want to move some of the objectives I write for session 6 to session 4 and align them with the appropriate tools. For example, I could discuss casting a circle in session 6, or I could move some of the objectives related to that to session 4, when I'm discussing the wand or athame (which are often used to cast a circle).

Once you've written your objectives, follow the remaining steps for fleshing out the core and creating an introduction and closing. Soon you'll have a full syllabus.

Good teaching is one-fourth preparation and three-fourths theater.

GAIL GODWIN

CHAPTER 7

Preparing to Teach an In-Person Class

Creating the content for a class or series of classes is essential, but it is only the first step in putting together and presenting a great class. Preparation and presentation are as important as planning out what you're going to say and what activities or teaching techniques you're going to include. You can have the best material on the planet and still be tripped up by preventable problems like faulty audio-visual equipment and poor presentation skills. This chapter covers some tips you can use to prepare for your class and present your material in the best possible way. Like chapter 6, the focus is more on formal than informal presentations, but many of the concepts you can apply in the classroom can be used in your living room too.

MEDIA

One way to break up your class and keep things interesting is to include media in your presentation. Media—such as video, audio, and slide presentations in PowerPoint or other software—can help grab and hold the attention of your students, and it might help them understand concepts in ways that lecturing can't. Ellen Evert Hopman told me about some of the challenges involved in keeping students interested:

I have spoken on college campuses, and the professors tell me
that because the current students in colleges were raised on
video games and television, they literally have a five-minute
attention span, because every five minutes there is a commer-
cial. So they have to bring all kinds of props and things to look
at, and every five minutes they have to do something, otherwise they lose the audience. Teachers have to compete with
television and videos. They have to have all kinds of bells and
whistles.

Brian Rowe points out that using media is a great way to "bring" extra
teachers into your class:

Using movies really allows us to take an expert on something
like mythology—Joseph Campbell—and bring him into the
discussion in our home, and then use that as a starting-off
point to talk about different references of mythology.

It's still possible to teach without much media, and many of the
people I interviewed told me that they were pretty "low tech," including
Ellen Evert Hopman:

I don't have a laptop. I don't do PowerPoint. I don't do any of
that stuff. It's just me with a blackboard. Sometimes I'll put up
a map I have of Celtic Europe that I've been hauling around
since the 1980s. It's getting pretty wrinkled.

However, I encourage you to try to include media, as long as it's relevant to your class and helpful to students. Don't do it just for the sake of
having a few bells and whistles.

Get to Know Your Media Technology

There are a lot of different kinds of media and media-related equipment you can use to teach a class. You might already own some of these

items, such as a laptop. Other items might or might not be provided at the venue.

If you are teaching in a place that might provide equipment, such as a convention in a hotel, call the event organizers or venue ahead of time and find out what equipment they can provide for you and whether you can reserve it. Don't just show up with all your material on a USB flash drive and expect there to be equipment ready for your use.

Unless you are already a pro at using the equipment, ask someone at the venue to help you set it up. Venue staff should know how to do this efficiently, although you can't always bet on it. They can also often warn you of potential glitches with each particular piece of equipment ("The cord on this projector falls out if you bump the table" or "The scan button on the DVD remote sticks") because they've either used the equipment themselves or seen others do it.

If you are teaching in a place that you don't think will provide equipment, you will need to find your own or go without. You might want to consider investing in some of the pieces you don't have if you think you will be teaching a lot, although it's expensive. If you get a business license for teaching (see chapter 2), it's possible equipment can be written off as a business expense.

This might not need saying, but I'm going to say it anyway: if you are planning to use a certain type of equipment in a presentation, such as a digital projector, *know how to use it before you show up at the venue.* Twenty minutes before your class begins is not the time to learn how to play a video from a PowerPoint deck or project things on an interactive whiteboard. Know what kinds of cables are required, how to connect one piece of equipment to another, and how to use the remote, if there is one. Here is some of the equipment you're most likely to use:

Laptop: You can store all of your media here or use it as a glorified DVD player. It's a good idea to bring your laptop's power cord to your class so you don't need to rely on the battery.

Speakers: Built-in laptop speakers are usually awful and are not adequate for projecting sound to a large (or even medium-sized) room. External digital speakers are a must for good sound quality.

Digital projector: There are many kinds of digital projectors, and they all seem to have their quirks. If you are borrowing one or bringing your own, make sure that it includes the power cord and the cord to connect it to your laptop or MP3 player. With some digital projectors you need to turn on the projector and get it running before you turn on your laptop and open your media file; with others this isn't an issue. Be sure to practice setting up and using the projector well before your presentation. The bulb in some projectors can get very hot and crack, so it can be a good idea to turn off the projector but leave it plugged in so the fan can run for a while after you're done using it.

DVD player and monitor: Always, always, always test the remote.

MP3 player: Not necessary if you've got a laptop, but if you just want to play music, this is a great option because it's so portable. Don't forget the speakers.

CD player: Feels a little like a trip back to the '80s, but if it works for your purposes, who cares?

Microphone: There are many different kinds of microphones. The stand-up kind, lapel mics, digital mics for use with computers, and headset mics are probably the most commonly used by educators.

Interactive Whiteboard: A common brand is the SMART Board. You project media onto it using a digital projector, and you can highlight text, take notes right on the board, print out content from the board, and open and use various applications. They are astonishing tools for educational purposes, but it takes a little time to get the hang of using one. There are some great tutorials on using interactive whiteboards on websites and YouTube. Once you understand how the features work and what you can do with them, you can create class content specifically for interactive whiteboards.

Using Audio and Video

Back in the dark ages when I started teaching Paganism, there was very little Pagan-friendly audio or video readily available, short of a few Gwydion Pendderwen or Kenny and Tzipora albums and bootleg copies of *The Wicker Man*. Things have changed, and now you can find Pagan-friendly music and video, to purchase and for free, on websites such as iTunes, Amazon.com, and YouTube. As with anything else on the Internet, some of the material is excellent and some of it is absolute crap. If you are interested in incorporating audio or video into your presentation, make sure to listen to or watch the piece in its entirety before you show it to students to check the quality and ensure that it covers the material you need it to. Many websites also display user comments or reviews, so you can get an idea of what others think about a video before downloading or buying it. Remember, too, that you don't have to show an entire video; you can show only the part(s) pertinent to your class.

Using Digital Slide Presentations (PowerPoint Decks)

Another media tool you might wish to consider if you are teaching a more formal class is a slide presentation using software such as PowerPoint or Keynote. Although these tools might feel too business-y for some Pagan teachers, they can still be useful for displaying important information, main points, and photos; projecting instructions or questions for small-group work; posting definitions of new terms (so students can both hear you define the terms and read them for themselves and thus have a greater chance of remembering them); and many other functions.

These types of slide presentations have gotten a bad rap because people who create them sometimes rely on them too much during their presentations, cram too much text onto each slide, or overuse the templates that come with the program, so all of the presentations start to look the same. If you want to try using PowerPoint or Keynote and you're not a designer, there are still ways to make your presentation readable and useful.

So why should you care if your PowerPoint slides don't look professional? Confusing, jumbled slides are hard to read and will not convey the information you need them to—in fact, students might even infer the *wrong* message from a lousy slide. Remember too that students might be reading your slides from the back of a classroom. And your students will get an impression of you and your knowledge from your slides, so you want them to be clear and professional-looking. Here are a few tips for making clean, readable slides.

Use "boring" fonts and stick to one or two at most. Don't make your slides look like a cut-letter ransom note or a letter from the Unabomber. Slides with too many fonts are jumbled, unprofessional, and confusing. Using one font in several sizes, using all caps and italics, or using light text on a dark background can look almost as crazy as using too many fonts. When it comes to fonts that you are going to project, boring is good! Commonly used fonts such as Times New Roman, Arial, Verdana, and Helvetica might not be thrilling, but they're easy to read. Serif fonts—the ones with the little "feet" on them, such as Times New Roman—usually convey a more conventional style, while sans serif fonts, such as Verdana, appear more modern. If you might be projecting your slides using a computer that's running a different version of the software than you created your presentation in, using commonly available fonts— fonts that are likely to be included in older software—should help your presentation render better.

Don't fill your slides completely with text. Consider using the 6 x 6 rule—a maximum of six lines of text per slide, six words per line. Personally I think this is way too much type, but this is a common guideline.

Avoid cutesy clip art. There is a lot of free clip art on the web or available on CD-ROM, and most of it is free for a reason—it's cheesy or ugly or both. It's better to have no art than bad art. Your art, like your font choice, conveys a message to your students; don't turn them off with it. If you are an artist or know an artist that you can sweet-talk into doing some work for you, consider using custom art instead of clip art. If you have your heart set on using clip art, choose pieces that are very relevant to your material. If people don't see the connection between your art and text immediately, the art will distract them. Try also to use the same style of art throughout your presentation.

Consider photos. Photos run the gamut from good to terrible, but in my experience you're more likely to find a decent photo than you are a decent piece of clip art. Although people frequently "borrow" photos from the Internet to use on everything from school projects to Facebook profiles—and chances are nobody is going to come after you if you do the same in your slide presentation (unless you package it and start selling it for profit)—it's best and most fair to the owner of the photo to stick to photos you can use legally. One way to find photos that are okay to use is to do a Creative Commons search on Flickr. (Creative Commons is a nonprofit which provides free licenses to artists, writers, and photographers that allow them to retain copyright while giving others permission to repurpose or share their works.) You can also find Creative Commons photos on other websites. Photos with a Creative Commons license can usually be used as long as you credit the photographer at the end of your slide presentation. Some of Creative Commons' licensed photos have other restrictions, so if you go this route, be sure to determine which kind of license the photo you're considering has.

Leave margins. This is especially important if you're using a computer, monitor, or projector you're not used to. If the display properties of your computer are different from the projector, it's possible the slides will be cut off at the edges. Leaving a margin around the edges makes it less likely that this will obscure any of your text or graphics.

Preparing Your Materials

Title and Course Description

The title and description of your presentation or class can attract potential students, give them a good idea of what they're going to learn and what kind of teacher you are, and help them decide whether the course is right for them. The title and description can also turn potential students off completely.

Writing a title and course description that are appealing and informative without being intimidating or off-putting can be harder than writing the presentation itself. Think about the kinds of people you'd like to have at your class, or the kinds of people who might be interested, and try to write for those groups. Play around with multiple titles and descriptions. Get input from friends. Find course descriptions for similar classes online and try modeling yours from theirs (without plagiarizing, of course).

If you are teaching at a specific venue, such as a bookstore or a Pagan conference, ask the owner or organizer what kinds of descriptions appeal to the people who usually attend classes there. Ask to see course descriptions from past events, or check them out online. Many event organizers will list course descriptions on their websites. In some cases it's appropriate to talk about your background and experience in the class description, but in some cases it isn't. Again, ask the organizer what the standard for the event or store is.

If you are teaching a basic class, keep the description simple, avoid jargon, and make it clear that yours is a 101 class. If you are teaching a higher-level class, you might want to include some more specific terms—which can signal potential students that the course is not for beginners—but still avoid using too much jargon.

Humor in titles is okay as long as it's still clear what the topic of the class is. It's better to be a little serious than to be unclear. Stephanie Raymond told me about recent experiences using humor to name a class:

The title can make a big difference in your attendance. I remember for Beltane one year we wanted to do one that was about sacred sexuality. And we could have called it Sacred Sexuality, because just the fact that it had the word "sex" in it is probably attractive to enough people that we wouldn't have to worry about attendance. But we also thought, "Well, if we just say sacred sexuality, that could also be really a snore." So we called it Sex: Now That We Have Your Attention… just to kind of play light with it. It's kind of like Skiing the Magical Bunny Slopes [the 101 class taught by Our Lady of the Earth and Sky]. Why do we call it that? Because we wanted it to be a compelling title, yet be a nonthreatening course title.

Syllabus

If you are teaching a class with more than one session, it helps to hand out a syllabus to students that includes:

- Dates and times of each class session

- The learning objectives for each class session

- Assignments that will be given at each class session (if appropriate)

- Your contact information, and how and when (or if) you prefer to be contacted

- Any texts, equipment, or materials that students will be required to provide for themselves

Handouts

Handouts can be very useful references for students both during and after your class. Before you go through all the work of creating them, however, make sure that you know exactly how each one will be used and if it's really necessary. Unnecessary handouts can be distracting, and we all want to use less paper and save more trees, right? Many of the "rules" for slide presentations also apply to handouts: limiting the number and sizes of fonts, not cramming too many words on a page, and keeping the graphics simple. Other things to consider are:

Break up the text for easier reading. Use heads, subheads, and bullets.

Number the pages. This is especially important if you will be referring to the handouts during your class.

Consider making handouts that go with your activities. If you give students a handout with instructions for an activity as well as give the instructions verbally, they have a reference to go back to during the activity. If you're having small groups answer a question or series of questions, putting the questions on a handout will help them remember the questions while they are doing the activity.

Provide references. A list of references can be very helpful for students who want to follow up and learn more about your topic after your class. A recommended reading list is a great idea, too.

Decide when you want to pass them out. Some people pass out handouts all at the beginning, while others pass them out as they're used or keep them until the end. The advantage of passing them out at the beginning is that it takes up less time than passing out each individually (this is more of a consideration for larger classes than for smaller ones). The disadvantage is that if students have all the handouts up front, they might flip through them and stop listening to you. For this reason, it's best to pass out reference handouts that won't be used in class at the end of the session.

Homework

Ah, the dreaded homework. Yes, the idea reminds us all of late-night cramming for our high-school biology test, and yes, you're (probably) teaching adults, not children, who might not take too kindly to the idea of assignments. But don't be afraid to assign homework. Homework is one of the best tools in your teacher toolkit.

Homework is a way to extend your teaching beyond the bounds of your class time. Like handouts, homework and take-home activities give students a concrete reference to remind them about what they learned in the class and a chance to practice and review skills and concepts (and therefore have a better chance of retaining them).

Brian Rowe told me why he assigns homework:

> Sarah and I attempt to have some type of a takeaway from it. We've found that a lot of people are able to learn better if they have something to reflect on, so if we do a worksheet, or if we do an activity on shielding, we might have a physical piece of paper that they can take away and write their thoughts on. If we've done a series of chakra meditations, we might ask them to create a physical item that represents each chakra and bring that back to the next class—something that tries to make it more substantial or physical, so that it's not all just in the mind.

If you have longer-term students, homework and take-home activities are ways for students to stay connected to you and to the class material between classes. When students bring completed homework back to class (this is far from guaranteed, but don't let that stop you), you can discuss their work together as a class, which gives students immediate feedback and allows them to hear each other's answers and ideas, and therefore teach each other.

T. Thorn Coyle talked about the assignments she gives to her long-term students and why she does it:

> My long-term students all have the following requirements: daily spiritual practice; weekly or monthly homework; a personal project such as a painting series or rune study; community service; a physical exercise program appropriate to their

particular body; some reading and intellectual study; monthly astral work. They are also required to check in to our online forum. The homework requirements, of course, fill in many aspects of human spiritual development, including self-examination, psychic skills, and work with the Gods. Our primary goal is full human health and integration, leading to consistent union of our divine nature with all of our facets.

As Thorn points out, the continuity, opportunity to engage with the material, and practice of skills that homework assignments provide help students integrate the material into their lives.

Here are some tips for assigning homework:

Vary your assignments. Just as you include opportunities for both active learning and listening in your class, make sure that the homework you assign allows students to learn and practice in multiple ways, to meet varied learning styles. You don't have to cover every learning style in every assignment—you can hit on the kinesthetics one week and the visuals the next—but do provide variety.

Make sure assignments are relevant. Don't add a bunch of subjects you're not planning on covering in class. Assignments should reflect what the student is learning in your class and provide opportunities for practice or further study. Adult learners do not like to waste time with activities that they feel aren't relevant.

Make sure your assignments are doable in the time allotted. This takes some practice, but try to find the sweet spot between giving assignments that are too large to do in the time frame between classes and those that don't take enough time. You want to make sure your students have some success with the homework (and to adult learners, part of success is often completion), but you want them to have enough to do so that they will engage with the material more than once between your class sessions.

Always give feedback. Whether you're discussing homework as a group or responding to each individual student, always remember to let students know how they did and provide suggestions for improvement if appropriate. Students don't like to do homework without getting credit for it ("credit," in this case, being feedback and/or praise).

GETTING READY

Practice Makes (Almost) Perfect

In teaching, there is no such thing as being overprepared. Any time you spend getting ready to present your material is time well spent, and it will pay off during your class. Being articulate is very important, and practice is the best way to accomplish that. As Patrick McCollum put it, "People don't give a lot of time to someone who doesn't appear to be able to explain what they're trying to tell you."

One thing to consider before you start to teach is to take a public speaking or theater class. It isn't necessary to do this, and many great teachers never do it, but if you're nervous or soft-spoken, it can be a very big help. Doing improvisational theater helped me immensely with presenting confidently and reacting to students' needs in the moment. Stephanie Raymond states:

> If you don't have that background [public speaking], I think it's worth it to learn a few techniques, do some instructor methodology research, or even theater sports or the kinds of things that make you comfortable standing up and speaking in front of a group of people. Because if you don't present confidently, or if you're reading a paper instead of presenting a workshop, that really can turn your audience off. And finding ways to engage your audience—finding ways to make it relevant, make it interesting, making sure you have vocal inflection—I mean, there are some really basic mechanical

things that don't have anything to do with the topic you're presenting that are pretty critical to capturing your audience and making sure they're not going go to sleep on you.

When I asked T. Thorn Coyle about how her theater background has influenced her as a teacher, she made an excellent point about projection of energy:

> Theater helped me learn voice modulation and how to work with presence. These both come in handy when I need to bring a group to focus quickly and also assist with pathworkings. My theater training included music, staging, and props, which come in very handy for running ritual. Combining theater with energy work and group participation can make for a powerful ritual experience.

> The thing I had to *unlearn*, or retrain myself from, was projection of a presence that was too far from my core. This sort of glamoury can unbalance the priest or teacher in ways that distance us from other ritual participants or students, making the whole experience less authentic and causing some of the rifts we see in Pagan communities sometimes, where someone might be a great ritualist but doesn't treat her people very well. The core is too far removed from the projected presence. I've had to work hard to unite the two, becoming more fully myself on many levels. This helps my teaching now, I think.

Projecting your energy too far from your core is one of the biggest pitfalls I believe teachers encounter, and it is one of the easiest to slide into accidentally. Always make sure you check in with yourself during a presentation. Are you grounded? Are you extended too far? Are people responding to your energy, or is it dissipating because it's disconnected or distant from your core? Really take some time to experiment with keeping your energy and core in sync. Consider having some friends sit at the far end of a room while you do a trial presentation, and ask them to give you feedback about your energy. If you project too far, it's easy to get lost or confused, or lose control of your class.

And if the theater thing isn't for you, you might also want to consider joining Toastmasters. I know what you're thinking—it's for old, boring businesspeople—but actually I have several friends who are neither old nor boring who have gotten a lot out of the program. But whether you take a class or not, there are some other things you should definitely do:

Rehearse. Practice in front of some friends. Get their feedback. Can they hear you? Do they understand what you're saying? Does the order of the material make sense to them? Are they able to do the exercises you have planned? Are they bored?

Time yourself. It's an unofficial rule of thumb that a rehearsal is 20–25 percent shorter than doing the presentation in front of an actual audience. Time yourself, and use this information to adjust your content. Remember that when you're actually teaching the class, people will be asking questions, shuffling papers, and moving into and out of groups, so allow time for those things.

Make a video. Have a friend make a video of you rehearsing. Watch it and notice where you are clear and where your presentation can use some work. Notice your body language. Are you being welcoming and engaging, or are you doing things that will turn off your students?

Before Your Class
Organize your notes. If you are using any kind of notes to guide you through your class, such as a script, PowerPoint, or note cards, prepare and number them.

Prepare for questions. Think about the parts of your presentation that students are most likely to question or have questions about. Ask the friends you practice in front of if you can't think of any. Get backup information or references to support the points you think students might quibble with, and prepare answers to questions you anticipate them asking.

Gather materials and equipment. Make or get handouts, slide presentations, and video(s). If you're teaching somewhere other than your own home, find out if the space you'll be teaching in already has the media equipment you'll need, such as a projector, screen, speakers, DVD player, or computer. If it doesn't, make sure you can bring these yourself, or rework your class to avoid using them.

Consider putting media on a USB flash drive. If possible, put any audio, video, or slide presentations you're going to use on a USB flash drive or your computer hard drive and play them from there rather than streaming them from the Internet. This way, if you don't have Internet access in your presentation space, or the Internet is slow, you can still use your media. If you're using PowerPoint, you might also wish to load the free PowerPoint viewer on the drive so you have that available.

On the Day of Your Class

Check equipment. Test any audiovisual equipment you are planning to use. Have a backup plan in case it doesn't work.

Check your media. If you are using a video or a slide presentation such as PowerPoint, run through it before students arrive to make sure it works. Set videos to the correct starting point, and check the volume on the speakers or DVD player.

Get a feel for the room you'll be teaching in. If possible, have someone stand at the back while you practice the opening of your presentation and tell you if he or she can hear you.

Create a welcoming environment. Check the lighting and temperature of the room. Adjust it if necessary (and if you can; you might not have access to the thermostat). Arrange chairs and tables.

Take a deep breath. You're ready to go!

Teachers should unmask themselves— admit into consciousness the idea that one does not need to know everything there is to know, and one does not have to pretend to know everything there is to know.

ESTHER ROTHMAN

CHAPTER 8

Giving a Great Presentation and Interacting with Students

The way in which you interact with your students can be as important as the information you're passing along; in some cases, it can be even more important. This chapter is about putting on a great presentation to maximize student learning, using ethics and boundaries to create healthy relationships with students, and fostering a positive class climate.

TIPS FOR MAKING AN EFFECTIVE PRESENTATION

There are several things to think about when you're presenting in front of a class, from how you speak to students and hold your body to how you monitor what's going on in the class. Here are some tips to help you interact effectively with students during a class and knock your presentation out of the park.

Communicating with Students

Use names. Students will feel more at home with you and respond to you better if you learn and use their names. Learning and remembering names is difficult for some people. (I know it is for me!) Cheat, if you have to. If you're doing a one-off class, have students fold a sheet of paper in half (into a "tent"), write their name on both sides, and place it on the table in front of them. Use the table tents to learn names quickly. You can also bring a drawing of the layout of the chairs in the classroom and write in names as you learn them.

Use active listening. See chapter 5.

Don't pontificate. Talk *to* your audience, not *at* them.

Define terms. Be sure to define any terms in your presentation that your audience might not be familiar with. If you're teaching something with a lot of jargon, like astrology, you might want to write definitions on a flip chart or pass them out as a handout.

Get personal. If you can, and if it's appropriate, add some personal anecdotes or stories to your presentation. People like to know that their teacher has "been there" and understands what it's like to be a student. Brian Rowe talked about the importance of sharing personal experiences with students:

> I also think it's important to relay personal experiences about how different aspects of the path have worked as part of teaching. And those might be some very private thoughts or memories that you're opening up to a new student, and you don't know how they will react yet. But I think the only way that you can create long-term trust is through that sharing and openness.

Use repetition. Reviewing and repeating important concepts throughout the class can be very helpful for students, especially if you're teaching a multi-session course. Don't expect students to fully "get" the more complicated stuff after hearing it only once. Christopher Penczak states:

> I find myself using repetition more and more. I think previously I assumed once I taught it, people got it and were using it, but I realize that's not always true, so I review more, and make each previous building block a little more noticeable in review.

Attend to your body language. Students learn almost as much from your body language as they do from what you say. Keep your hands at your sides when you're not writing or gesturing, but make it look natural, not stiff. Avoid fidgeting or pacing. This takes practice. Making and watching a video of yourself will help you see what your body language is saying to students.

Speak slowly and smile. Remember to breathe!

Monitor and Adjust

In teacher-speak, "monitor and adjust" means to observe your students while you are teaching and change course if you notice something that indicates you need to. You can go into a class with a great plan, but if the students don't have the background to understand what you're talking about, or if they need you to deliver your information in a different way than the way in which you'd planned, your detailed outline and copious notes won't do you any good. It's not enough just to deliver a great class; you also have to keep your eyes and ears open and notice if students need more information or help. Ellen Evert Hopman spoke to me about shifting midway through a class:

> One thing I can say is no matter how well you plan, you have to be able to adjust to your audience. Like you might plan this gorgeous lecture talking about Indo-European cosmology and find out that that's not what they want to talk about. They want to talk about how you became a Druid, what is a Druid, what kind of robes do you wear, something like that. So you have to be able to adjust.

A huge part of monitoring and adjusting is listening. As teachers, sometimes we're so focused on talking—on saying the right things— that we forget to listen. Brian Rowe commented on the importance of listening:

> Listen to students for feedback. No matter how wonderful you believe a recent discussion went, until you find out a week

or two later whether a student got it and is able to implement it, you might just be talking to yourself. So listen to students and learn from them.

Sarah Davies mentioned the importance of:

> … making sure that you're really listening to them and not pushing them too far, or that they're not quietly freaking out and uncomfortable, and that what you're doing is helpful and challenging.

Remember, it's much, much easier to throw your plan out the window and improvise a new one in response to student needs or feedback if you are well-grounded in your material. This is one area in which preparation really pays off. And as you become more comfortable with teaching, your class structure can become much looser, and you can respond in the moment to students' needs. T. Thorn Coyle told me about being flexible and responsive to the audience:

> I feel out what the community I'm visiting might need and check in with the local organizers. So theme comes first. Then I try to make sure there is a mix of meditative work, time to share insights and experiences, some music and movement to engage the nonverbal parts of us, plus energy workings or ritual to round things out. My lesson plan used to be much more structured when I began. These days, there are some things that need to be covered, but the rest can flow according to the needs of the group and inspiration from my guides or the Gods.

Handling Questions

Student questions can provide excellent "teachable moments" or be challenging enough to throw you off your game—or both. Here are some tips for handling questions:

Listen. Really listen to what your student is asking you. Don't jump the gun and assume you know where he or she is going. T. Thorn Coyle told me about how she tries to listen:

> I try to listen a lot, both in order to follow the energy better and to sense the questions beneath the questions. This is an ongoing practice for me, and not something I could have done when I began teaching. I needed to learn to slow down and trust the process.

Tell participants when the best times to ask questions are. Some teachers answer them along the way, while others wait until the end. Use the parking lot (as described in chapter 5) as necessary.

Postpone questions. It is sometimes best to postpone answering questions that only apply to one person or involve solving a personal problem until the end of the class. Getting wrapped up in one person's question can take up valuable time and throw your agenda off track. On the other hand, sometimes one person's question pertains to the whole class, so monitor your class to see whether you should answer immediately or wait until the end. Poll the class if necessary. According to Christopher Penczak:

> Finding the boundary between course questions and sharing and personal healing is also important. A large group class is not the place for one individual to get the healing support they need unless that is the purpose of the gathering. Many people in public classes will fail to get private personal [help] but try to use class as a forum for their own emotional and psychological help. Strong verbal boundaries, and sometimes energetic boundaries, are necessary, and even a private talk on the break. I offer my services—or if in a store/center, there are a whole host of private-practice healers that might help them, depending on their need—but I emphasize the need to do it outside of the class.

Repeat participants' questions. This helps ensure that the entire class hears and understands them.

Ask students questions. Rather than just answering students' questions, pose some of your own to give them a chance to do some critical thinking. Ellen Evert Hopman uses this technique:

> I like to use the Socratic Method instead of me just pontificating. I ask them, "Well, what do you think a Celt is? What do you think a Druid is?" and then I let them all answer, and then I put in my opinion. I enjoy doing that because I think it helps people to stay on topic.

Asking the right number of questions at the right time is important, too, as Anne Marie Forrester pointed out:

> The goal is to get people thinking for themselves without looking for any predetermined "correct" answers. Ideally your students should develop critical thinking skills and confidence to explore ideas based on their own study and experiences. If you don't give them enough information up front, you can leave them floundering in the dark without understanding what you're asking. But if you give them too much, you're simply feeding them answers they can parrot back to you. The trick is finding that line for each student, even when in a group setting, because every student will require a different balance of information and questions.

Admit what you don't know. If someone asks a question you can't answer, be honest about it! You can always offer to find the answer after class and get back to the student later. You can also point them toward resources where they might be able to find the answers for themselves. Patrick McCollum has a philosophy about this:

> There is an old saying which I like to use a lot: "Wisdom is the recognition of the absence of knowledge." So I sign on to

that to be a teacher. And to be a person who's wise enough to share what it is that I know, I have to first accept that I know very little and be able to be humble enough to accept that.

Following Up

Pass out handouts. If you haven't already done so during the presentation, pass out any handouts you've created that summarize important information or terms from your presentation.

Provide contact information. If you're comfortable doing so, provide contact information that participants can use to ask you questions later.

Ask for feedback, either verbally or in writing. Remember that people are more likely to be honest with you if you give them an anonymous form to fill out.

STAGE FRIGHT

I think it's fair to say that most people get at least a little nervous when they're going to talk in front of a group. I've been teaching various subjects for a long time and I have a background in theater, so you'd think I'm immune, but it's not so. I'm a private, introverted person, and I still get nervous when I'm in front of a new audience. So don't feel bad about it, but definitely do something about it!

This is where it's really handy to be a Pagan. Pagans know how to work with energy and visualization. Before you begin speaking, there are some energy-related things you can try to help get rid of your nervousness.

Visualize yourself giving a seamless performance. If the image is in your brain, you're more likely to make it real.

Visualize yourself as relaxed and at ease. Then act that way, even if you don't feel it on the inside. Use what you know about energy to project calm. If you act calm, you will begin to feel calm. (This is some-times called "fake it until you make it.")

Channel your nervousness into an inanimate object. Some people carry a chunk of obsidian or hematite in their pockets and visualize putting all of their nervousness into the stone before they start their class. I keep a piece of jet for this purpose.

. . . .

One important non-energy-related trick for fighting nervousness is keep-ing the content of your class within the bounds of your knowledge and experience. If you're knowledgeable and comfortable talking about the subject, you'll be much more confident than if you go out on a limb. Experience makes some people feel more confident, too; the more you present, the easier it should get. But whether you're experienced or not, it helps to not focus on how you feel. Instead, put your focus on what you're saying and pay attention to your students to make sure they understand you. If you're thinking about that, rather than how scared you are, you'll do a much better job.

It's important to remember that most of the time when you're teach-ing adults, you and the participants have the same goal: for them to learn whatever you're teaching. They're on your side. They want you to suc-ceed. They've usually chosen to take the class, and they're (usually) not a hostile audience.

STUDENTS AT DIFFERENT LEVELS IN THE SAME CLASS

A challenge many teachers face—whether they're teaching Paganism or fourth-grade math—is having students with widely different levels of experience and competence in their classes. It can be difficult to meet the needs of the more advanced students and the less advanced students at the same time, and the "average" students can get lost in the shuffle.

One way to reduce the width of the range of ability of your students is to make sure your class description is very, very clear. Call out what students will need to know in order to have the appropriate background to participate in your class—books they should have read, energy work they should be able to do already, prerequisite courses, etc. This will give students some guidelines for determining whether or not they belong in your class. If possible, include an email address where students can contact you with questions about your class content and whether or not it's appropriate for them.

If you still end up with a wide range of abilities in your class, there are several things you can do to try to ensure that all of the students get what they need.

For partner and small-group activities, try to have less advanced students work with average and more advanced ones. The less advanced students will benefit from the more advanced students' knowledge, and the more advanced students can learn a lot from watching someone else learn something they already have some familiarity with.

Try to give assignments that can be done at varying levels of difficulty. Add extra components to assignments for more advanced or average students who want the challenge.

In some cases, you can also have advanced and average students help teach the less advanced ones. This is a way to give advanced students a little bit of exposure to teaching others.

Do not try to bring the difficulty level of the class "down" to the level of the less advanced students unless they are the majority of the class. Students will almost always try to reach the bar you set for them; it's better to set it a little too high and provide a lot of support to help them get there than to set it too low. As Sarah Davies put it:

> Brian and I found that the higher level of expectation we have
> for students, the more effort they tend to put in, and we were
> surprised at the great work they can do.

If you're comfortable giving out contact information, make sure students have a way to reach you between classes for extra support.

Handling Difficult Personalities During a Presentation

Most teachers have a war story or two about people who disrupted their classes, either on purpose or unwittingly. The last thing you need when you are making a presentation is someone being distracting or trying to pull the class off track, but it can happen to even the most experienced teachers.

One way to deal with difficult people is to simply decide beforehand that you're not going to tolerate disruptive behavior. This sounds obvious, but it is far easier said than done; in the moment, with an entire class watching, many people find it difficult to confront someone who is being disruptive or belligerent. However, your other students deserve to have a class session free from that person's negativity, so it's important to shut it down if you can. Ellen Evert Hopman said:

> In the past what I would do is I would try to be very nice. I would kind of suppress myself and let them talk, and hope that they would calm down, but as I have gotten older, I'm less patient. Somebody gives me a hard time, I just tell them to leave. It used to not be like that, but life is too short. There's not much time left, and as Oberon Zell likes to say, "If you don't want it, you can't have any."

Christopher Penczak doesn't tolerate disruption either:

> Those who are maliciously difficult or seeking to prove superiority aren't as much of a problem anymore. I feel I've been doing this long enough to be deft enough to usually take their legs out from under them. First you try to see if it's a genuine misunderstanding or question and respond accordingly, even

if it's from someone seeking counseling rather than education. But when it's purposely disruptive, I have no patience
for it. I am all for people having their own opinion, and if
someone approaches me before, after, or on a break, I might
even have coffee to chat about differences of opinion, training,
or philosophy, but when someone wants to turn a class into
their own personal forum to pontificate, argue, and receive
attention to the detriment of everyone else, I have to shut it
down. I've found that holding fewer publicly open and free
workshops cuts down on that, as not many problem-makers
want to pay for the pleasure of being an ass and being asked
to leave.

And T. Thorn Coyle gave me the following advice about dealing with
disruptive or rude people online—but the principle is a great one, and it
works in person too:

I often try firm kindness first. If that doesn't work, they are
blocked. There just isn't the energy to spare on people who
don't wish to make a positive contribution to discussion. Disagreement is fine, rudeness is unacceptable. The reason I try
firm kindness first is that sometimes the person is having a
bad day, and given the opportunity to correct themselves, they
will. That has happened many times—even garnering apolo-
gies—which is a teaching for me to not jump to too many
conclusions.

Patrick McCollum suggests that one of the best ways to handle disruption is to really know your stuff and to turn it back on the disrupter:

Know about what it is that you're teaching so that a person
actually can't disrupt you. Because if a person challenges
something that you're saying or trying to share, if you know
ten times more about it than the person who is challenging

you and you're a little bit diplomatic, it takes a very short period of time to have that person become less disruptive and more respectful and silent if you throw some questions back to them about what they're challenging and it's a question they can't answer.

Once I was speaking in a bookstore about using the moon in astrological timing, and I was describing the moon void-of-course. Many astrologers will speak about the planets as if they were people to avoid some of the technical jargon and explain the planetary movements in a way non-astrologers can relate to. I was doing that and referring to the moon as a "she." Most of the people in the room were following along, but one woman—whose friends had dragged her to the class, and who for the entire presentation had been crossing her arms and scowling at me under furrowed brows as if she were trying to kill me with her gaze alone—interrupted me and said sarcastically and with a dramatic eye roll, "Can you please explain that without anthropomorphizing?" I wasn't sure if she thought I was incapable of explaining it another way or if she felt my personification was insulting her intelligence, so I just said, "Sure! The technical explanation is..." and rattled off a nice jargon-laden definition, followed by "And another way of looking at it is..." followed by another explanation in lay terms, without the personification. That shut her up, and she even uncrossed her arms, relaxed a little, and asked me some non-sarcastic questions later.

If someone in your class is being a general nuisance, you can ask him or her outright what's going on: "So-and-so, I see that you're agitated/upset/fidgety/restless/talking to others. Do you have a question or a problem we should address?" Often you can stop people who are causing problems in a class by simply acknowledging them. If the person is questioning your authority or knowledge, you can back up your statements and give sources, if possible. This is one reason why I encourage you to try to anticipate questions students might have and come prepared with answers. If you do choose to address the person's issue during the class, don't let it derail you or take up too much class time. You can always offer to talk to the person after the class or put the question or issue in the parking lot to be dealt with at the end of the session.

One way to deal with people who try to throw you off balance is by unbalancing them back. Stephanie Raymond likes this technique:

> I also really like to break the scripts—like, what's the last thing that somebody expects me to say in agreement or in response to a confrontational question. That's a really good opportunity to say, "Let's have this conversation…why do people think this way, and where are your concerns rooted?" I just kind of unpack it a little bit, and sometimes that makes people more belligerent because they don't want to go any deeper than just trying to throw you off balance. So if you can throw them off balance back by saying something totally off the wall back at them that somehow relates to the topic, that often will make people laugh.… If the original person is just sort of trolling and wanting to make trouble, that's not the response they wanted, and so it tends to shut them down.

She also points out that challenging questions can be a learning opportunity for both her and her class:

> Very often I find that when somebody does challenge something, what they do is remind me of a piece of the topic I forgot to mention or wanted to include.… And then when they bring it up, I can thank them for reminding me of another piece that I wanted to add and get a discussion going. I think often when someone confronts you, and you're the expert, and nobody else in the room identifies themselves in that way, the people get really quiet and think, "What are you going to do? How's she gonna deal with this?" And to invite other people to participate on an equal playing field is a good technique to defuse things.

If you have two people side-talking, there are several things you can do. As with the single disrupter, you can address it directly: "Do either of you have a question or comment?" If you're in a classroom situation, you can simply wander around the room as you talk, linger right next to the side-talkers, and talk right over them; they usually take the hint. Another option—it's kind of the nuclear option, actually, but it works—is to stop speaking and look directly at the side-talkers while you wait patiently for them to stop talking. The rest of the class will start looking at them too. When they realize they're the center of attention, they will almost always stop immediately and usually have the good sense to be embarrassed.

It's possible—although I wouldn't count on it—that your students will take care of a disruptive person or people for you. Pete "Pathfinder" Davis told me a story about some of his students quieting a woman who was determined to ruin one of his classes:

> There was a woman who came and insisted on witnessing to us. I'm teaching from a stool in the front of the classroom, and I tried to address her concerns and wasn't getting anywhere, and finally I was getting a little frustrated, and I stopped, try-ing to collect my thoughts, and the students took off on her, and they started asking her embarrassing questions about "If this is the case, the Bible says that, then why do you do this?" and they pretty much got her to leave. When I realized what was happening, I just sat there on the stool and watched. They all said essentially the same thing: "If you want to teach your religion, talk to the front office and maybe they'll give you the opportunity as part of this program, but we've paid for *this* and we want to hear what *this* man has to say."

Of course, not everyone who asks difficult questions or is distracting in a class is doing it on purpose. Some people will simply not agree with you and feel the need to say so. Stephanie Raymond says:

While good instructor methodology means that everybody's going to get your message and understand what you're saying, that doesn't mean that they're going to accept it or believe it or agree with it, and that's okay.

And sometimes people are distracting because of a lack of social or self-regulation skills. Christopher Penczak told me:

Many difficult personalities are due to overenthusiasm and excitement. Some people can't control their sharing, or find the appropriate venue for sharing…. One class forced me to do a variation on the talking stick. We had a talking crystal ball, smoky quartz for grounding. It was for one particular person and the rest of the class knew it, but it gave me a mechanism for keeping her in line for a long-term class where she was otherwise thriving, without getting personal or hurting her feelings. She had the "me too" syndrome. As everybody shared, she would then share, so she had twelve turns to share and everybody else had one. After the initial seven-week session, we were able to discontinue the talking crystal ball for level two.

Humor is a great tactic too. Laughter is a great way to bring a group back together and enhance a sense of camaraderie—as long as you're not laughing at someone in the group.

ETHICS AND BOUNDARIES

So far in this chapter we've been talking about the more direct things you can do to interact well with students. But there are some less direct and more subtle—but equally important—things you can also do that will greatly enhance your ability to build healthy relationships with students. Two of these are (a) defining and following your own code of teaching ethics, and (b) creating and enforcing strong boundaries with students.

Ethics and boundaries help you build a philosophical base that can give you solid footing and smart, respectful guidance as you navigate the complicated experience that is teaching others in a spiritual context. Your ethics and boundaries create a code of conduct that will inform how you treat and communicate with students.

Your Personal Ethical Code

Everyone derives their ethics from somewhere, and often from several "somewheres." Some people try to live by the values their parents or families instilled in them. Others try to live by their personal interpretation of the Wiccan Rede or Threefold Law. And others simply try to live in a manner they believe would honor their gods. You probably have a good sense of your own personal ethics and values; they've probably been tested throughout your life through choices you've had to make and interactions you've had with others.

Before you dive into teaching, examine or reassess your own personal code of ethics and think about how it would apply in teaching situations. For example, if you have a personal rule that says you try to treat others as you would like to be treated, how does that work specifically in a teaching context? How does it apply to how you teach and interact with students?

As you're doing this, it's imperative to think about the power differential and how it adds new layers to situations in which you might have to apply your code of ethics. In teaching, the power differential refers to the imbalance in power between the student and teacher. The teacher is in a position of authority, and that makes the student at least a little bit vulnerable. Even if we are teaching people our own age who have similar knowledge to us or whom we know well, they are not exactly peers as long as we are in the teacher-student relationship.

I can almost hear some of you saying, "That won't happen in my class! Everyone in my class is my equal!" That might be true, but you are still the teacher; you are still in charge. In the back of their minds, students are ceding at least a little bit of authority and power to you, no matter how many times you tell them they don't have to. Even if you have a very egalitarian class where students' opinions are valued and there is a lot of respectful interaction and consensus decision-making, there is a power differential.

Recognizing and accepting that there is a power differential and considering it when you are looking at your own ethics will help you create a personal code that doesn't abuse it. This is a very slippery slope, though. In some cases, it's very difficult to tell where using power to help students shifts into the areas of micromanaging them, taking their power, or abusing the power.

Teachers need to be aware not only of the potential for accidentally abusing power but of the many ways in which it can happen. For example, teachers should keep in mind how much emphasis students place on their words and actions and how much influence those words and actions have, even if those teachers are trying to run an informal, democratic class. Sarah Davies commented:

> I think, especially with magical groups, that the leaders of the group have a lot of influence. Students know that you know something that they don't, so if you ask them to do something or tell them to do something, even if it's really weird, they probably will because they trust you and they're there to learn. That's something that I am trying to keep in mind as a leader.

There are many forms that abuse of the power differential can take. Teachers can exert an undue influence over students' beliefs, belittle students in order to bolster their own egos, or extract inappropriate "payment" for teaching. In my tradition, there are horror stories about teachers who used their power to force students to clean the teachers' houses before and after class, do their yard work and laundry, and basically provide maid service. And in my more than two decades of time in the Pagan community, I've heard far too many stories about teachers of various paths using the power differential to coerce students to have sex or insisting that students sleep with them as payment for teaching. This is an egregious violation of the power differential and of students' trust.

Personal Boundaries

Ever heard that saying "Good fences make good neighbors"? Well, good boundaries make good student-teacher relationships. Personal boundaries denote the amount of physical and emotional space you need between you and another person in order for each of you to be yourselves and not be unduly influenced by the other. They are the demarcation of where one person ends—physically, emotionally, energetically—and another begins. Good boundaries allow you to be separated from others enough that you don't become dependent or codependent, while being close enough that you don't feel completely detached from each other.

Creating and maintaining good personal boundaries is one of the best things you can do for yourself and your students. Demonstrating good boundaries, coupled with a professional attitude, can help students with poor social skills by giving them subtle guidelines about how to behave. Boundaries can help you keep a healthy distance from very needy students while still responding to their concerns. If you are shy or an introvert, boundaries can help you interact with students in a professional, courteous way that gets them what they need while still maintaining your personal space. Good boundaries can make or break a teacher, especially one who is prone to getting too involved with students or giving them too much of him- or herself.

Some teachers hesitate to create boundaries because they believe they should be emotionally available and not have artificial barriers between themselves and their students. The ironic secret is, of course, that boundaries allow you to "be there" for students without them inadvertently sucking you dry of time or energy, so ultimately you will be far more useful to them. Melanie Henry commented about this:

Teaching involves also being able to create space for yourself so you have your own life, so you aren't getting eaten alive by your students.

Boundaries are also helpful for dealing with students coming and going. If you're too enmeshed in your students' lives, or if your identity as a teacher is so reliant on how well your students do or whether or not they stick around, you are setting yourself up for a world of hurt. A few years ago, a student I was very fond of left our group. Another teacher asked me how I could watch her go without feeling sad or as if I'd failed. We'd spent a lot of time with the student, developed trust and affinity, worked hard together, and now she was simply moving on. I told the other teacher that although I was really going to miss the student, I thought her leaving was a good thing. She got what she needed, and she didn't need to be in the group anymore. She was going off to discover new things and continue wherever her spiritual and life paths were taking her. I don't take that personally at all; in fact, I consider it a success. Boundaries allow you to let people go when they need to go.

Just as you did with your code of ethics, think about the personal boundaries you want or need before you start teaching. Consider things like putting limits on how much time per week you'll put toward teaching, when and how much you're willing to help students with personal problems, and how you prefer to be contacted (email, phone, IM, text) in order to maintain your personal space. Remember, too, that it's okay for you to change boundaries if they aren't working. If you have informed students of your boundaries (kind of like posting office hours), be sure to let them know that things are changing. What you were willing or able to handle at the beginning of a class might not be the same as what you are willing or able to handle toward the end, depending on your personal situation and your students' needs.

Ethics and Boundaries Together

You can combine your lists of ethics and boundaries to create ways to interact with students in healthy ways to mutual benefit. Here are some examples of policies that you might come up with:

- I will only hold class on these days: *X, Y, Z*.

- I will answer non-emergency student emails within *X* amount of time.

- My weekends are my own unless I'm teaching a class; no student business on weekends.

- I will treat students as equally as possible and strive to avoid preferential treatment.

- I will not trash-talk about students, no matter how frustrated I get, and especially not to other students.

- I will ask everyone to bring food for ritual so the burden doesn't fall on one or two people.

- I will set up a sign-up list so people can take turns hosting a class or bringing supplies.

- Students aren't allowed to call or come over in the middle of the night. (This might sound silly, but you'd be surprised how many people need to be told this.)

- I will not abuse the power differential by sleeping with my students or encouraging them to form any romantic attachment to me.

If you're going to make only one ethical rule for dealing with your students, consider making it something along the lines of this last one. Pete "Pathfinder" Davis told me that he has banned teacher-student sexual relationships at the Aquarian Tabernacle Church:

> If you're going to be teaching somebody in a sort of semi-formal setting, there's a couple of things that you need to real-

ize, and one of them is that this is not a license to troll for bed partners. If you have a formal teacher-student relationship, you cannot have a personal intimate relationship until that is over.

It's true that the Pagan community tends to have a more flexible idea of what is okay in the arena of sex than the mainstream community does, and that the "rules" around sex are not black and white. But having open or flexible sexual mores and practices isn't an excuse to be predatory. If you are a teacher who is attracted to one of your students, you need to be thinking about what your motives are for entering into a sexual relationship with him or her. Sexual relationships with students can—and frequently do—plummet straight down the slippery slope of the power differential. Some students have a tendency to develop sexual attachments to people they look up to or whom they perceive to be in authority. Depending on the circumstances, these attachments might or might not be healthy. Some people believe that as long as there is a power differential, there is no truly consensual sex. I'm not sure I buy that, but I do think it's imperative to keep the power differential in mind.

There might be exceptions, such as if you were already lovers before you entered the teacher-student relationship, or cases where sleeping with a student is less of a taboo, such as within Pagan paths that practice sex magic or sacred sex. But in these latter situations, there are often also guidelines for circumstances under which the sacred sex is done, informed consent being high among those guidelines. Just remember: the power differential makes students vulnerable. The degree of vulnerability will vary with the student and the situation, but it's neither fair nor ethical to take advantage of vulnerability for sex.

Whether you adopt the sex rule or not, make sure you use the ethical and boundary policies you create as consistently as you can, so students learn them. If students are aware of your limits, they might even help you enforce them.

CREATING A POSITIVE LEARNING ENVIRONMENT

There are things you can do as a teacher to create a positive learning environment where problems are less likely to happen. Establishing yourself as a trustworthy leader and your class as a safe, respectful place where people can learn, express themselves, and walk further on their personal spiritual path will greatly enhance your students' learning experience and your teaching experience, and it might also help you head off some interpersonal issues.

Model and Expect Respect

As I've said countless times already, adult learners aren't the same as child learners. However, like child learners—and whether they're aware of it or not—adult learners look to teachers for cues about how to behave and what's expected of them in a class. The teacher's behavior sets the tone, so one of the most important things you can do to create a great learning environment is to model respect. This means doing some of the things I mentioned in the information on presentation: remembering to be friendly and courteous to students, greeting them as they come to class, listening to them carefully when they speak, and not interrupting. It also means dealing with disruptive people respectfully and swiftly, and not allowing students to disrespect each other. Don't complain to students about other students. Don't let your temper get the better of you. Be calm and level-headed.

The flip side of modeling respect is expecting respect. Don't allow students to disrespect you in front of other students. Defuse situations politely and quickly. Show students that courtesy is the norm in your class.

You can build mutual respect by using consensus for decisions that affect the class, when possible. Consensus isn't appropriate for all teaching circumstances, but using it even for small things, such as deciding jointly when to take a break during a long session, can help build trust and the feeling of respect. Consensus can also be challenging, both for teachers and students. Some teachers don't like to give up control, and students who don't trust others are sometimes reluctant to embrace a consensus model. Melanie Henry talked to me about consensus in her group:

> We just basically work through stuff by consensus. It can be really scary for people who don't have a high level of trust going on and don't necessarily trust us as a group, but I find that bringing everything to the table and getting everyone to talk through stuff—if people are willing to do the process—works. If they're not willing to do the process, they're with the wrong people.

Do Your Best to Create Stability

Over the years, several of my students have told me that they were surprised at how "normal" and stable my husband and I appeared to be when we met them for the first time, and that those qualities helped them trust us enough that they could begin studying with us. You don't have to be normal—whatever that means—to be a good teacher. As a matter of fact, I don't think my husband and I are that normal at all, although we can pass for mainstream with a little effort. However, stability—or perceived stability, anyway—*is* important. Being fairly stable and creating a stable learning environment will help your students feel that they're in a place that's safe enough where they can be vulnerable and try new things. Paganism deals with a lot of subjects and concepts that mainstream society thinks are pretty weird. Teachers who project stability by being patient, consistent, and reliable help give students the sense of security and confidence they need to explore things that are unseen or intangible, such as deities, magic, and energy.

Patience with students is vitally important, and it's one of the hardest things for many of us to achieve. Some students have annoying habits. Others don't move forward as fast as we want them to. Still others ask endless questions or seem to forget everything we've just told them. The trick is not to stop yourself from feeling impatient; rather, it's not letting your impatience show (well, not too much, anyway). When you feel impatient with students, or when you want to hurry them along faster than they're ready to go, breathe, count to ten, and remember what it was like for you when you were learning. Think of a teacher, parent, friend, or mentor who helped you learn something important by being patient, and try to do what he or she would have done. Use self-talk. Tell yourself to chill, get over yourself, relax, or knock it off. You don't have to be perfect and stuff your feelings in situations with students that make you feel impatient, but try to calm yourself down. You'll feel better, and so will they.

Consistency, like patience, is a crucial teacher quality and one that's hard to maintain. Consistency for teachers means things like keeping your behavior and emotional reactions fairly constant so students know what to expect, treating your students with the same level of respect and applying the rules the same way to everyone, and having the same expectations of all students. There will be exceptions to the consistency rule—for example, one student might need to do extra work that others don't need to do because he or she has fewer skills than the others in that area and needs to catch up to the others—but it's important to try to treat everyone similarly and fairly and try to keep your own behavior fairly constant in order to build trust.

Reliability is a kind of consistency. Being a reliable teacher means showing up on time and prepared, making yourself available to students, and generally doing what you say you will do. It's hard to expect them to be reliable if you can't be reliable as well. And you will lose students' trust if you exhibit erratic behavior and frequently go back on your word without a good reason.

There will be times as a teacher when you screw up in the patience, consistency, or reliability categories, or all three. In those cases, the patient, consistent, and reliable thing to do is admit you messed up, apologize if necessary, and show students that you continue to strive to achieve these characteristics.

Be Open and Honest—Maybe Even a Little Vulnerable

While you're projecting respect, you should also try to project open honesty. You don't have to tell everyone in the class your deepest secrets—and, as I already mentioned, you should maintain some professional boundaries—but showing students a little of yourself and making yourself available and receptive to students can really help build trust. Trust is important if you want students to come to you with problems, respect what you have to say, and be receptive to learning in your class. And it's vital if you ever find yourself needing to talk to a student about a problem he or she is having or creating.

Sarah Davies talked to me about learning to open up and:

> ... admit to your personal feelings—to go really deeply into yourself with someone who you might not know all that well—because it's important for them to understand where you're coming from.

And Sylva Markson talked about being open and giving students the benefit of the doubt initially, even when you know it's possible that you might get burned:

> One of the things that my former high priestess would say— and my high priest even more so, I think, that I don't like and I don't really want to believe—is that you can never really know a person until they have nothing more to gain from you.... It's only then, when you see what they do, that you know their true nature. You can't know a person—really know them— until they're at that point.... But I don't want to be that jaded person who comes to the Craft saying I can't really trust anybody until we are completely on equal footing and I have nothing to give them, because until then they're just playing a game with me or they might just be playing a game with me. I don't want to think that about people, and I won't, and the consequence of that is I might get my ass handed to me once

in a while, but I'd rather get hurt than be totally jaded about everybody and never give anybody a chance.

Markson also talked about owning your mistakes and being honest with students about them:

> You're going to make mistakes … probably some big whoppers. And to be honest with your people and tell them, "Hey, you know what? I'm learning here too," and be forthright and don't try to pull power plays on them, and don't try to bluff your way through it, but be human. I think that they'll respond well to that. They will be a partner for you instead of peons that are feeding from your hand, which is not how I think it should be.

Again, you don't have to tell students your life story, but it can help build trust if you're honest about problems you are facing that might have an effect on your class. Sarah Davies told me a story about a teacher who wasn't honest with students and how it hurt credibility:

> I had a teacher who was obviously exhausted and had not made time in their life for teaching and did not want to admit it, and so told the class, "Oh, well, you know, I just moved a bunch of stuff, and my house is full of boxes, and so we can't meet tonight." And then someone else who lived quite near them volunteered *their* house, but then the excuse changed. I forget what it changed to—"We can't do that because of some other reason." It was clear that they were not being open and honest with their students, and I understand the desire to save face and try to have some semblance of authority, but it really ended up making them lack all credibility.

Once you lose credibility, it can be difficult to impossible to regain it. Adult learners approach learning critically, and they're less likely to continue working with a teacher they no longer trust or feel they can rely on.

Don't Be Dogmatic

If there is one thing I have learned in more than twenty years in the Pagan community, it's that there is rarely one right, true, and only answer to *anything* in Paganism. Creating an atmosphere of exploration, not dogma, helps facilitate learning; rigidity shuts it down. Sarah Davies commented on being dogmatic:

> I think a lot of our philosophy is *not* to impart our philoso-phy—to try really hard not to be dogmatic and not to tell them what's right and what's wrong and what they should be doing, but more to help them find themselves and find the path that's functional and fulfilling for them.

Sylva Markson also talked about teaching with flexibility:

> The bottom line is someone's spiritual path is *their* spiritual path. It's not mine. And yes, they might very well be walking that path alongside me for a time in their lives, because I'm their teacher and that's the way it's going to be for the time being.... I certainly don't want to force my viewpoints down someone else's throat if it's not a good fit for them, because it's their spirituality, not mine. I go to great pains to under-score the thought that we can have different viewpoints; that we don't have to all agree; that we're all adults—every one of us in the group is an adult—and we all have our own life expe-riences, we all have our own personalities, and we all have our own thoughts about things.

Nobody likes being told "it's my way or the highway," and adult learn-ers are particularly turned off by that kind of inflexibility. Brian Rowe talks about putting aside the dogma to make space for exploration:

> A lot of my philosophy around learning is creating an envi-ronment where individuals can explore, learn, and even fail, and then iteratively try again. The experience, to me, is more

important than esoteric, abstract facts, and the more opportunities that are given to try, the more that can be gained or
gleaned out of what happens.

As Brian points out, sometimes the experience is more important than
the facts. The difference between facts and experience is similar to the difference between believing in something and knowing it. I have often said
that one of the great things about being Pagan is that we participate in
the world around us—the cycles of the earth, the patterns of nature. We
don't have to have faith and belief in the Divine around us because we
know—we experience it. This doesn't mean facts aren't important; one of
the most basic things teachers do is pass along facts. But if we're too rigid
and dogmatic, we don't leave space for experimentation and gnosis, two
things that are inherent in Paganism.

If that isn't reason enough to chuck the dogma—or at least the dogmatic attitude—here's another: teaching is one of the best ways to learn,
and if we as teachers think that we have the world all figured out—that
we are "right"—we miss out on the opportunities to learn that teaching
and our students present us.

Don't Expect Perfection—Yours or Theirs

If you want to create a positive learning environment, it's important
as a teacher to let go of the idea that you have to be—or pretend to be—
perfect. It sets you and your students up for disappointment and creates
an unnecessary barrier between you and them. If you're going to teach,
get realistic about who you are and what you are doing. If your students
wanted to learn from saints, they'd go to church. Sylva Markson commented about perfectionism:

> Don't expect perfection out of yourself, and don't try to
> pretend to your students that you're perfect. You're human.
> You're on a journey as much as they are. If they're going to
> be in your group, they are partners with you on your journey,

and you are a partner with them on theirs. So get off your high horse and just be a human being.

One thing teachers of adult learners—especially teachers who like to be perceived as perfect—need to come to terms with is that their students might very well know more about or be better at something than they are. Melanie Henry commented about this:

> You have to be willing to look at what you're not good at and get that there are going to be people who are good at every single thing you're not. Especially if it embarrasses you. You are going to have students good at that, because that's just the way it goes. And you've got to be okay with that.

T. Thorn Coyle's advice for new teachers works well for teachers who want to be perfect: "Listen. Come from your core. Connect. Don't try to teach everything. Try to pass on one thing." The closer you stay to your core—to your true self, with all its glories and limitations—the more accessible and effective you'll be as a teacher.

The job of an educator is to teach students to see the vitality in themselves.

JOSEPH CAMPBELL

CHAPTER 9
Taking It Online

Teaching via the web offers some awesome possibilities for Pagan teachers. It can provide greater flexibility than in-person classes, especially if lessons are not delivered in real time—students can take the classes when their schedules allow. It also allows you a greater reach as a teacher. Not only can you teach more students, you can teach people who are not living in your area or any area in which you are likely to travel. T. Thorn Coyle told me about her experiences using online teaching to reach a wide variety of people:

> I love the variety of people that get to interact via online classes. The wealth of experience they bring and the perspectives from living all over the world make the discovery of our commonalities all the more poignant. Plus, it is a great way for people to spend time studying according to their work or family schedules, it being less tied to real-time events, with the exceptions of things like chats or in-person weekends if it is that sort of a class.

As I mentioned in the introduction, there are far more people seeking teaching than there are teachers, so another great benefit of online teaching is that one teacher can reach more people online than he or she could in person. This can be especially good for students who live in an area where there are few or no other Pagans, or for students who can't find the "flavor" of Paganism they want in their local area.

And Thorn mentioned another benefit—networking:

The other helpful aspect to online classes is that we can access a variety of teachers and share ideas readily with people of many traditions. This, of course, can become a distraction from settling into deep work, but it doesn't have to be.

Of course, online teaching has its challenges, too. One big challenge that teachers face online is that online students usually don't get the face to face interaction that they would in an in-person class, which can make communication more difficult. Christopher Penczak commented:

> I find that it is harder to evaluate the energy of a situation online. I'm going on people's direct feedback written down, but I don't have a sense of facial expression and energetic expressions. I realize I rely a lot on energy and auras when I teach, so I've had to follow my gut or ask internal questions about homework assignments to give the proper feedback.

Another challenge is that it can be harder to build strong bonds with your students if you never meet them face to face. This is not such a big deal for one-off classes or short series, but it is a bigger issue for people who are trying to establish long-term student-teacher relationships. It's hard to build those bonds over the web.

And Thorn pointed out that some kinds of teachers and learners—especially the more self-sufficient ones—do better with online courses than others do:

> Also, if students are really in trouble and don't speak up, it can be hard to offer the best sort of help. My students have learned to be pretty self-sufficient because of things like distance, but also, nurturing is not my nature. It is more my way to offer some techniques, insights, or ideas, and let people explore them on their own. For other teachers or students this would not work at all, and I acknowledge that. Friends of mine only teach one-on-one or in very small groups and find that to be best for them and for their apprentices. That is not my strength, nor did I ever expect that from my teachers. Even

though I was sometimes taught one-on-one or in small groups, I was still expected to go off and just do the work myself, with minimal support. That worked for me.

I also asked Holli Emore about the differences between teaching online and in person:

As a teacher myself, both occasionally at Cherry Hill Seminary and in my consulting profession, I would say that it's really not very different. As mentioned before, I'm not going to have the visual cues that one has in a site-based classroom, but then we are not working with undergrads or grade school. Our students bring, in some cases, a whole career's worth of experience with them, and I've seen classes that practically ran themselves, so eager were the students to dive into the material and discuss it with others.

Oberon Zell-Ravenheart, co-founder of the online Grey School of Wizardry, also commented on the differences:

Well, online teaching requires many of the same skills as classroom teaching, but also the ability to express oneself extremely well in writing—and for different ages. Also, online teaching isn't time- and space-bound the way classroom teaching is. Lessons and assignments come in around the clock, from throughout the world, rather than in a fixed time and place. In many ways this is much easier, because teachers can sit at home, don't have to dress up, and can respond to students' questions and grade assignments at their own convenience. Since the teachers aren't seeing the students face to face, there's no question of favoritism based on appearance, race, sex, age, clothes, etc. But by the same token, all the visual cues we so depend on for daily communications and feedback are entirely absent online: facial expressions, body language, etc. So teachers have to be able to deal with that.

Communication issues do arise on the web, but Holli Emore points out that correspondence courses have always had that issue:

> Obviously, we have little in the way of visual or audio cues. That said, we are finding that Cherry Hill Seminary is actually out ahead of most universities in the country, who are still very tied to the older distance-education models. Some of us might remember taking home a box of audiocassettes or videotapes and, basically, working through something more like an old correspondence course. I know that I took courses in the 1980s in which I never knew who my instructors were.

Ways to Teach Online

There are many ways to teach online, but most people who are teaching Paganism online seem to follow one of these three models:

- The "If I Post It, They Will Come" approach: Posting videos, podcasts, or complete lessons online but not interacting with students who use them, except maybe by enabling the comments feature and reading the feedback.
- The "Kitchen Sink" approach: Teaching using a variety of web technologies (webpages, chat, Skype, video, email, IM, podcasts, blogs, interactive web workspaces, etc.), some interactive and some not, pieced together to make a complete experience.
- The "Full Monty" approach: Using an LMS (learning management software) program, frequently also incorporating several of the technologies from the Kitchen Sink approach.

The "If I Post It, They Will Come" Approach

Posting material for people to find online is a good way to get started teaching, get feedback before developing it into a full class, or supplement a full online or in-person class. Posting text lessons, videos, or podcasts (podcasts are non-streaming audio or video files on the web) is a great way to reach a lot of students all over the world. You can create a lesson, video, or podcast on a single topic or multiple topics, or spread one topic across several segments.

Podcasts and videos give students a chance to listen to a real person instead of reading a blog or website, and they give you an opportunity to practice modulating your speech for times when you might be in front of live students. Podcasts and videos are usually released serially, and they are sometimes syndicated. You can also work with Pagan bloggers and website owners to syndicate your podcasts or videos and/or get the word out about them. A great example of a podcast series is T. Thorn Coyle's *Elemental Castings* (www.thorncoyle.com). Thorn talked to me about her podcasts:

> *Elemental Castings* has turned out to be a great way for people to not only access my work, but the work of all of the incredible authors, magic workers, and teachers I have as guests. People from all over the world tune in to those podcasts, which feels so gratifying.

Proud Pagan Podcasters is a website dedicated to using podcasts to enrich communication in the Pagan community. If you're interested in learning how to make a podcast, check out their Getting Started with Podcasting page for tips (http://paganpodcasting.org/resources/get-started-with-podcasting).

The "Kitchen Sink" Approach

The majority of online Pagan teachers, at least for now, seem to structure their classes to distribute their lessons via a website as lecture MP3s, videos, or podcasts, and using chat rooms, Skype, and email lists to interact with students. Christopher Penczak's web classes follow a similar model:

> We don't have a specific time to teach together online in a chat room. I send out a recording of the lecture and additional notes that are not in the [Temple of Witchcraft] books we use as a text, along with a syllabus and assignments. Students email their completed questions and experiences for critical feedback

and evaluation each month. We have a Yahoo group for group discussion and sharing, and community support.

By cobbling together several technologies, Pagan teachers can create a rich learning experience online.

The "Full Monty" Approach

Some Pagan teachers (such as T. Thorn Coyle) and Pagan organizations (such as Cherry Hill Seminary) are using the "Kitchen Sink" technologies in conjunction with learning management system (LMS) software. LMS software, such as Moodle, can help you create a fully interactive website that allows you to chat with students in real time, post lectures and assignments, and even give and grade tests. Moodle is open source (meaning the code is free and users can alter it). T. Thorn Coyle uses a variety of technologies together, including Moodle, Google+ hangouts, and Skype's online long-distance service:

> I teach stand-alone online courses with homework, discussion groups, and chat rooms. I also use things such as Moodle to supplement in-person training. There is a lot still to learn about using these systems effectively, but even at a basic level, they work pretty well.

Cherry Hill Seminary, which teaches Pagan clergy, also uses Moodle to run its online classes. Holli Emore, executive director of the seminary, explains how this works:

> Each student, upon registration, is given login to the Moodle classroom for that course. In that classroom, the instructor will have posted a syllabus, a beginning-of-the-semester greeting and orientation, and lots of other resources. Each instructor approaches the mechanics of the class a little differently, but most will post a written lesson, sometimes an audio file lecture, sometimes a PowerPoint presentation, etc., followed by assignments, discussion questions for the forum, links to other

resources, etc. Most classes have required texts and periodicals to read. Some classes "meet" regularly by chat or audio call (we use Skype at this time), though some only communicate through the forums.

Depending on your web experience, Moodle can have a learning curve when you are beginning to use it. However, some of the Moodle users I talked to thought it was a breeze. I asked Thorn if she had help setting up and maintaining Moodle:

> I do have help with a lot of the technology I use, partially because my schedule is so packed. I'd rather call upon those who have greater skills instead of learning systems myself. However, Moodle and Skype are really quite simple to learn. Were I more skilled, I could likely do more with Moodle than I do, but it is a very functional system, and Skype is dead easy.

Pete "Pathfinder" Davis commented on the size of the Moodle setup he is using for the Woolston-Steen Seminary and some of the complexities the Aquarian Tabernacle Church dealt with in getting it running:

> We had no idea of the complexities of putting together an online teaching program. There's some basic software with the strange name of Moodle, but it requires an enormous amount of server space, and so the seminary programs are spread out over six different servers—six different actual websites—but you don't know it when you go to wiccanseminary.edu and it redirects you to the other places, depending on what you want to do. It's spread all over the place because it's enormous. Thank god for geeks, because to me that thing is just a fancy typewriter.

Like Cherry Hill Seminary and Thorn, some Pagan teachers use Skype to enhance their web teaching and give students a chance to interact with each other via group voice chat or video chat. This helps them personalize their teaching and give students a face to put with their teacher's name. You can also use Skype to do one-on-one student mentoring. Others use interactive broadcast platforms such as Ustream to show students events or classes happening in the moment.

Beyond the Full Monty

You know that phrase "Time stands still for no one"? Well, technology never stands still either, and most of the time it doesn't even slow down long enough to catch its breath. Although LMS and the other technologies I've discussed will probably be with us for quite a while, educators are beginning to look to cloud computing (usually referred to as "the cloud") to provide learning experiences online.

The general idea of the cloud is that software applications, servers, content, and databases can be accessed via a web service rather than locally, as is the case for a software program on your hard drive or a server in your office. The owners of the web service provide access to many different people or organizations, so resources are shared. The cloud is often likened to a utility service such as gas or electricity. You pay for the service monthly rather than owning all the software or hardware (you'll still need a computer, of course).

The benefit of the cloud for educators is that their online courses don't have to be contained in an LMS or other software structure, and it might be possible to use the cloud to provide a much more personalized learning experience for each student. LMS technology emerged in the early days of the web, and thus it was born from older ideas about the ways people could and should learn online. But both the web and online learning have evolved since then, and educators are looking to the flexibility of the cloud to help them meet the rapidly changing needs of students and the education market.

As a Pagan teacher, however, the important thing to remember with any of these technologies—from podcasts to the cloud—is that you should choose the tool that's right for the job rather than going for the one with the most bells and whistles, just because you can. Some teaching is best accomplished with a simple, uncomplicated delivery. On the other hand, if you are tech-savvy, your options are broadening every day.

SOME GENERAL GUIDELINES
FOR ONLINE CLASSES

Best practices for online teaching are changing rapidly as we learn about the many ways people interact with the web and the effect the web has on assimilation of information. (A recent book about this that you might find interesting—and a little scary—is *The Shallows* by Nicholas Carr.) And not many online teaching practices have substantial scientific validation behind them (so far). Without knowing what technology you might use to teach your class, it's impossible for me to make specific recommendations for your course. However, there are some general overall guidelines you can use to design and teach an online class that apply to many of the technologies you might use. For more specifics, I highly recommend you visit the eLearn Magazine website (http://elearnmag .acm.org), which contains very helpful in-depth information on teaching online and designing online classes. There are also some sites and books listed in the resources at the end of this book that can provide more specific guidance for your particular situation and needs. And if you think you'd like to try Moodle, there's a strong Moodle support community online.

Course Description and Course Syllabus

The course description and course syllabus are important parts of any class, whether it's online or in person, but they are particularly essential in an online class, where students can't ask you questions quite as easily as they can when they're standing right in front of you. Use the tips in chapter 6 for creating a course description and syllabus for a traditional course. If students will be required to use any particular technology to access or participate in your class—email, IM, chat, video streaming, Skype, camera—list it up front, along with the version, if applicable.

When writing a syllabus for an online class, follow the guidelines for an in-person class syllabus from chapter 6, and also consider the ideas below. Remember that in a traditional classroom, you would probably explain a lot of these things on the first day in person:

- Post or email the syllabus well before the class.

- List any passwords students will need to access the class content.

- As with a traditional syllabus, the syllabus for an online class should be detailed and outline what you hope to accomplish with each class session (if your format has sessions), including learning objectives. The general wisdom is that since you won't be interacting with students as directly, it's best to make an online syllabus even more detailed than you might make a regular syllabus.

- List any texts students will be required to use. Sometimes online students like to have texts to refer to, especially if they weren't raised with the web. "Texts" can also refer to URLs for online texts or content.

- Include your "attendance policy," if you have one (for example, rules about participation in a chat room with the rest of a class at a certain time), and what your overall expectations are for student participation.

- Make sure the syllabus contains your contact information and your online "office hours," if you have them. If you have preferences about how and when you should be contacted, state those as well.

- Include in the syllabus the format(s) in which you would like students to submit homework or assignments, and how soon they can expect to receive feedback.

- Include information on what students should do if they encounter technical issues—contact you or a specified technology help person, refer to a troubleshooting website you create, etc.

- It helps to post the syllabus in multiple places and also email it to students. Students will invariably lose it (as they often do paper ones in traditional classes), so having the syllabus in several places is a good idea.

Getting Students Used to the Technology

Students might or might not have experience using whatever technology you're using to deliver your class. Here are a few things you can do to help them get used to the technology and feel more comfortable with it:

- Provide or point students to documentation or video demonstrations about how to use the technology.

- Make sure you understand the technology thoroughly yourself so you can help students troubleshoot if they have problems. Another option is to have a tech-savvy friend on call to help with problems.

- If possible, provide students with access to the technology or tool before the class starts so they can explore it a little.

- Consider making your first assignment one that will require students to use the main types of technology you'll be using in class.

- During class sessions, remember to allow download time for videos, etc. Not everyone will have a rocket-speed Internet connection.

Interacting with Students Online

Since you usually can't rely on facial and body cues when you're teaching online, the general wisdom is that you need to compensate for that in other ways. Here are some tips for communicating with students online:

- Give feedback quickly, constructively, and frequently. Students need to know there's someone there if they can't see your face.

- Use whatever tools you have at your disposal to foster communication between students so they can support each other and trade ideas. Use technology such as chat rooms, streaming video, and private email lists to help the group interact and bond.

- Make sure your expectations for everything—homework, class participation, respectful behavior between students, etc.—are very, very clear. Post them and restate them. Students can't ask you about expectations face to face, so they need extra support here.

- Even in this day and age, some students might not be used to interacting online, so you might need to teach them a little netiquette.

- When you're about a quarter of the way through the class— enough so that people are settling in but not so far that you can't change direction if you need to—ask for student feedback about the class and what, if anything, you could do differently to make it work for them.

- Set boundaries as you would if you were teaching in person. In certain situations you might need to explain these rather than model them, since you're not face to face.

- Positively reinforce well-reasoned answers and posts by students, either privately or "in front" of the group.

- Refer to students by name, as if they were in the room with you.

- Don't use sarcasm or irony. It doesn't translate well online, and it's possible people will misunderstand or be offended.

Leading Online Discussions

There are many ways you can lead a discussion online. Below are just a few ideas, which I hope will inspire you to come up with your own. As you would in an in-person class, be sure to model and reinforce respectful discussion and shut down non-constructive arguments or flaming. Remember, too, to give adequate reading time and think time after posing a question. Since many online discussions are in text (unless you're using video conferencing or Skype), people need time to read the question, think about it, and type a response.

- Have students post discussion questions, rather than you suggesting them. Consider having the student who suggested the question moderate the discussion about it.

- Raise an issue with two or more possible "sides." Use the polling feature of an LMS or Survey Monkey (a website that allows you to build online surveys) to find out which position students agree with most and why. Use the results to discuss the topic.

- Break students into groups and give each group a few questions related to the topic to answer together. Have students post their answers.

- Post a question or issue for a particular class session several days before the class, using an LMS or blog. Have students use the comment feature to answer. You can use this technique by itself or to prepare them for a full-group discussion.

Organizing Your Content

Although the technology used to teach online varies from what you might use in the classroom, the basic principles and best practices for organizing the two types of courses often overlap. Using the class creation technique described in chapter 6 can serve as a starting point. Write your SMART objectives, place them in a reasonable order, and determine how you will teach each one, whether it be through a video or podcast, an interactive quiz in an LMS or discussion or activity staged in a chatroom. How you present your content will, of course, depend on the technology at your disposal.

One place where online course creation is very different from creating an in-person course is that depending on the technology you use, your students might have the option to navigate through your class material in an order that's different from what you intended. They might skip around, try different sections and return to them later, or simply go through the material in an order that makes more sense to them than the one you chose. This isn't always ideal, since sometimes topics build on each other and students need to understand a foundational concept before they can grasp a more complex one, but where the order of instruction is less crucial, technology can offer more flexibility to students to choose to learn or absorb information in the way that makes the most sense to them. Online teachers handle this in a number of different ways, including but not limited to setting things up so the content has to be read in a specific order, making suggestions of different effective ways to navigate through the information, and/or creating modules of information in the course that stand alone and aren't dependent on the others.

One generally accepted (but hardly unanimous) principle about online content is that it should be presented in smaller chunks than you would use if you were presenting it live. For example, a lecture that you might give in person would be tedious in type on the web (although it might work as a video or podcast), so you would break apart the lecture content into small, easily absorbed sections, and place them on multiple pages if you are presenting the content in text or find more dynamic ways to present them. Some other general guidelines for organizing the content of your class and choosing the appropriate technologies (or, in some cases, the other way around) are:

- Organize the content in a progressive way that makes sense to you, with one topic building on another, but when the nature of the content makes it possible, create navigation that allows users to use the content out of order or in an order that makes more sense to them.

- Don't use every technology at your disposal just because you can. Consider carefully whether the technology you want to use will be effective for teaching the particular objective you are working on. Don't use so many technologies in one class that you confuse people.

- Remember that not everyone will have the latest processor and fastest Internet connection. Some of the more bandwidth-hogging technologies might make it difficult for some students to complete your class.

Don't forget that although you have many options, simpler is sometimes better. At my day job we recently released two online trainings. The first consisted of a set of video modules, with the idea that a group of teachers would gather together, watch the modules, and have a discussion after each one. The other was a full-blown Moodle setup, complete with online quizzes, games, and other interactive features. Guess which one the teachers use? The relatively simple, uncomplicated video modules.

TEACHING TECHNIQUES AND ACTIVITIES FOR ONLINE CLASSES

Here are a few general guidelines for online activities:

- Most activities you do online will take longer than they would if you were doing them in person, in part because of the time lag due to technology, and also because people can't see each other and interact directly. Plan accordingly.

- Try to use both synchronous (activities that students do at the same time or together) and asynchronous (activities done separately) techniques.

- As with in-person teaching, use a variety of large- and small-group activities, and try to choose activities and techniques that touch on multiple learning styles. It's harder to include hands-on activities online, but if all else fails, you can always assign them as homework or independent study to be done away from the computer.

- As you might have guessed already, many of the teaching techniques listed in chapter 5 for an in-person class need to be modified if you are going to use them online, but most of them are usable if you have an interactive online workspace or if you do some of the synchronous activities asynchronously.

A Note About
Web Accessibility

Making a website "accessible" means using certain practices to ensure that people with disabilities can use the site. For example, there are ways to tag images and links to make them more compatible with software and hardware used by the blind to convert text to speech or Braille. Explaining accessibility best practices is way beyond the scope of this book, but if you are interested in making your site accessible, there are a variety of websites detailing how to do it, as well as YouTube tutorials. Following accessibility guidelines will add another layer of complexity to setting up your class, but it might be worth it to you if it means a wider variety of students can access your teachings. Accessibility is considered very important in the professional teaching community.

Reconciling Nature and the Web

As I was writing this section about teaching online, I thought about the nature orientation of many Pagan paths and wondered whether it was possible to reconcile use of the web and other modern technologies with our love of the natural world. I am very interested in online education technologies—I use them constantly in my day job—and am very excited about the possibilities they have for teaching Paganism, but I also agree with what Patrick McCollum said in chapter 2 about teaching outside, or at least in a place where you can feel connected to nature. I suppose you could haul your laptop outside and take a Pagan course (as long as you could get wifi), but it just doesn't quite seem right to me.

I asked T. Thorn Coyle, who frequently teaches online, if she ever found that she had to reconcile a love of nature and teaching on the web for herself, and if so, how she did it. I thought her comments could be illuminating for any Pagan who is considering teaching online:

Humans are part of nature, and therefore these technologies were made by animals. Some human activity helps support the health of nature, and some activity is detrimental. In this way, we are not dissimilar to termites or beavers, for example. I have more of an issue with my expenditure of jet fuel for my out-of-town workshops than I do with teaching via computer. Since I have chosen to teach in these ways, rather than teaching five people at a time in my home, I have to reconcile myself to the fact that I do harm. I simply work with the hope that the good my work provides outweighs the harm.

The other thing I do, however, is emphasize the importance of the physical in our practice, the importance of recognizing nature in all her forms, and honoring that with more than our words. By becoming more integrated, it becomes more and more difficult to not recognize when our choices are disconnected from our ideals. We learn to eat healthy food, to exercise and rest, to recycle, to compost, to not drive so much, to work for clean water, to lobby for better treatment for animals, and to save trees.

In addition to the environmental ways Thorn suggests for connecting our choices and ideals, your online class can also include assignments that involve meditating or exercising outside to tune in with the rhythms of nature. It's important to encourage online students to get out of their chairs and away from their screens and interact with the "real world" whenever you can, otherwise what you're teaching them online is purely theoretical. Wiccan and Pagan traditions tend to be very hands-on—we have physical and mental connections to our gods and nature's cycles—so make use of that to give students ways to balance screen time with other priorities and align with what you're teaching them in a physical way.

Teachers who inspire know that teaching is like cultivating a garden, and those who would have nothing to do with thorns must never attempt to gather flowers.

AUTHOR UNKNOWN

CHAPTER 10

A Few Possible Pitfalls

There are some traps that even the best teachers are vulnerable to falling into, and many of them sneak up on us when we're distracted and looking the other way. Often, as teachers, we're so busy dealing with the little things—the details, the day-to-day issues that arise—that we don't look at the bigger picture, and we don't see problems brewing until they've taken a firm hold.

However, as grandmothers are fond of saying, an ounce of prevention is worth a pound of cure. If you know about some of the possible problems you might encounter, you are more likely to be able to avoid or minimize them. The point of this chapter isn't to frighten you away from teaching but rather to help you recognize and ward off problems before they get out of hand.

YOUR BEST DEFENSE: NOT AVOIDING CONFLICT

The challenges you might encounter as a teacher might be simple, or they might be complex and complicated, but almost all of them will require you to communicate clearly with students about the problem and not avoid conflict. These situations usually require that most dreaded of teacher-student communications: the "difficult conversation," otherwise known as calling them on their crap (or them calling you on yours) and coaching them to work through whatever the problem is. And it's your

job as the teacher to make sure that the difficult conversation happens
and things aren't left to fester.

For the record, I *hate* having this kind of conversation. I always figured
that was a result of my personal baggage, because I'm a proper passive-
aggressive Midwesterner who dislikes confrontation. But it didn't take
me long to discover that a lot of teachers—maybe even most teachers—
hate it as much as I do. However, we can't bury our heads in the sand and
avoid confrontation with students. For their benefit, and for the sake of
everyone else in the class, we as teachers have to get over our reticence in
this kind of situation and be the leaders our students need and expect us
to be. And that means having uncomfortable conversations.

Sarah Davies talked to me about the value of getting past your fear
and initiating this kind of talk:

> I'm the kind of person who doesn't like to have personal con-
> versations and will avoid conflict, but I definitely see how if
> we end up with a difficult personality it's way better to have
> that difficult conversation early. It's easier for me to have that
> difficult conversation having been on the side of the dedicated
> student who would really do anything to make this work.

Anne Marie Forrester told me a story about getting past her own fears
of confrontation in dealing with the problems caused by a student and
stressed the importance of having the conversation with kindness and
respect:

> The trickiest part—and I think this is true whether it's the
> coven or workplace or personal relationships of any kind—
> is that you have to confront people and be very up front and
> honest with them, which is really hard. But at the same time
> you have to do it in a respectful way that's kind, if possible.
> We've had to do this with a couple of people now. It's impor-
> tant to take the time to talk with them in private, not in front
> of the whole group. Then we can say things like, "We've

noticed that you're not always respectful to the other members of this group, and we would like you to work on that" or "We work by consensus here, and some of your behavior has caused hard feelings among some of our other members. We can't tell you who or why, and we're deeply sorry about that, but you have to go." Not being afraid of confrontation has been a really difficult lesson for me to learn; however, it is the most honest and respectful way to be, and it saves a lot of unnecessary pain in the end.

I've personally found the compassionate approach to be very helpful. Sometimes when you point out a person's disruptive behavior to them, they appreciate being talked to because they didn't even know they were behaving that way. Sometimes your compassionate and calm handling of the issue defuses the behavior immediately; the disruptive person picks up on your calm energy and responds in kind. And sometimes the compassionate approach encourages them to behave when they see the contrast between their behavior and the way you are treating them when you are dealing with it. If you want them to change their behavior and not leave the class or group, the compassionate approach—rather than an angry or accusatory one—allows them some dignity and you the opportunity to coach them on what better or more acceptable behavior might be.

Being compassionate doesn't mean being a doormat, being passive-aggressive, or letting the student manipulate you if the problem you're having is with a student. It means standing your ground and handling the situation with respect and empathy, and getting tough if the compassion doesn't work. If you are teaching online, you can still use the compassionate approach via chat, email, phone, or however you communicate with students. Just remember to word what you're saying carefully, and keep in mind that email can be forwarded, so don't write anything in frustration that you don't want the world to see.

It's important to keep the upper hand. By this I don't mean "beat students into submission," no matter how tempting that might be at times. I mean keeping things flowing smoothly and not letting students take control of your class. Melanie Henry talked to me about this:

> One always has to keep the upper hand, but keeping the upper hand doesn't have to be just the main show of force.... It's energy perceptions and keeping a good idea on where your leverage point is; like the philosopher said, "I know I can move anything if I know where to stand."

Good Pagan teachers use all of the tools at their disposal—both the "regular" senses like sight and hearing and energetic or psychic senses— to make sure they have their thumb on the pulse of what's going on in their class.

Some Specific Challenges with Students

Students Who Don't Get Along

Nearly everyone has been in a class where another student drove them nuts—the person who won't shut up, the person who is rude, the person who demands the teacher's attention all the time, the person who won't do his or her share of a group project—and most people deal with it by gritting their teeth and bearing it or talking to the person they're having a problem with in order to try to solve the problem and get the most out of the course without detracting from anyone else's learning. Sometimes, however, one student's irritation or anger at another affects the whole class.

To me, the commonly used Wiccan phrase "perfect love and perfect trust" doesn't mean that you completely love and trust each person you're going to be in a circle or room with; it means that you have the perfect—or right—amount of "love" (or regard for) and trust for them so that you can put aside any beefs you might have with them at least long enough to do your circle or class, and keep your feelings from tempering the experience for yourself and others. Stating that perfect love and perfect trust (or just plain respect and good manners) are expected in your class is a very good ground rule. If students can't seem to get along anyway, you have several options:

- Encourage students to talk to each other if they have problems. Often they'll mediate their own problems.

- If they can't solve the problem themselves, take one or both parties aside privately—together or separately—and have one of those "difficult conversations" I mentioned earlier.

- If the conflict appears to be a no-fault situation, you can ask the people involved to go into a separate room and come back when they've sorted it out, with or without you mediating.

If you believe one of the parties in the dispute is being bullied by the other—adults can bully as well or better than kids can—try these steps:

- Take the two people aside separately. The person being bullied will be much more comfortable and up front about what's going on if the person who is bullying is not there.

- Reassure the person being bullied that you've heard what he or she has to say about the situation, you understand, and you are taking action.

- When you talk to the person who is bullying, try to find out why he or she is doing it.

- If there's a reason—he or she is upset or nervous or just doesn't have great social skills—you might be able to coach him or her through it.

- If there's no reason, or if the person is just a jerk, don't hesitate to boot him or her.

Keeping an unrepentant bully around is one of the best ways I can think of to sabotage your class by destroying morale, peace, and trust.

Your students come to you for spiritual teaching, not to be traumatized. You're not their parent, and you're not running a nanny state, but it's your responsibility as a teacher to try to create an environment that is safe and conducive to learning. Trust me: if you notice there's something going on, students in your class who are not involved in the conflict have noticed it too—and probably before you did. The teacher is often the last to know.

Students Who Get Along Too Well

Naturally, you want your students to bond. These bonds make communication, energy flow, ritual, and magic smoother. But sometimes problems can arise when two or three students like each other so much that they form a group within your group, something like a high-school clique. If it's just a mini mutual-admiration society and the members are still doing their work and not disrupting the class, it's not necessarily a big deal. But sometimes cliques become a bit like black holes in the middle of your group: they focus inward rather than on whatever the greater group is doing and they pull people off track, first within the clique and then other members of the class.

There's also the issue of exclusion. If there's a tight-knit group within your group, the students who aren't members of the clique might feel alienated and left out. Of course there's no rule that says everyone has to like or be friends with everyone else. But when students come together to learn, things work better if each person can treat the others in the group relatively equally, at least during class.

The other potential danger of cliques is when and if they break up, the fallout can affect the whole group. Friendships that happen quickly and deeply sometimes blow up equally spectacularly. Two BFFs who suddenly decide they can't stand each other can disrupt and divide your group.

Here are some ways to reduce the impact of a clique or discourage cliques from forming:

- Encourage students to socialize as a whole group outside of class.

- Plan in-class activities that require working with a partner or small group, and keep mixing up the participants so everyone gets a chance to work with everyone else.

- Online you can encourage students to chat or email with everyone in class.

And of course if a clique does form and it's starting to disrupt your class, you can pull the members aside and have yet another one of those difficult conversations. Stress that you're glad they're friends, but that their relationship is a distraction to others, and ask them to leave it at the door when they come to class.

Students Who Don't Do Their Work

Having students who don't do their work regularly—whether it be assignments you give, at-home spiritual practice, or work on their personal issues—can be a big problem. At first it seems like they're only hurting themselves when they don't do their work, but if you have a couple of people who constantly refuse to do their work, it can reduce the morale of the overall group and hold everyone else back. Students not doing their work can really suck the energy out of a class, and it can also diminish the respect the other students have for you as their teacher, especially if you let the ones not doing their work get away with it.

If it's just one or two students who are not doing their work, take them aside privately and ask them why. It might be that they don't understand the assignments, or there could be other things going on that are preventing them from finding time. It might also be that they aren't getting what they wanted to out of the class or they are having a problem with your communication or teaching style. If that is the case, ask them what you could change that might help them get more out of the class, and incorporate their suggestions if you can. Adult learners often have a good sense of what they need in order to learn; it's possible that you can learn a teaching trick or two from them in these situations.

Some other options are:

- Be sure to give students reasonable assignments and enough time to do them. Adult learners have a lot of other things going on in their lives.

- Offer help. Sometimes students—even adult students—don't do their work because they're confused or overwhelmed and afraid to ask for assistance.

- Make it clear to students that you're not assigning busywork; the assignments you give are designed to help them on their spiritual path.

It's a good idea to make it clear up front that you expect people to do their work, and if they don't, that might hold the whole class back. It's especially frustrating if you give them an assignment and plan to have a group discussion about the work in the next class and some people don't do it. Sometimes just saying that out loud will encourage people to follow through, if only because they don't want to incur the wrath of everyone else in the class.

A few times when I've had students show up without doing their work I have asked them to do it orally in front of the class. Being put on the spot generally deters most people from not doing their work again, although some people actually seem to enjoy making an impromptu presentation more than doing whatever the assignment was.

Another option is not to base your lesson on students having done their previous assignment. The problem with this is that students generally learn more from doing follow-up or going over assignments in class with their peers. Just collecting the work from those who have done it and giving the eyebrow to those who haven't doesn't give students the chance for peer feedback and interaction.

Whatever you do, do not allow the number of incidents of students not doing their work to escalate. It will drag your class to a screeching halt. My student group has been together for many years now, and during that time there have been periods of ennui where students didn't feel motivated or were too wrapped up in whatever was going on in their personal lives to make the class a priority. Groups that stay together over long periods of time ebb and flow in terms of motivation. It's important to address the issue openly with students if you hit one of these lulls, whether your group is long-term or not. It's possible that there is something you can change in the way you're teaching, making assignments, or presenting information that will help motivate them again. It's a two-way street; they have to do the work, but you need to continue to provide them with work that is meaningful to them and good reasons to do it. If they've really lost their motivation, it might be better for them to take a sabbatical and spend some time thinking about what they really want or need.

Students Who Are Chronically Late or Absent

Like students who don't do their work, students who are frequently late or absent can have a big impact on the morale of your class.

To minimize this problem:

- Make sure you're clear up front about your expectations about attendance—what you'll put up with and what you won't—and stick to your guns.

- Set up a policy that people need to contact you a certain number of days or hours before class to tell you if they won't be there.

- Make sure everyone is aware of the class schedule, and let everyone know about schedule changes as far in advance as you can.

- If you are running a long-term group, such as a coven or grove, involve everyone in creating the schedule so their needs are more likely to be accommodated.

- Consider posting the schedule online, so people can see it anytime, or using an online calendar, such as Google Calendar. People will still call you at the last minute to ask, "Do we have class tonight?" even if it's posted online in blinking neon lime-green 24-point type, but this should at least reduce these annoying calls.

If students are late or absent anyway, it's best to address these issues privately with the students in question. If they've just lost motivation, ask them if they know what might help them get it back. And if they don't think they can recapture it, suggest that they leave the class until they can make a commitment to being there regularly and participating fully.

Although it's best to address the issue privately with students, it's good to let the remaining students know you've done something about it once you have. Students who are responsible and on time get frustrated when they think their teacher isn't dealing with issues of absenteeism. After all, why should they make time in their schedule to be somewhere and put in the effort to be on time if others aren't doing the same thing?

My husband and I asked one student to leave because of chronic absenteeism, and we waited far too long and put up with far too much before we did it. The student was in a period of transition, and we tried to be accommodating, but we bent over too far, and it frustrated and angered some of our other students. They finally ganged up on us and asked us to cut the other student loose—and they were right. Don't let it come to that in your own class. The students shouldn't have to school the teacher.

Emotional Baggage, Disclosure, and Crisis

Let's face it: teaching means dealing with people—and all of the good, the bad, and the ugly that implies. Your interactions with people as a teacher can be limited to presenting information and answering questions, but sometimes when you are teaching spiritual topics, deeper issues rise to the surface.

Students might disclose to you relatively simple things such as anxiety all the way up to revelations of rape, violence, abuse, and neglect—and the events might have happened in the past or could be happening at the time of disclosure. Don't think that because you're working with adults you're less likely to have a student spill deep, dark secrets to you. These issues can come up for any person at any time, regardless of age. And spirituality classes, for better or worse, can be very conducive to encouraging people to talk about their most troublesome problems. Personally I think it's at least partly due to the fact that if you are working your spiritual path, you are trying to better your life, and really doing that means dealing with—or at least letting go of—the unsavory things in your past or present. For some people, moving forward means that those issues will rise to the surface. When this happens, people look to their teachers for support.

When people are deep into exploring their spirituality, just about anything can be a catalyst for unresolved stuff to come to the forefront. For example, when we are working in light trance and accessing different states of consciousness, the part of our brain that keeps everything (seemingly) under control is distracted and/or bypassed, and all sorts of things—both good and bad—can surface.

Melanie Henry told me about meditation bringing up people's issues:

> People in our class work up to meditating an hour a day, which in itself will bring up a lot of stuff, plus there are various exercises. We tell people that if they take the class to expect to have your stuff come up—have big things happen. This last class was pretty intense because it was even bigger than usual. One woman went through a divorce. One woman's eldest daughter had a baby that she ended up taking temporary custody of. And a third woman had really severe health problems, unfortunately. Generally the kind of intensity that comes up is that their psychological stuff confronts them because of the meditation.

Along those lines, a student of ours once had a frightening experience during a pathworking meditation. Instead of going to a forest glade or wherever our pathworking led, the student ended up in a bedroom where she had been sexually abused by a relative. We stopped the pathworking while the student was in trance and talked her through it. She couldn't go out the door, because the abuser was in the hall, and she couldn't go out the windows, because they were too high. We told her that in folklore mirrors are sometimes considered doors to other worlds, and that if she climbed up on her dresser and crawled through the mirror as if it were a door, she would end up back in the room with us, and the abuser couldn't follow her. She made it back from the pathworking safely, and we did a debriefing to make sure she and the other students were okay. It was a little scary, but we were proud to see how well she dealt with it.

Please note that I am not saying you shouldn't use meditation and pathworking because it will cause traumatic things to happen. It has actually almost always been the opposite for me; I have found meditation and pathworking to be powerful tools for bettering students' lives. I am merely using them as examples to show the kinds of emotional issues you might have to work through with students.

Chances are at some point you'll end up finding yourself in the role of counselor, whether you're qualified for that or not. You can make it clear, as we have in our classes, that you don't take the "ritual as therapy" approach, where a class or ritual is designed to help students overcome problems they might normally deal with in a therapy session, and that students are expected to handle their emotional issues in a healthy way outside of class, possibly with a therapist. As Melanie Henry put it:

> I try to make the point that it's not group therapy. The whole point of this is to work on your own stuff for the purpose of doing ritual.

But even if you draw that boundary, the lines might blur from time to time. Unless you have a background in counseling or therapy, however, it's important to make it clear to students that you're not qualified to counsel them beyond what a knowledgeable friend or family member might do, and to know your limits when it comes to dealing with others' issues. It's crucial to draw this boundary both for them and for you, as Melanie Henry points out:

> Teaching takes being able—being willing—to talk endlessly to people who are freaking out, as needed. And also knowing when you have to be able to say no to people. Because while it is important that you be able to counsel people, it can't suddenly be your job to counsel them through x, y, and z. If they need professional counseling help on an ongoing basis, you're not going to be that person for them.

Sometimes there is a personality trait or teaching style that one teacher has that seems to unlock answers for a student in crisis or a "difficult" student, and it appears that that student and that teacher are "meant" to walk their paths together for a time. I have known many Pagan teachers who have been catalysts like that for a student or students, willingly or unwittingly. Although it might feel that you are destined to help a particular student in crisis, don't let that feeling disarm you and cause you to set aside common sense. It might be that you are just the right person present at the right time to help a particular student. But it might also be that your conviction that this is the case gets you in far over your head, and you do more harm to yourself and the student by preventing him or her from getting more experienced help.

As you develop as a teacher, you will learn more about your own strengths and what you can and can't handle in terms of your students' problems. It might develop that you have a knack for dealing with a particular kind of student that others find difficult. But until you learn what your particular area of expertise in dealing with people is—and even afterward—I highly recommend that you keep resources handy to help you handle crises and emotional situations.

It can be very helpful to keep a list of people or organizations you can refer students to, such as the non-emergency police phone number for your area, the local emergency room, crisis hotlines, women's health clinics, shelters, Child Protective Services, drug and alcohol support groups, and Pagan-friendly therapists. Sometimes when someone is distraught, giving them the phone number of someone who can help makes the difference between them seeking help and not seeking it. When you're in crisis, it can seem overwhelming to find help or even look up a phone number yourself. Check out therapists or other mental health professionals before adding them to your list.

In addition, if you know anyone in the Pagan community or outside of it who is used to dealing with people problems and who can serve as a sounding board or mentor for you as you handle a student in crisis, do not hesitate to call on him or her.

Drugs, Alcohol, and Mental Illness

Students who are recovering from drug or alcohol problems or who have mental health issues might benefit greatly from your class, especially if they are working on those issues and trying to get healthy. Spiritual learning or guidance might help keep them on a positive path. There are lots of recovering addicts and people living with and managing mental illness in the Pagan community, and many of them will tell you that their Paganism makes their struggle easier.

On the other hand, addicts and people with mental illness might also ruin your class or destroy your teaching group, depending on how their particular issue affects their behavior and how their behavior affects those around them.

Your personal experience with drugs, alcohol, and mental illness (and by "personal experience," I mean literally your own experience with those things or having had close friends or relatives who dealt with them, or both) will also color your interactions with people dealing with those issues. Personally, I've had to deal with a lot of addicts in my life. I have the deepest and most profound respect for people who manage to recover from addiction. I believe it is one of the hardest things on earth to do. On the other hand, the behavior of addicts when they're deeply in the throes of addiction—lying, extreme secrecy, emotional withdrawal, erratic behavior, theft, and physical, emotional, and verbal abuse—is extremely destructive, and I don't want to subject myself or my students to it, so addicts who are currently using are not allowed in my group, and we expect everyone to show up for events sober. We consider taking on students who are in recovery and who are not using on a case-by-case basis, just as we do for all students.

We also have some rules about mental illness. Because we have a tight-knit group and we teach out of our home—and because I have seen a few mentally ill individuals wreak havoc on their own lives and the lives of those around them—we ask potential students if they have any mental issues that they need to be taking medication for, what they are, and whether or not they are taking the medication. Our rule is that if a doctor has prescribed you medication, then you need to take it and continue to be under the doctor's care—and to take care of yourself—to be in our class. After that, we take students' mental health issues on a case-by-case basis, based on if or how their issues affect them and the rest of the class.

My husband and I have been presented with more than one opportunity to test what our boundaries are about dealing with students' mental health issues. Once we interviewed a potential student who disclosed that she was schizophrenic. She was very honest and straightforward about it. She was following her doctor's regimen closely, and she was extremely high-functioning, so although we had some reservations, we decided to take her as a student and see how it went. She was a great student—funny, smart, and willing to (gasp!) do her homework—and we liked her a lot and really enjoyed having her in class. But as we got to know her better, we began to wonder if what we were teaching her might actually be harmful to her.

Schizophrenics can have hallucinations and a hard time telling the difference between reality and illusion. When she saw something that she wasn't sure others were seeing, our student used a complex protocol she had created to determine if it was real or a hallucination. We became concerned that what we were teaching—basically using pathworking, energy work, and visualization to sense stuff that doesn't appear to be there when you are using only mundane senses—might confuse or degrade that protocol and make it more difficult for her to function; that what she was doing with us would further blur the line between illusion and reality for her. The more we thought about it, the more frightened we got that we would contribute to making it harder for her to deal with her condition, and that we were not equipped to help her if that happened. So we reluctantly and with great sadness asked her to leave the group.

Some other teachers told us they believed we'd made the right decision, and some told us we were cowards. I suspect the truth—if there is a truth here—is somewhere in between. But I think the important thing was that we recognized that we were in over our heads, and we did what we thought was best to protect our student and our group. The good news is that by releasing that student from our group, we freed her up to find a group with a structure that was a better fit for her situation and needs. She was initiated into a local coven and is thriving as a member of that community.

If you have had a bad experience with someone who has drug and alcohol issues or a mental illness, try not to make the assumption that everyone who has the same condition as the person you had a problem with will also cause problems. For example, if you had trouble with a bipolar student, it doesn't mean that all bipolar students will act exactly the same way or be problematic. When you are thinking of taking on students, consider each one individually as a whole person with unique strengths and challenges, and try to look at the big picture when you make your decision. It doesn't mean that you shouldn't listen to your instinct or past experience when considering working with someone with addiction or mental health issues, but it's important to know that each person is much more than his or her problems and consider them on their individual merits.

As with dealing with students in crisis, it's good to have a list of places where you can refer students with addiction or mental health problems for help. It's also good to know what you can handle and what you can't. I know from long, hard, heartbreaking experience that there is absolutely nothing I personally can do to help addicts who are still using and refuse to stop except kick them out of my class and hope that this is one of the many acts of "tough love" that eventually inspires them to go to rehab.

If you take on a student with known addiction or mental health issues because their behavior is normal, and that behavior changes after they're in your class, talk to them as soon as you can after the behavior change. If the person has a mental illness and has stopped medication, make their participation in your group contingent upon them seeing their doctor and resuming medication right away or, if the medication was problematic, starting another doctor-prescribed treatment regimen. Whether it's a mental health or addiction issue, do not allow the behavior to get out of hand. Be firm with the person and make it absolutely clear that they must follow your group's accepted rules for respectful, consistent, reliable behavior. If they can't or won't keep their behavior within acceptable limits, ask them to leave. It might feel very cold to boot them—after all, nobody signs up to become an alcoholic, and mental illnesses are not the patient's fault—but that doesn't mean you can save them or that it is your job to try.

And it's likely your other students didn't sign on for that either. You need to think of them and their well-being too. Melanie Henry told me, "The people I've learned the most from have often been the most disturbing." She is absolutely right, but don't let that learning come at the expense of your other students. Remember, too, that if you really want or need to help someone with mental health or addiction issues, you can always find ways to do it outside of class and the student-teacher relationship.

Trolls

The sad truth is that the Pagan community has a certain appeal for people who thrive on conflict. Our community tends to encourage everyone to explore his or her own personal spiritual path and ethics. We tend to be tolerant and accepting of personal differences. And although we have some large umbrella groups, we tend to avoid centralized authority. These are wonderful traits for the most part, but they also make the Pagan community very appealing to people who like to cause problems for the sake of causing problems and getting attention.

People in the Pagan community who wreak havoc in groups—setting fire to the city just to see it burn—are often called trolls. This term is particularly used online for people who enter a discussion group or online community and purposefully derail the discussion, start fights, or insult and flame others. But it also applies to people who do the same things in person. Trolls are often very likable at first—charming, even, with the gift of glamour (meaning the ability to make themselves seem to be something other—and more appealing—than what they are). They are also often excellent liars. Frequently they have a personal set of "ethics" that either changes to suit their purposes or otherwise doesn't mesh with others'. They can be very good at playing the victim in a situation and making you believe it, even if they actually instigated the problem, and nothing is ever "their fault." They're also often very good at making you question your choices as a teacher and a leader.

Several of my interviewees told me stories about trolls. Melanie Henry told me about a student she worked with who tried to "glamour" her whole coven:

> She was just a huge liar. I mean, she would say three opposing things about the same thing, like, for example, why was she wearing the wedding ring—there were three different stories within about six weeks. It wasn't the thing you would catch on the first instance. The story would be internally consistent during the interview, it just fell apart pretty quickly afterward.

Sylva Markson also told me a story about a woman who created a sub-culture of secrecy within their coven, and whose lying and manipulation blew up the group from the inside:

> As all of this started coming out, we realized that we had all been part of it unwittingly. She would say things to me—"Well, don't tell anybody, but..." and then she'd tell me something that she had heard or something that she believed or whatever, and then she'd do the same to other people. When we started talking to each other, we realized that there was a whole kind of underground culture of silence going on inside the group—that we all had little bits of secrets of things from her that none of us knew that everybody else had different versions of.
>
> She was kicked out of the group.... She brought it to the larger community and besmirched our trainers in a lot of ways that were completely wrong and unfair and outright lies. And some of the ways in which she was not completely wrong she at least grossly mischaracterized or exaggerated the reality, and basically hurt everybody in the group horribly. And it was all politics.
>
> I don't think most people would have the kind of agendas that this person had. But again, I'm left feeling like I'm questioning my own judgment because I adored her. I did not see this coming at all. Nobody saw it coming.

Trolls are in a whole different league from regular disruptive and needy people or people who don't get along. Most disruptive people can change their behavior when they find out it's a problem, or at least tone it down. Trolls don't have any incentive to change, because their behavior gets them the attention they crave. Their goal is chaos. If you ask them to stop their behavior, they might take it underground, say you've misunderstood them, or accuse you of being a bully—but they will not stop.

215

Like the woman in Sylva Markson's story, they will turn friends against each other, bring your dirty laundry out into the greater community, and make you question yourself as a teacher, a Pagan, and a human being. The only way to truly deal with a troll is not to feed it—meaning stop giving the person your attention, boot him or her out of your group or class, and cease all contact. It's possible that the troll will badmouth you in the community, but dealing with that is better than having him or her destroy your group from within. The "difficult conversation" doesn't work at all with trolls. Don't waste your breath. Save your compassion for someone who will benefit from it.

So how do you tell if someone is a troll or just behaving badly because they're having a bad day or in a crisis of some kind? This is tricky, because trolls are masters of what I like to call the "theater of one." They always show you, the teacher, exactly what they want you to see, and nothing else. If they were actors on a stage, you, as the teacher, would always be sitting front and center. If you moved, the trolls would move to maintain the position directly in front of you. They will avoid letting you see them from the side or behind the scenes at all costs. They will always put forward their most charismatic face. The good news and bad news about that is if trolls have you in the theater of one, it's possible that maintaining that is taking up enough of their attention that others might be able to see "backstage." If you think that someone might be playing you or is simply too good to be true, you can ask a friend or another teacher to observe the person as you teach. It's possible the friend will be able to see a side of the maybe-troll that you can't, because you're busy teaching.

Melanie Henry told me she likes to have another person around to help her see through the glamour:

> I am really bad at seeing through glamour, so I try to have someone who's good at seeing through that stuff. One thing you learn as a teacher is that it's good if you can identify things you're bad at, not because you'll suddenly become good at them, but if you can find someone else who's good at that who can watch your back, that's a really good thing.

I generally don't ask students to be that person watching my back, because it's unfair to ask them to "spy" on one of their peers. But sometimes other students are the best eyes and ears you can have, and if it's a matter of putting a student in what could be an uncomfortable position versus having a troll destroy your group, you might decide it's worth it to ask the student to be uncomfortable. It does put an unfair burden on the student, however. As with most interpersonal things, this is a judgment call, and no two situations are the same.

As Melanie Henry points out, it's important to listen to students, too, if they approach you with concerns about another student or about anything class-related, for that matter:

> One of the key things there is, too, is if somebody says that there is a problem, listen…. People are doing a great favor if they disagree with you and tell you why. They could be wrong, but there's generally something going on.

They might be wrong about the other student or they could be seeing trollish behavior that you are missing. I once booted someone from one of my classes for a reason other than being a troll, and afterward several of the remaining students came up to me privately and told me that the person had been doing things behind my back that could have done a lot of damage to my class if left unchecked. I had no idea, I felt like an idiot, and I wished that my students had told me earlier, but I understood why they didn't. The person in question had them in thrall too, to a certain extent, but they also just weren't sure they should speak up. I could tell in retrospect that the student we booted was very good at the "theater of one" routine.

If the person appears to be extremely self-centered—to the point of having a very different reality from "consensual" reality—or not to care about the feelings of others, keep an eye on him or her. Part of the reason trolls succeed in causing so much trouble is that they just don't care who they hurt in the process. They will say and do just about anything to perpetuate their version of reality and make themselves appear to be the victim if you start to get wise to them. Another telltale sign is people who give different accounts of the same event to different people. You won't necessarily know this is happening unless your students or someone else tells you, but keep your ears open. Sometimes the troll will tell the same story differently in your presence, or at least within earshot.

One of the best ways to deal with trolls in your class is to not allow them to get there in the first place. The screening techniques in chapter 3 aren't foolproof, but they can help you weed out some potential trolls beforehand. There is absolutely nothing wrong with asking potential students for references. If they've burned a previous teacher, be careful. It's possible the teacher was at fault—and there are certainly cases where a student leaves a group because he or she doesn't get along with the teacher and then gets along fine in a new group—but it's also possible the person is a troll.

Some Teacher-Specific Challenges

Students are only human, but so are teachers, and teachers can have as many problems as their students do. The bad news is that the pitfalls in the section below can happen to nearly any teacher. The good news is that using the ethics and boundaries section of chapter 8 and the self-care tips in chapter 11 can help you avoid some of them and recover from others.

Hubris and Believing Your Own Hype

As a teacher, it can be easy to slip from a more modest place—where you take pride in knowing that you're facilitating others' learning—into an arrogant hubris, where you erroneously think that the good stuff happening for your students is all about you. It is particularly easy to do this if you have been teaching for a while with success, or you've begun to make a name for yourself, or if you haven't found anyone who knows more than you do (yet).

Oberon Zell-Ravenheart told me a story about hubris:

> In my earliest days of teaching Paganism and the Craft (in my
> late twenties), I was stunningly arrogant in my assumption of
> how much more I knew than anyone else. I recall a particu-
> larly embarrassing (in retrospect) incident when I had really
> only been studying the Craft myself for a year or so. Since this
> put me way ahead of everyone else in the Nest, they looked to
> me to teach them and expected me to know all the answers.
> One time they brought in a young guy who wanted to meet
> me, having heard of me as a great teacher. He said he was a
> Witch, so I started asking him questions. But I was so igno-
> rant that I didn't know anything about his tradition (Alexan-
> drian, as it turned out), and I cut him down mercilessly when
> his answers differed from what I had been taught and learned
> through my own studies—which was heavily based on Crow-
> ley and Leland. Later on, when I learned about Gardnerian
> and Alexandrian Trads, and realized he had been perfectly
> right, I felt like a total fool. It was a very humbling experience,
> and I've always wished I could have tracked that guy down
> and apologized profusely to him. Many years later I even
> wrote a cautionary editorial about this in *Green Egg*.

Falling into hubris can happen to beginning teachers too, who mistake
the powerful feeling that teaching can give you for actual power or who
think that because they've got a few students, suddenly they are mov-
ers and shakers in the community. Ellen Evert Hopman told me a story
about a young teacher who thought she was a bigger fish than she really
was:

> I was at Pagan Pride Day a couple of years ago, and they said
> they were going to have a panel of elders to speak to the audi-
> ence. I was invited to be on the panel of elders. I thought,

"Well, that's cool." So I'm up there with a bunch of other people—we're all in our fifties, sixties, seventies, right? And then there is this seventeen-year-old sitting there with us. And I just very innocently turned to her, because I had no idea why she was there, and in a friendly way said, "What are you doing here?" Because I didn't know why she was there—to wait on us? Bring us water? What, actually? And I couldn't figure it out. She replied, "Oh, I'm an elder." And I said, "Oh, really?" and then she immediately ran to find her mother. She was in tears and all upset because I had challenged her.

And the mother came back and was furious. She said that I had destroyed her daughter's self-confidence. How dare I question her daughter? And I was just flabbergasted, because everybody else on the panel was an elder. To get to the status of elder you have to go through hell, literally—I mean years and years and years of teaching and dealing with human frailties and conflicts and initiating people and marrying people and having people die. And, I mean, to really be an elder, it's a lifetime of work and experience—for no pay, of course, because Pagans won't pay for this kind of thing—you dedicate yourself and with very little reward. We have no pensions, we have no health insurance, no retirement, nothing.

And then to have a little seventeen-year-old say that she's an elder because she had founded a coven and she had kids under her—I guess fifteen-, sixteen-year-olds—so we were supposed to respect her. It's difficult. We were supposed to respect her on equal footing with people who are in their fifties, sixties, and seventies. I found that a little difficult, the fact that she had to go running for her mother. I wanted to say—but I didn't—I wanted to say, "Well, look: if you have to go running for your mother, that shows you're not quite there yet."

Obviously, hubris turns people off, since nobody likes self-important people who bask in their own awesomeness. But worse yet, hubris is almost always built on a false conception of reality—where you think you're more important than you really are—and living in that false place cuts you off from your center and whatever grounds you, and also from the real world and what's going on around you. Teachers who are cut off are ineffective at best.

People wrapped up in their own hubris are distracted by the needs of their own egos and therefore incapable of living up to their hype. We've all seen it: actors, directors, musicians, authors, and athletes who crank out some really great work and are showered with accolades. Then they buy into the image of their own greatness created by the praise and are unable to produce any new work that's as good, because they lose touch with whatever made their work great in the first place.

Hubris can also lead teachers to pull power plays on their students, boss them around, belittle them, and engage in all sorts of other behaviors that are more about controlling students and/or feeding the teacher's ego than about teaching and helping others.

It's good to have some people around who are willing to be straight with you and tell you if they think you're getting too arrogant. Keeping close to your core and revisiting why you teach and what you want for— not from—your students are good hubris antidotes too.

Guru Syndrome: The Cult of You

Be they Pagan, Wiccan, Christian, or any other path, spiritual communities seem predisposed to creating gurus. I am not referring to gurus in the Hindu sense or in the general sense of "teacher." I am using the term to mean teachers who are perceived as having great spiritual wisdom and knowledge—more than the average teacher—and who acquire followers, disciples, or devotees. A cult of personality builds up the teacher, and the teacher becomes symbolic of and then synonymous with the spiritual teachings followers hope to gain. Followers feel they are dependent on the guru, rather than on their own initiative and intuition, to achieve their spiritual goals.

Sometimes teachers become gurus out of their own hubris, gathering students around them who follow them like ducklings and feed their egos. Sometimes students "create" a guru out of a teacher by putting the teacher on a pedestal and deciding that the teacher will somehow "save" them or give them all the answers they need. And sometimes teachers buy into the inflated, unrealistic image students have created of them, and knowingly or inadvertently set themselves up as gurus with students' enthusiastic help.

It is very important as Pagan teachers that we not allow our egos to make us gurus or allow students to make gurus of us. We are here to help facilitate students' spiritual growth, and although we might guide them, it's crucial that they own the process themselves, or they will fail. Paganism and Wicca are, among other things, ways to claim one's own power. For students, claiming and owning their own power is their means to walking their path and achieving their spiritual goals. When students make you their guru and become your acolytes, they are essentially handing you their power, thus abdicating their responsibility for their own learning and spiritual growth. This can feel great to unwitting teachers— students are putting their faith and trust solely in your hands, and you feel important and needed. But for their sake and yours, it's crucial that you hand students' power right back to them and resist the urge to take on responsibility that should be theirs.

Teachers should be on the lookout for students who might be developing an unrealistic image of them. Melanie Henry commented:

I don't like people looking at me all starry-eyed and getting "teacher crushes" on me. That drives me a little crazy. I can be flattered, but if your eyes are glazed over like that, you're not seeing me.

Another thing to watch out for, especially if you're working with one group of students over a longer period of time, is whether your students are beginning to exhibit cultish behaviors or overdependence on you as the teacher. Magical groups can get very insular, to the point where members spend an inordinate amount of time together and allow other relationships to suffer or fall away. It's important that your behavior as a teacher doesn't encourage students to do this, not only because they're building their own mini cult, but also because they're building it around you.

To avoid the guru syndrome, you also want to nip other codependent behaviors in the bud. If students begin to rely too much on your opinion or help rather than their own ideas and initiative, find ways to put the responsibility for decision making and action back on them. A friend recently told me a story about a teacher of alternative healing whom she greatly admired but hadn't seen for a long time. When she did see the teacher again and observed her with clients, my friend noticed that several of the teacher's clients had become dependent on the teacher, coming to her weekly for up to a decade to make sure they were energetically "in tune with their higher selves." The teacher was so good at doing this for her clients that they resisted doing it for themselves, even though they could. And the teacher was unwittingly perpetuating this dependency by not cutting the cord and telling students they needed to do this work for themselves.

Students seem to be especially vulnerable to picking up codependent behaviors or putting unrealistic expectations on teachers who have helped them have life-changing realizations or discoveries. When students have these epiphanies, they are sometimes overcome with what I call the "fervor of the newly converted"—the belief that this discovery they've just made is so awesomely powerful that it will work for everyone, and that they must immediately go out and evangelize about this incredible, life-changing realization which, in addition to solving everyone's most pesky problems, will put an end to famine, halt global warming, save the whales and the polar bears, and make all the peoples of the earth embrace each other in peace and harmony. Students in the midst of the fervor of the newly converted might transfer their enthusiasm for their epiphany to the teacher who helped them have it. Remind students who have these revelations in your class that it was they themselves who climbed Mount Everest and made the discovery. You simply provided them with supplies, and maybe a Sherpa.

Another way to pop the guru bubble is to be very open with students. Don't hold back and keep things a mystery. The more mysterious you are, the less "human" you are, and the more students might think that you have some sort of mystical, magical power or arcane knowledge.

Exhaustion and Burnout

Exhaustion and burnout are often insidious. In most cases, they don't overcome you overnight. Becoming exhausted and/or burned out is a gradual process that sneaks up behind teachers slowly. Often they don't realize how fried they are until they are whacked over the head by some cosmic clue-by-four because they were so tired they weren't paying attention. The clue-by-four can be a smallish-but-embarrassing thing, such as a friend or another teacher telling them they're slipping, or it can be much bigger, such as a health crisis brought on by stress.

It can be very difficult to recover from exhaustion and burnout if you let it go too far. I can tell you this from hard personal experience. For the past three years, I have been working on a huge project at my day job that has consumed an enormous amount of my time, including evenings and weekends. On top of that, I've battled a set of serious health problems. My health is improving and my deadline will be met soon, but I know it will probably take me months to get all my energy back again. During this time, it has been very difficult to find the energy or even desire to teach. My class has met much less frequently, and my students haven't gotten the attention they need. And my teaching has really suffered.

Exhausted and burned-out teachers are not inspiring or effective. It is very difficult to motivate or facilitate students' learning when you are exhausted, and it's also hard to drum up the enthusiasm for your subject that you need to teach it well. Students can tell when you're exhausted or burned out, and they're less likely to be engaged and get what they need to out of your class if it appears that you yourself have lost interest.

There are several things teachers do—often with the best of intentions—that can accelerate their own exhaustion and burnout. The most obvious is simply taking on more than they can handle time-wise or energy-wise.

Taking responsibility for students' learning or actions will also drain your time and energy resources very quickly. It's important that they hold the reins of their own spiritual education and journey. If you try to do it, you are robbing them of owning it themselves, and you're also taking on a burden you can't possibly carry.

Trying to control students' learning—the pace at which they learn and internalize the information, how they learn, or whether they learn it at all—can also lead to exhaustion and burnout. Although you will help students gain knowledge gradually by waiting until they have some understanding of a concept before building on it with new, more challenging material (this is called "scaffolding" in teacher-speak), you can't control how quickly students grasp concepts, or at what level. If you are expecting them to come to conclusions at a certain time—or, worse, in the same way as you did or as your other students do—you will be disappointed. Don't wear yourself out trying to make this happen. Most students will "get it" at their own pace and in their own time.

Martyring yourself—throwing everything you have into teaching, getting over-involved in students' personal lives, and/or sacrificing your own needs for those of your students—is a one-way ticket to exhaustion and burnout, as is expecting students to reciprocate to your martyrdom with gratitude and thanks. Many students will appreciate what you do for them, but don't expect them all to say so, and don't expect to counteract your exhaustion with positive feedback from students that might or might not ever come. The sad truth is that although there are exceptions, our society in general takes teachers for granted. Don't depend on student kudos to revitalize you. And if you're sacrificing enough for your

225

students that you could be called a martyr, you're giving up much more than students could ever reciprocate, even if they were inclined to do so. Some of the symptoms of exhaustion and burnout are:

- Finding yourself caring less and less about teaching, your students, and/or your class
- Feeling tired at the mere idea of teaching
- Slacking on your prep work
- Dreading an upcoming class
- Losing patience and/or getting irritable with students on a regular basis
- Procrastination of anything having to do with the class (my personal favorite)

It's best if you can determine that you're heading for exhaustion and burnout before you start having these symptoms, but most teachers don't realize they're in trouble until some of these begin to manifest. Don't knock yourself if you don't notice you're exhausted or burning out until you're in the thick of it, but do try to be aware and catch it before it gets to the point where you either can't reverse it or it affects your physical or mental health. Many of the symptoms are reversible—although it isn't easy if you've gone a long way down the path. Some practical steps you can take if you think you are beginning to burn out are:

- Taking a break or sabbatical
- Reducing the class schedule
- Teaching fewer classes at a time
- Changing up the overall syllabus or the individual activities and lessons you use to teach to make them more interesting to you
- Delegating responsibility for some teaching to capable students
- Team teaching—ideally, if there are two of you, you only do half the work, although you do have to take some time to coordinate with the other teacher

There are also things you can do to rejuvenate and try to bring the spark back. The techniques I mention in chapter 11 help to fight off and recover from exhaustion and burnout.

Facing Your Own Demons

Earlier in this chapter, I talked about handling crises and situations when people's personal issues surface as a result of learning. But what about your own baggage?

Becoming a teacher is an initiation of sorts. Initiation, by its very nature, is not comfortable. The point of initiation is to induce change in your life and transition you from one state, or point, to another. Teaching other people can do that too. Once you have stepped into the teaching arena, you will never be the same as you were before you did it, even if you never teach again. It will be a catalyst to your own learning and spiritual growth, but it might also cast a harsh light on your own baggage or issues you didn't know or remember you had.

And if that wasn't enough, students' crises or emotional responses to their experiences can trigger your own issues too. In fact, it's commonly said in my tradition that when you initiate someone, you go through initiation yourself all over again. It's true in the sense that you are participating in the ceremony again—albeit as the initiator, not the person being initiated—but also in that you are affected by it and change as a result. Melanie Henry talked to me about teaching making you face your own demons:

> If you're squeamish on whatever level, believe me that the teaching will confront you with your own shit. So you'd better have some idea of that, and know how to face it. Especially it will make you face your shadow. Your students will for sure show you that you've got to be willing to deal with the scary, icky stuff that's part of the human condition.... If you set yourself up as a teacher of Witchcraft, you will not be able to avoid that, because you're a doorway—a doorway of

initiation. People coming to you for Witchcraft are going to be people who do have at least a nod to dark stuff. You have to be willing to look into the darkness. You have to be able to have some of your strength come from that…. I think if you embrace Witchcraft as a spirituality, you have to make your peace with darkness—I don't mean darkness in terms of evil, I mean in terms of night.

Making peace with your darkness can mean many things, among them knowing your own weaknesses and less-healthy tendencies and devising ways to handle them. For example, if you are prone to taking things personally, it's good to know that and have a way to talk yourself through it if such a situation arises. It can also mean accepting the fact that without dark there is no light, and vice versa, and that we carry both within us at all times. As Pagans we don't have to accept a good-versus-evil mentality. Embracing and understanding your darkness can mean accepting that there are many shades of grey, both in you and in your students, which is easier said than done but important nonetheless.

Having your personal issues come up while you are teaching can be subtle and (relatively) easy to deal with, such as having doubts about your teaching or feeling insecure. These types of problems are among the most common, and often you can talk yourself out of them or have a friend help you do so. Issues of identity that make you do a lot of soul-searching can also come up. You might question why you're on your own path, whether you think you're "good" enough to teach, and your purpose in life. These questions aren't comfortable, but they're important questions to explore, no matter how they come up. In this way, teaching can be a catalyst for healthy stuff to surface in addition to all that emotional baggage.

It's important to have your own support system in place before or in case something happens. In many cases, it's not appropriate to rely on your students for emotional support, even if something happens while you are in class. Exceptions might be if you are co-teaching or if you have close friends in the group. Have a short list of friends, mentors, or family members in mind whom you can call if you need help or to talk. And, if you are going through a period of depression or anxiety or have unresolved issues from relationships or family history that might be triggered by students' problems, it's not a bad idea to "get your house in order" by doing some work with a therapist or counselor. You will be far better at helping students handle their problems if you are dealing with your own in a healthy way.

Try as much as possible to prevent whatever is happening to you from affecting the quality or atmosphere of your class, and keep any freaking out to a minimum while you're in students' presence. If you need to leave the room or cancel a class, do so, give them a reason, and reschedule later if possible. You don't have to be specific about the reason. "I'm very sorry, but I need to deal with a personal crisis/issue" is sufficient. It's crucial that your students know you are not perfect and that you have feelings, but they don't need to see you have an emotional meltdown. If you do have one in front of them, apologize and take responsibility for it.

It's also important not to blame students for what's happening or associate them with it if something they did or experienced in your class contributed to your issue surfacing. It's not their fault. Sometimes these things just happen. On the positive side, with the right support you can get a great deal of learning and healing out of these incidents, and you'll be more understanding and have more experience to help others handle problems that arise for them.

The self-care tips in chapter 11 can help you handle this sort of problem too.

I had a terrible education.
I went to a school for
emotionally disturbed
teachers.

WOODY ALLEN

CHAPTER 11

Care and Feeding
of the Teacher

Self-care is essential for a long and happy physical life, and it's equally vital for a long, happy, successful Pagan teaching career. Strong ethics and boundaries provide a great foundation for self-care, but there are a lot of additional things teachers can do—and in some cases *should* do—to keep themselves physically, mentally, emotionally, and spiritually healthy while they are teaching. I have been teaching on and off for two decades, and whenever I have slacked off in any of the areas on the self-care list below, it has had a negative impact on my efficacy as a teacher. Do as I say and not as I do (did). Teacher, heal thyself!

I've divided the information below into long-term self-care—the preventive stuff you can do to try to keep yourself healthy and ward off problems—and short-term self-care—some ideas for how to recover from more acute situations where you need help *now* and the long-term stuff will take too long. If you follow the ideas in the long-term care, you should be able to significantly reduce the chances you'll end up in one of those acute situations, but, as we all know, the universe doesn't always follow our carefully laid plans.

LONG-TERM SELF-CARE

Find and Stick to Your Core

Your core is your purpose—your true will—and whatever connects you to it. Your core drives and fuels everything you do, to one extent or another, and it influences your will to teach and your teaching phi-losophy. It might or might not be tied to your spirituality, but for many Pagans the two seem to be intertwined, if not one and the same.

When you're busy teaching, working, doing the laundry, raising a fam-ily—just plain living—it's easy to lose touch with your core and forget why you're doing all this stuff in the first place. But your core is what nourishes you and makes everything else possible, so you need to recon-nect to it regularly to stay in harmony with your purpose.

It's important to take time out from the daily grind to discover what reconnects you to your core. It might be that you need to spend more time by water or in nature. You might reconnect through meditation, physical activity, talking to loved ones, or music. The mechanism is dif-ferent for everyone, so you'll need to discover it for yourself. And there might be more than one way for you to do it. Almost all of the methods above work for me.

Once you know what helps you find your core, make time to do it as regularly as you need to in order to keep in touch with your will. This might feel selfish, since you're taking precious time away from something else, but in fact it's not. You will function better and be happier if you are connected, and that will have a positive impact on the other areas of your life. You should not think of this as optional or unimportant. It is prob-ably one of the most important things you can do.

Once you are connected, examine or re-examine why you started teaching. Look at how (or if) teaching is related to your true will. Remembering why you do this important work and how it supports your true will can help inspire you to be a great teacher and help you find the motivation to kick exhaustion, burnout, and a host of other problems.

Nurture Your Personal Practice

If you're teaching Paganism, chances are you are (gasp!) a Pagan, which means you have some path or tradition or ritual that you follow to express and experience your Paganism. It's very easy to neglect your own personal practice when you're helping others find theirs; it seems like there is never enough time for both. But you need to make time. Keeping in tune with your own spirituality and keeping up on what's going on in the community make you a stronger, more effective teacher.

I asked several of my interviewees if they had been taught to teach. T. Thorn Coyle discussed her various teachers but ended her statement with this: "Above all, though, daily spiritual practice is my teacher."

Your personal practice also provides you with the space to continue making your own spiritual discoveries and communing with your gods. You are not expecting your students to be static, and neither should you be. Being open to spirit makes teaching from your core easier and more rewarding, and it can help keep you on track too. Christopher Penczak commented:

> Really be open to the service of teaching, be open to guidance. Be able to work with spirit as you teach. That's the most important thing to me.

In addition, your spirituality nourishes you, and you need that nourishment to help others find their way. Plus, if your gods are anything like mine and you ignore them for too long, or if you act all hypocritical by teaching others Paganism but neglecting the gods yourself, they'll give you a cosmic boot to the head to get your attention. (As a result of my considerable experience on the receiving end of the divine boot to the head, I can attest that the gods really, *really* don't like hypocrisy.) A boot to the head from the gods is no laughing matter, so I encourage you to keep up your spiritual practice, even if it's just to avoid divine heel marks on your forehead.

Get a Change of Scenery

As I've mentioned already, we all get wound up in our daily lives and stuck in ruts. As spiritual people and teachers, however, it's important that we break free sometimes from the day-to-day so we can meet new people, get new information, or simply look at our lives from a different perspective. If we are not dynamic and constantly seeking new information and experiences, we become static—and boring—people and teachers. And we're much less likely to have these new experiences and insights if we rush like rats through a maze in the same pattern every single day. It's sometimes said that the definition of insanity is doing the same thing over and over again but expecting different results. When I feel like I've gotten myself stuck in a cycle of sameness, I know I need a change of scenery to rejuvenate and find inspiration.

For me, physically getting away from the places I see every day—my office, my home, my neighborhood—and going somewhere, anywhere else, whether it be in my own city or far away, is essential for sticking to my core and keeping the teaching spark alive. There is absolutely nothing like travel—even inexpensive, short-term travel—to reset your clock, so to speak; to give you time to take a breath and think about the world a little differently. Recently I saved up some money and took a solo trip to Crete. Wandering among the ruins of Knossos and Gournia and climbing down into the Dictaean Cave—places of power with a long spiritual history—reconnected me to the earth and the gods. And traveling around the island, talking to complete strangers and trying to speak a little Greek, gave me a peek at a lifestyle very different from own, which in turn gave me insight into my own world. A trip to Crete is expensive and probably a once-in-a-lifetime thing, but I have found that I can get similar benefits from simply leaving the city and going anywhere that is different enough from the places I see every day to allow me time and space to pause and reflect.

If travel isn't your thing, you don't need to go somewhere to get a change of scenery. Taking a class or volunteering with people you don't know can also give you a fresh perspective. The skills you learn and the people you meet can help you look at your life in a different way. The idea is to break your usual pattern, not spend a lot of money. And if the class or volunteer work is related to something you love, then you're feeding your core too.

I encourage you to do these things for yourself—this chapter is about care and feeding of the teacher, after all, and I want to emphasize that self-care without the thought of your students is essential—but you can also do something to get a change of pace with your students. Just make sure you're also doing solo work. In Washington State, the Aquarian Tabernacle Church holds an event each year called the Spring Mysteries, where they re-create the rites of Demeter and Persephone that were held at Eleusis in Greece. As part of the event, the organizers build shrines to the Greek gods. Three or four times my husband and I have gone with our students to help build shrines and experience the mysteries together. The process of planning, getting the materials for the shrines, decorating, and then experiencing the space we helped create in ritual not only gave each of us individual insights and fresh ways to look at our personal spirituality, but it also gave us some rich shared experiences to bond us as a group.

Find a Mentor

Everyone needs support, especially new teachers. When you go to formal teacher school and learn how to teach elementary or secondary students, you student teach for at least a semester with a trained, experienced teacher. It shouldn't be any different for Pagan teachers, but it usually is. If you can't turn to your own teacher for support, or if you didn't have one, consider finding people in the community who can mentor you and answer questions, or who you can "shadow" by watching or participating in their class to learn how they teach. Don't be afraid to ask for this kind of help. Your students will benefit from you sticking your neck out to get answers. Melanie Henry commented:

> Ideally you have someone at whose feet you can sit for a while to model, so you can sort of student teach. At the very least, have someone you can ask questions of, and don't be embarrassed. I started out by being embarrassed when I had questions. Please ask your questions of somebody, because nobody knows everything, especially when you first get started. It's okay not to know everything. The more I do, the less I realize I know.

You don't have to meet your mentor in person, either. Online will do in a pinch.

Take on a Physical Practice

One of the things I highly recommend, both for self-care and for keeping connected to your core, is taking on a physical spiritual practice such as tai chi, yoga, or sacred dance. I have been doing tai chi for about fifteen years and dance on and off longer than that. Both practices greatly enhance my understanding of energy and how it moves through and with the body and how the physical and spiritual worlds connect. There's something about picking up my tai chi sword, moving it through the air, and feeling the energetic connection between the tip and my *dantien* (the energy center behind and slightly below the navel) that makes it seem like my world is in harmony. Or maybe I'm just happier when I'm holding a weapon. Anyway, I'm not alone in this opinion. T. Thorn Coyle appears to derive a great deal of her spirituality from physical practice. I asked her where her teaching comes from:

> My teaching is informed by my practice, the way my mind and heart put things together, my understanding from the Gurdjieff Work, Sufism, Buddhism, and mysticism. It also is informed by my own guides and the particular syncretism of my path, which includes emphasis on the body and physical health and engagement.

If the spiritual benefits aren't enough, physical practice is also therapeutic and great exercise. Both of these make me feel better, which in turn helps me with everything else I do, including teaching. I feel so strongly about physical practice that I make my students choose and do a physical practice too (and they do, with a lot of grumbling and eye rolling).

Get a Life

It's very easy to get wrapped up in teaching and allow friendships and your social life to slip away. But friends are essential to your mental health. Having fun and laughing with friends is one of the strongest antidotes I have ever found to burnout and other teacher problems. As I said before, you shouldn't be relying on your students for social or emotional support. There are cases in which they might help you—especially if you are more or less peers or you were friends before you became teacher and student—but you really need a group of non-student peers who can support you, help you problem-solve, and make you get out of the house and do something frivolous and fun, just for yourself. It's important to have hobbies and interests that are your own and separate from your students too. This helps you retain your sense of personal identity and keeps you engaged with the world outside of teaching.

Don't Beat Yourself Up

Teachers can be their own worst critics. We know how important teaching is for our students and our community, and we want to do it well, so we are very hard on ourselves when we mess up. But teachers who are self-flagellating over a mistake aren't focused on what they need to be focused on: their students.

It's important that you treat yourself with the same compassion you show your students, or you're not going to last long as a teacher. You will make lots of mistakes, and you won't have the time or energy to beat yourself up over every single one. Besides, while you're wasting time doing that, you're missing out on everything else that's going on in your class, both good and bad.

Anne Marie Forrester commented: "Be kind to yourself. It's not always going to go perfectly." Don't invest the mistake with more power by dwelling on it. Own it, apologize if necessary, learn from it, and move on.

There is an easy cure for beating-yourself-up syndrome, but it's not a pleasant one: simply make a really huge mistake and survive it. Making a mistake and realizing that the world isn't going to end as a result gives you a much healthier perspective. As Pete "Pathfinder" Davis pointed out, "You know, we learn best from blisters and scars."

Don't Take Yourself Too Seriously

As I've said, teaching is sacred work. But that doesn't mean that it always has to be serious work. Allow yourself to find joy and humor in your situation, your students, and even your mistakes. We all know that "with great power comes great responsibility," but don't think that because you're a teacher and you're in charge that you have to be serious and authoritative and suppress your natural personality. One of the great things about teachers is how diverse they are. They come from different backgrounds, different perspectives; each has something unique to offer. Don't stuff everything that makes you different to fit some sort of ideal you hold in your head of what a perfect teacher should be. Christopher Penczak told me how he learned not to take himself too seriously:

> In an effort to illustrate not taking yourself too seriously, in one class healing ritual, I accidently set my long hair on fire.... I wasn't hurt. It went out, and I don't think anybody really noticed, but hey, I learned to laugh at myself after that.

Get Out While the Getting's Good

Sometimes, no matter what you do, the desire to teach is extinguished, and it isn't going to come back. In these cases, the right self-care to administer is often to decide you're done teaching and retire. There's no shame in that. Teachers are just people, after all, and people's lives, interests, and needs change.

If you think you're in this situation, don't let it drag on too long. We've all seen professional teachers who hang on and keep teaching long after the passion is gone in order to keep their retirement or because they don't know what to do with themselves next. These teachers are often ineffective at best. Don't be one of them. Retire gracefully.

If you are going to discontinue your classes, make sure you give students adequate notice. Try to help students who are in the midst of proj-

CARE AND FEEDING OF THE TEACHER

ects finish, or refer them to other teachers who can help them complete their training. You can also hand your class over to another teacher, if one is available. Transition out of the teaching role respectfully, and then take a good, long break before jumping into something else. You've earned it.

Short-Term Self-Care

Even the best teachers can reach a point of crisis. Maybe they have been pushing themselves too hard and it's finally caught up with them. Maybe they've expended a lot of energy helping a student through a personal crisis. Maybe something crazy has happened in their personal lives that has derailed their teaching. The point is, acute crisis situations arise, and you'll need immediate, short-term self-care to handle them.

In my experience, unless something is literally on fire *right now* or you're dealing with someone in immediate crisis—such as a suicidal student—the best way to handle an acute situation is to get away, calm down, get some perspective, and make a plan.

Get Away and Calm Down

It's difficult to make rational decisions when you're freaking out. Your amygdala—the part of your brain that just reacts—gets overwhelmed with panic, and your cortex—the thinking part of the brain—can't do its job to get you out of the situation. The best thing you can do when this is going on is remove yourself from the situation, either physically or mentally, and calm yourself down. The idea is to break the stress feedback loop so you can move forward in a more constructive way.

Once you've removed yourself from the immediate situation, try one of these ideas to calm down and take care of yourself:

- Do something you consider therapeutic. Personally, my go-to stress relievers are bad rubber-monster movies, the mugwort bath at the local women's day spa, and live drag shows, but you're free to find your own.

- Get some hard exercise. Hike, run, or dance away your stress.

- Get outside. We're Pagans, right? We derive energy from the earth. No better time for that than when you're in a crisis.

- Get under or into running water. There's something about the negative ions released in falling water that seems to release tension. A medicine woman I know likes to do healings in waterfalls when she can for this reason, but the shower will do too, or a bath with Epsom salt and/or soothing herbs.

- Meditate. Make sure you include deep breathing.

- Do grounding and centering exercises.

- Play with your pets. Animals are great for shifting your perspective. We have a very talkative parrot, and when we get upset, she says "it's okay" over and over. I'm not sure if she's trying to soothe herself or us, but when she does this, we make sure to calm down just so we don't upset her.

- Go to a movie. Sit in a dark theater, trance out a little, and allow your mind to let go of the problem for a couple of hours and be wrapped up in something else.

- If your crisis is less a "trip to the emergency room" situation than a "crisis of faith" about a teaching situation, make a list of all the great experiences you've had teaching and/or the reasons why you've enjoyed it. Remembering these things and reliving them in your mind can help pull you out of an acute morale crisis.

Remember that it's okay to get away from the situation and calm down. You're allowed to take care of yourself and handle the problem thoughtfully and calmly. Unless someone is on the bridge, ready to jump, don't allow yourself to get sucked into others' stress about the problem. Find your center.

Get Some Perspective

Once you're calm and you've detached enough from your emotions about the problem that you can begin to think clearly, ground and center (if you haven't already) and try to get some perspective on the problem that's not colored by your feelings. Talk to your friends or mentors. Do a meditation or a pathworking about the problem. Talk directly to your gods and ask for insight. Do some divination, or have a friend do it for you if you think you can't be objective.

Make a Plan

When you've thought things through and gotten insight from outside (or inner) sources, make a plan for dealing with the issue. Brainstorm a variety of possible solutions. Pick two or three that seem the most reasonable, and think of any consequences they might have. (Chances are they'll all have them; if this problem were easy to solve, it wouldn't be a crisis.) Choose the one you think will solve the problem with the fewest negative repercussions. Check in with your gods or guides, and put your plan into action. Take some comfort in knowing that you have really thought this out, and you didn't just jump at the first solution that presented itself.

After you've executed your plan, don't dwell on the problem. Use some of the "getting away and calming down" techniques to let the problem go. It's possible you'll need to go back and tweak a few things after you've done your plan—clarify things with people, soothe hurt feelings, comfort or reassure someone—but for the most part, it's important to move on and not feed the problem any more of your energy.

A true teacher defends his pupils against his own personal influence. He inspires self-distrust. He guides their eyes from himself to the spirit that quickens him. He will have no disciple.

AMOS BRONSON ALCOTT

CHAPTER 12

From Teacher to Clergy

As I've mentioned already, being a teacher of Paganism doesn't mean that all you do is teach. Sometimes you're a mentor. Sometimes you're a counselor. Sometimes you're a traffic manager. Sometimes you're tech support. Sometimes you're a herder of cats. And sometimes, by accident or design, Pagan teachers are asked to take the next step and serve as Pagan clergy. As a matter of fact, some Pagan teachers—many of those who lead covens, for example—are clergy from the start. The point is, in the Pagan community, the line between teaching and being a clergy-person isn't just thin; it's porous. So it's helpful to know a little about being a Pagan clergyperson even if you're not planning on going that route. I never planned to do it, and I've been ordained twice. This chapter is about supplementing your teaching with clergy work and some of the incredibly important ways you can serve the Pagan community as a teacher/clergyperson, including interfaith work and prison ministry.

BECOME AN ORDAINED PAGAN CLERGYPERSON

Becoming an ordained clergyperson (or at least "legal to marry and bury") can be a large undertaking because of the time it takes to go through the training and jump through the legal hoops, and also in terms of the time you might end up spending teaching and serving as clergy, but it is also an essential service for the community.

In the past, the idea of "official"—especially professional—Pagan clergy could be a divisive topic in the Pagan world, and for some people it still is. Some Pagans felt that the only way we were going to be treated with any respect by non-Pagans was if we had professional teachers and clergy, and schools or seminaries in which to train them. Others believed that the autonomy of the various Pagan traditions (and eclectic practitioners or those with no established tradition) was absolutely sacrosanct, and having professional clergy in particular, but also professional teachers, was a one-way ticket toward becoming a hierarchical, monolithic, bureaucratic religious institution, not unlike some of the religious institutions many of us left to become Pagan in the first place. And still others just resented people setting themselves up as authorities in a community that prides itself on its lack of centralized authority.

About fifteen years ago a woman moved to the city I was living in at the time, declared herself a professional Pagan clergyperson, tried to set up a church with herself as a salaried Pagan minister, and expected the community to fall in line behind her. Some people in the community got pissed at her hubris, audacity, and presumption for thinking she could swing into town and have the community acknowledge her authority over them, but most of us just yawned and ignored her. It didn't take her long to move on.

However, times have changed. A lot. More and more Pagans are finding ways to get legal ministerial credentials, and for those who want structured ministerial training, now we have Pagan seminaries and training programs. We've come a long way.

Getting ministerial credentials is essential if you want to perform legal weddings. Getting credentialed might also allow you to officiate funerals, work on certain interfaith councils, and visit sick people in the hospital as a clergyperson. Unfortunately, as Patrick McCollum has discovered, being Pagan clergy will not necessarily get you into prisons to minister to inmates (although it might). Patrick has been fighting in court to challenge the "Five Faiths" rule in the California prisons, which states that only Catholic, Protestant, Muslim, Jewish, and Native American clergy can be hired to represent and work with inmates. And without a clergy-person present, inmates are often not allowed to gather to worship together at all.

Some Pagans sign up online with multi-faith organizations, such as the Universal Life Church, to get credentials. Others join Pagan umbrella organizations like Covenant of the Goddess, which also provide credentials. And still others have formed actual Pagan churches. I've talked to many Pagans who have been intimidated by the idea of jumping through the hoops to get credentials, but it's not necessarily as difficult as it sounds. Sylva Markson told me about her experience getting credentials. Her first set of credentials came from an already existing Pagan church, so all she had to do was file a certificate of ordination with the county. Later, she and a different group decided to establish their own church. This, of course, was a little more complicated:

> The most difficult part of this process was simply finding what was needed by the state—there is no nicely laid out, step-by-step process, so we waded through the statutes. In my state, there are several different ways that a church can be legally established, largely based on the amount of money we anticipated the church would bring in annually. Since our plan was for the church to bring in *no* money, we chose the simplest set-up. We had to draft a certificate of incorporation and file it with our county.

Just a decade or two ago, if you were Pagan and you wanted to learn how to minister to and counsel other Pagans, you wouldn't have had many options beyond joining an established Pagan group or coven and hoping they could give you some guidance, or studying materials aimed at training Christian clergy and adjusting them for Paganism. Now we have workshops and online courses for clerical training, and we even have full Pagan seminaries, such as Cherry Hill Seminary and the Woolston-

Steen Theological Seminary affiliated with the Aquarian Tabernacle Church. Holli Emore told me how Cherry Hill Seminary got its start:

> Kirk White, of Church of the Sacred Earth, originally conceived of Cherry Hill Seminary as a correspondence course with occasional retreats on his land in New Hampshire. An early collaborator, Cat Chapin-Bishop, suggested that courses be offered online through an open source program called Moodle. Laura Wildman-Hanlon was another person involved in the early years. The initial brainstorming by this trio quickly identified a need for training beyond one's tradition. Today, about a dozen volunteer staff comprise the team (and one paid executive director) which maintains the Cherry Hill Seminary organization and continues to implement our vision.

I also spoke at length with Pete "Pathfinder" Davis about how the Woolston-Steen Seminary came into being:

> It was clear to me that one of the major problems in Paganism is that pretty much anybody can stand up and declare themselves a priest or priestess, and maybe they're good at it, and maybe they're not. I have seen people offer counseling services, who if you took counseling from them you might be more inclined to go home and hang yourself in your closet, because they don't know what they're doing. I just felt that we needed to do something to professionalize the clergy in my tradition. I'm not saying that everybody else has to do this, but I want the people who decide to be clergy to others to be properly trained.

I asked Holli Emore if there was any such thing as a "typical" Cherry Hill student and what kind of person the seminary attracted:

As you have already guessed, Cherry Hill Seminary students, just like the entire Pagan world, are diverse, if nothing else. We have many students who come to us with graduate degrees already earned but who wish to go further in developing skills and knowledge for ministry. Even those with no college background tend to be individuals who have been leaders in their communities for some time. One trait which I see almost universally is that they value education as a means to their spiritual ends of service and personal growth.

Of course, the benefits of getting some ministerial training go far beyond the rights you are granted by law as clergy. There are opportunities for a great deal of personal development as well. Holli Emore spoke to me about this:

> I will share with you what I have gotten out of my experience, since I've been a Cherry Hill Seminary student for the past five years. I have gained a great deal of knowledge, of course, on the topics studies. But I've also worked through and developed my own personal code of ethics. I've integrated every single class I've taken with what was going on in my life at the time and ever since. I've gained new friendships and connections all over the country and in some other countries, too, and have people to whom I can reach out when I need help—and I've done that quite a few times. I feel supported in a way I never did before. And learning in the company of diverse Pagans gives me a perspective I might not ever develop in my own community or group of friends and peers. Finally, I feel validated and affirmed in my work, something which rated highly in a recent survey we conducted.

Starting a Pagan Organization

Starting a Pagan organization that provides teaching, clergy services, or both can be very rewarding and a valuable service to your community that's a step beyond simply teaching. There are legal issues to consider, as well as writing a charter, finding other members and a location to meet, holding meetings, and putting together the services you are planning to provide.

Pagan organizations can have a huge impact. I asked Oberon Zell-Ravenheart about the founding of the Church of All Worlds and *Green Egg Magazine* and Green Egg Online Forum, all of which were seminal in forming the Pagan community:

> As pioneers, I think it can be fairly said that Church of All Worlds and *Green Egg* established early templates that have served as models for many groups and, to a great extent, much of the entire Pagan movement. Certainly much of our CAW liturgy has been widely embraced and circulated throughout the Pagan community—such as our handfasting rites, water sharing, theatrical rituals, Gaean thealogy, etc.

I also asked him what he thought the role of the Church of All Worlds is today:

> Well, I guess I see our work as continuing to seed and tweak the evolving community in the direction of our very "green" vision and mission; specifically: "To evolve a network of information, mythology, and experience to awaken the Divine within and to provide a context and stimulus for reawakening Gaea and reuniting her children through tribal community dedicated to responsible stewardship and the evolutions of consciousness." Thus we sorta add our little influences here and there, like working on a bonsai tree.

Most of this we've done by subtly encouraging (through *Green Egg*, workshops, interviews, books, rituals, art, music, our personal lives, etc.) things we think should be part of the new world we are creating (such as inclusivity, cherishing diversity, the Gaea Thesis, polytheism, immanent divinity, sacred sexuality, feminist values, freedom of choice, equality, environmentalism, seasonal celebrations, nature worship, honesty, integrity, wisdom, service, cooperation, community, tribal values, ordaining priestesses as well as priests—and acceptance of personal lifestyle options such as different sexual orientations and identifications, polyamory, and social / ritual nudity). And of course, to not-so-subtly discourage aspects and attitudes we don't think should be part of the Pagan community, such as exclusivity, bigotry, dominance, competition, contempt for other ways, homophobia, racism, classism, sexism, "one-true-right-and-only-way-ism," environmental desecration, manipulation, dishonesty, stupidity, abuse, and buggering choir boys.

INTERFAITH WORK

Interfaith work—working with representatives of other religions to increase religious tolerance and mutual understanding—is something of a controversial topic in the Pagan community. Some Pagans believe we need to reach out to Christians and people of other religions to dispel some of the myths about Paganism and further establish Wicca and Paganism as legitimate religions with the same legal standing as other faiths. Other Pagans feel that outing ourselves to represent the Pagan community can be dangerous. Still others believe that if we do interfaith work at all, it should be within the Pagan community, since there are so many paths that fall under that umbrella, and—let's face it—we don't exactly coexist in peace and harmony. Personally, I think we need to do interfaith work both within our community and with people of other paths, and that it is a great way to teach. The ultimate goal of interfaith work is, after all, peace.

Interfaith work is a big commitment, but not in quite the same way as running a coven or teaching a class. Some Pagans sit on formal interfaith councils, working with Christians and others to advance tolerance. Others act more as ambassadors for their paths, speaking at interfaith or other non-Pagan conferences and venues to try to expand awareness and tolerance for Paganism. Interfaith work usually doesn't require planning classes and dealing with students' problems (although it might require giving some speeches or presentations and answering questions). It's more of a diplomatic role, and it requires a slightly different skill set. Reaching out to others and acting as a representative of your tradition or community—whether it's inside the Pagan community or outside— takes a lot of time, energy, and patience. However, it can be a great fit for people looking for a way to teach but who would prefer not to do so in some of the more conventional ways.

PRISON MINISTRY

One of the biggest Pagan teaching commitments you can make is to do prison ministry. This means going into prisons and providing clergy services and education to Pagan prisoners. This is extremely valuable work helping some of the people who need it most, but it's not to be undertaken lightly.

Prison ministry is not my area of expertise, so I interviewed Pagans who have done this work, including Patrick McCollum. McCollum serves as a statewide correctional chaplain for the California Department of Corrections and Rehabilitation. He has been working with prisoners for more than fourteen years and is well known in the Pagan community for his work on behalf of incarcerated Pagans and for his extensive interfaith efforts.

In 1997, a California Wiccan inmate won a court case and the right to have religious and chaplaincy services, so the attorney general contacted McCollum and asked if he could facilitate these services. What started with one student soon escalated, and now McCollum is working with 2,000 inmates at 33 different institutions, as well as facilitating chaplaincy services across the United States at both the state and federal levels.

Prison ministry serves some of the people who can benefit most from counseling and support, and who are least likely to get it. McCollum describes his first realization about how important this work can be:

> I realized how much difference you can make by going into a prison. If you start by recognizing the high value of one human life and spirit—what that is really worth—you really begin to see the great work we can all do in our community by just taking on one person and supporting their spirit, whatever that is, in some positive way.

But this work isn't easy. One of the things Pagan teachers worry about when considering prison ministry is the potential danger. McCollum agrees that Pagan prison chaplains need to be careful:

> You've got to learn the ropes if you're going to do that work. You have to have a lot of empathy, and you have to be pretty sharp and on your feet, because prison is a dangerous place. There are inmates who will do bad things to you, there are staff that will do bad things to you, and you just have to be really careful all the time and really be thinking a step ahead. You also have to be someone who can command respect. Inmates know weakness. They're trained from the moment that they get in prison that you take advantage of the weak, so you can't walk into prison acting like you're afraid or that you don't know something or you're worried about what's going

to happen to you. You have to come in there totally confident that you are in charge, and all those inmates will see that and they will follow what you say. But it takes a period of time to build a relationship with them to where you're really safe, so you have to learn your stuff.

I asked McCollum what it takes to do prison ministry successfully.

It requires a lot of fortitude—ability to stand up against a whole system that is stacked against you—because there are a lot of people in the prison system, even with all the positive steps we've made forward, who really don't want you to be there. So you have to start first of all by being willing to take some level of abuse and come out on top.

The fortitude McCollum is referring to is not just the strength to teach Paganism. It's also the strength to stand up for people who don't have much of a voice and deal with pushback from corrections personnel who didn't want Pagans to have access to chaplaincy services:

I have a certain stubbornness. When somebody starts push-ing, trying to stop me from doing something good, I push back harder than however hard they push. And I just keep bringing together as many resources to push back until in the end I hopefully can succeed.... I've gone into prisons, I've been beaten up, I've been thrown in a cell and arrested and charged with false charges and had people spit on me. I mean, you would not believe the kinds of things I've had happen to me. And every time they do something like that, I just decide that that behavior can't continue. The next person who comes in can't be made to have to deal with that. And so I take 'em on, and so far I've done fairly well.

The work that McCollum has done in California and elsewhere to allow incarcerated Pagans access to religious services has paved a path for others who wish to do the same.

Like clergy of any other faith, Pagans doing religious services in the prisons need to be very professional and set a good example. McCollum states:

> Up until three or four years ago there were a lot of people who just assumed that because they are high priest or priestess or something of some small group that started a year ago, that all of a sudden they're also qualified to walk in and be a spiritual leader or something in a prison. That's not really the way it works.

He also told me a story about the importance of acting like a professional in the prisons:

> You have to not do things, especially while you're in the prison, that would reflect badly on Paganism in general or on the work that you're doing....Sometimes Pagans feel that their spirituality puts them outside of social responsibilities, and so, for example, they think, "There are rules in the prison that don't apply to me because what I'm doing is somehow sacred." I once worked with a man working as chaplain who felt it was appropriate to bring illegal substances into the prison because he believed that they had a spiritual component to them and were supportive for the inmates and good for them, even though the law said that he couldn't. The person actually believed he was doing something good by doing that, and he justified it by saying [the substances] were part of our religious practice, which of course then shut down the religious practices for every Wiccan in the institution, because the institution said, "Well, we're not going to let that happen

here, so we're not letting any Wiccans in here." There have been many, many of those kinds of instances.

McCollum stresses two important messages with inmates: the idea that the gods love them and the idea of their inherent sacredness:

> When I started doing this, inmates were pretty much exposed only to Christianity and almost entirely Protestant Christianity. There was a little Judaism and Catholicism thrown in there, but it's really minimized in the prisons. And what those particular kinds of faith groups teach the inmates is that you are evil, you are bad, you are evil from creation, from the very beginning, because of the sins of Adam and Eve and such, and that you can never be redeemed until you actually die and stand before God and be judged. I go into the prisons with a different message.
>
> I'm primarily a Goddess worshiper, so I go into them and I say, to begin with, our Creator/Creatrix, whatever it is, is like a loving mother. She never abandons her children. You could do all kinds of terrible stuff, and she might really be ticked off about it, but she's never going to cease loving you or trying to help you. That really resonated with the inmates, because the largest number of inmates in institutions typically do not have a role model as a mother or a father. Many of them live on the streets and have had all kinds of social issues, come from broken families and things like that, so just the concept that there might be some sacred holy mother up there who cares about them becomes really important to them.
>
> The other thing I teach is that our particular tradition is as much about creating community and acknowledging and recognizing the sacredness in each of us. I tell them that every one of us, according to our belief system, all originate from

the same source that created everything, and so we have, like, a piece of God inside of us. So there is no one who can be entirely bad or useless or unable to contribute, because we are all sacred. And once we know that, we as a community come together and acknowledge and recognize the sacredness of one another … all of a sudden all these men and women come together as a family, which is something they never had.

We talked a lot about the difficulties associated with doing prison ministry, so I asked McCollum about his successes too. He told me about a woman he worked with:

She never wanted to be anything, never wanted to do anything, was on drugs and every other kind of problem. She came to Wicca to just sort of check it out and got more and more involved, and I saw her all the way through prison and her getting out, and got her into a halfway house in Long Beach, California. That woman, it turns out, was illiterate. She had to learn to read things in order to do her part of rituals. People would give her something, and she'd act like she knew what it was, but she had no idea what it said. So she struggled to teach herself to read enough to be able to learn how to do her parts of the ritual, and gradually got better and better.

When she got out, she shared that and said she wanted to dedicate herself to the Goddess and teach other women how to become literate.… She was successful in the halfway house, but she decided to stay on as staff and teach all the women who were illiterate how to become literate. And she in fact did that, but she went way beyond that; she began to write poetry and won a number of poetry awards and actually became this very well-known poetess. And she is still doing that today. So we can have such a huge effect on someone like that.

I asked McCollum for some final words of wisdom for Pagans considering doing prison ministry:

> You really have to have a spiritual desire to do the work. You have to be a person who is connected to whatever source spirit or divinity is, because that's what it will take to support you to actually do the work. You can't just be somebody who says, "I think it will be cool to go into prison. It'll make me look good to do this." That doesn't work, but if you're inspired by your own spiritual path to go do the work, then you'll do well.

. . . .

As you can see, Pagan clergy work is very nuanced and requires a great deal of self-confidence and diplomacy, so it is probably best done by teachers with some experience under their belts. But these services are also needed desperately by our community, so if you feel called to become a Pagan clergyperson, try not to be discouraged by the complexities. If you have any aptitude and interest in this work, and you feel it is something you must do, I encourage you to help others by walking this path. However, I also encourage you to seek training and mentorship—and maybe even an internship—from those who have walked the path before you. Good clergy, like good teachers, are not created in a vacuum, and a supportive network is a must for this kind of work.

Conclusion
Okay, Now Go Change the World!

When I try to distill all my years of teaching into a simple sound bite or idea—something upbeat to leave you with as you begin your teaching journey—what I come up with is that teaching, to me, means hope.

I remember my first day of student teaching English to tenth-graders. I was just a few years older than they were, I was pretty sure they would eat me alive, and I was scared to death. It's a generally accepted (if not scientifically supported) fact that kids can smell fear like sharks smell blood in the water. But what helped me conquer my fear was hope—hope that I could help these kids, many of whom were disadvantaged. Hope that I could give them a safe space to learn, away from whatever problems they had outside of class. And hope that maybe I could inspire them to like reading and writing and expressing themselves, even just a little bit.

Teaching means hope not only for the students right in front of you, but also for the future. Teachers have a unique opportunity to have an impact on the world around them. They can help shape thought and influence future generations. They can be role models and set examples of being a positive force in a community. They can help a community be more interconnected. They can inspire. And teachers can be agents of extraordinary and powerful change.

Patrick McCollum told me:

> You can change the world. I mean, many Pagans are concerned about many different aspects of the world we live in: pollution, the ecology, human rights, equal treatment, and

pluralism.... Here is a place to walk your talk, to actually get
in on the ground floor and do something to bring about the
things you believe in.

Envision the world you want to live in. Envision a positive future for
the Pagan community. Teaching can help make it a reality.

I don't want to blow sunshine up your skirt here. If you teach, there
will definitely be challenges. There will be situations that freak you out,
make you cry, and maybe even make you question yourself and your purpose. But don't let that stuff throw you. There will also be moments of
gnosis and sublime beauty, epiphanies and breathtaking discoveries, and
communion with the Divine.

Patrick McCollum commented to me on how when you're working in
tune with the Divine, the Divine tends to look out for you:

> I would say that in our traditions teaching is a sacred thing,
> and I think that people who are interested in wanting to teach
> can put a lot of store in that—that the work they're doing isn't
> just work, it's sacred, and that if they will give themselves over
> to that idea, they'll not only shift and change for the better,
> the people they work with and help will too....
>
> There seems to be a force that takes care of you and makes
> sure you're okay if you put yourself in line with the sacred-
> ness. Our whole religion and spirituality is about that. That's
> something that people really want to think about and really
> want to try to move into it as a priestess- or priesthood. Not
> so much "you have to be a high priest or priestess of a group"
> or something. Take it on as a walk on the sacred path. That's
> what your particular sacred walk is going to be.

Teaching is a rich, rewarding way to align your spiritual beliefs deeply
with your daily life and walk the path of your gods. And when you're

aligned and walking that path, you're truly following your bliss. Remember that your work is vital and desperately needed by our community. And remember that as a teacher, you are an agent not only of learning but also of hope.

Never doubt that a small group of thoughtful, committed people can change the world. Indeed, it is the only thing that ever has.

MARGARET MEAD

Appendix A

Screening Questions

Here are some questions you might want to use when screening students. They range from simple to complex, not very personal to very personal. I have never used some of these questions, although I know others who have. Teachers should alter them to meet their specific needs and situations or use them as springboards for creating their own questions. And obviously, if you think a question is too invasive or it makes you uncomfortable, don't use it!

One thing that I've found very helpful is asking open-ended questions rather than yes-or-no ones. Open-ended questions give potential students a chance to elaborate, and you can learn a lot about them by the way in which they explain their answers. So if you just get a yes or no answer to a question, consider asking a follow-up question to tease out more information. Not all questions have to be open-ended, of course.

At the end of the interview, be sure to ask potential students if they have any questions for you. This gives you an opportunity to clarify things for them, but what they choose to ask about can also tell you a lot about them.

Pagan "Résumé" Questions

Interest

- Why are you interested in exploring Paganism?

- What would you like to get out of this class? What are your goals?

- Why do you want to study specifically with me/us?

- How did you hear about this class/us?

- What will you do with the information you learn in this class? How will you apply it?

History

- How long have you been Pagan?

- Tell me about your past history/experience with Paganism.

- What other Pagan classes have you taken?

- Have you ever taken a Pagan class online?

- Have you had other teachers in the past, and if so, who?

- How long did you stay with your past teacher(s)?

- Why did you leave your past teacher/teaching situation?

- Have you ever been initiated into a Pagan, Wiccan, or occult tradition? If so, which one(s)?

- What is your pre-Pagan religious background (Christian, atheist, etc.)? What impact has it had on your life? How has it informed your worldview?

- Have you ever been a member of a cult? If so, how was that resolved?

Preferences

- What is your favorite Pagan-related book, and why?

- What Pagan books have you read?

- Are there any particular deities you work with regularly? How did that relationship come about?

Experience

- What is your experience with magic?

- How would you characterize your expertise with magic?

- What is your background in mythology?

- How would you characterize your ability to use energy?

- What do you already know about (class topic)?

Relationship to Community

- How many other Pagans do you know?

- How would you characterize your relationship to the Pagan community, either local or online?

- Have you ever been to a large Pagan event such as camping, public ritual, etc.? How was that experience?

Philosophical and Ethical Questions

General Religion/Spirituality

- What are your feelings about religion in general?

- In your opinion, what is the difference between spirituality, religion, and belief, if any?

- What do you think is the function of religion in modern society?

- How important is spirituality in your life?

Paganism

- What does the word *Paganism* mean to you?

- What aspect of Paganism appeals or resonates with you most?

- What importance does Paganism have in your life?

Deity

- What is your view of deity, if you have one?

- What does the Goddess mean to you?

- What does the God mean to you?

- Would you consider yourself a dualist? If so, what does that mean to you?

- Would you consider yourself a pantheist? If so, what does that mean to you?

- Would you consider yourself a polytheist? If so, what does that mean to you?

- How do you feel about working in a matrifocal tradition? (If applicable)

Nature

- How would you characterize your relationship with the natural world?
- How important is nature to your personal spirituality?
- How do you feel about animals and animal rights?

Sex and Nudity

- What is your philosophy about sex?
- What is the place of sexuality in religion, if any?
- Do you feel that your sexual orientation has an impact on your spirituality?
- How do you feel about homosexuality? Bisexuality? Transgenderism?
- How do you feel about practicing skyclad?

Ethics

- Do you follow any particular ethical code (such as the Rede)? If so, how does that affect how you handle the situations in which you find yourself?
- Give an example of an unethical situation you found yourself in. How did you handle it?
- In your view, what is an example of an ethical "grey" area? Why?
- How do you feel about doing magic for someone else without telling him or her?
- If you have a romantic partner, have you told him or her that you are exploring Paganism? Why or why not? What was the response?
- Is it okay to do a love spell on someone? Why or why not?
- How do you feel about lying? Are there circumstances under which it is okay to lie?

Politics

- What are your feelings about being in or out of the closet about your Paganism? Which are you?

- Do you think it's okay to "out" other Pagans? Why or why not?

- How do you feel about Christianity?

- How do you feel about Islam?

- Do you consider yourself more liberal or more conservative?

- How do you feel about war?

- How do you feel about feminism?

- Do you have any causes you are particularly dedicated to? Why?

Personality Questions

General

- What do you think your personality strengths are? Weaknesses?

- Do you consider yourself an extrovert or introvert? Why?

- What things in life give you the most satisfaction? Happiness?

Learning

- How do you learn best (hands-on, lecture, group work, independent study, etc.), and why?

- Which do you prefer: working in groups or working alone? Why?

- Under what conditions or circumstances do you learn best?

Interpersonal Stuff

- Tell me about a time when someone challenged your credibility. How did you handle it?

- Tell me how you would deal with a fellow student with whom you were having a problem or personality conflict.

- What one person has been most influential in your life, and why?

Stress

- Are you nervous about joining our class? Why?

- In general, what scares you most? Why?

- What stresses you out, and why?

- Tell me about your self-care: what do you do to handle stress?

Schedule and Logistical Questions

- Our class schedule is X. Can you fit that in with your regular schedule?

- Do you live close enough to get to class regularly?

- Do you have or need transportation?

- What other commitments do you have that might conflict with class?

- Are you in a place in your life when you can devote the necessary amount of time to this class?

PHYSICAL AND MENTAL HEALTH QUESTIONS

Physical

- Do you have any allergies to animals, foods, perfume, bee stings, incense, etc., that we need to be aware of?

- Do you need any special physical accommodation to do the activities covered in the class?

- Do you have any health issues (epileptic seizure, insulin reaction, etc.) that might arise in class that we should know about?

Mental

- How would you characterize your current state of mental health?

- Is there anything you would like us to know about your mental health?

- Have you experienced any trauma in your life that might have an impact on your experience in this class?

- Are you on prescribed medication for a mental health issue? If so, are you seeing a doctor and/or a therapist regularly?

- Do you have any psychological issues you think we should know about?

- Have you ever had a nervous breakdown or psychological break? Please explain.

- Have you ever been diagnosed with a personality disorder? If so, which one?

- Have you ever been institutionalized, and if so, why?

Drug and Alcohol Questions

- How would you characterize your drug or alcohol use?

- Have you ever had a problem with drug or alcohol addiction?

- Are you in recovery?

- Have you had any kind of drug or alcohol treatment, and if so, was it successful?

- Are you prone to binge drinking or drug use?

- Are there any modifications you might ask us to make (for example, juice instead of wine in ritual) to accommodate your recovery?

Background Check Questions

- Have you ever been charged with a crime? If so, what was it, and how was the situation resolved?

- Have you ever been incarcerated? If so, for what crime, and for how long?

- Have you ever been violent with others? What were the circumstances?

APPENDIX B
Sample Syllabuses

Here are some simple example syllabuses you can use as a starting point for creating your own. I have listed objectives for each class session. Unless stated otherwise, the objectives are meant to be met within the class section under which they are listed.

SYLLABUS A: USING ENERGY

Session 1: Energy Introduction

What is energy? Types of energy. How energy is used in ritual and magic. Etiquette for using energy.

Session 1 Objectives

- Students will be able to name and define three different types of energy.
- Students will be able to describe at least three ways energy is used in ritual and magic.

Session 2: Grounding and Centering

Why grounding is important, and why you should know how to do it before you raise energy. Grounding techniques. What centering is, how it is different from grounding, and how and why to do it.

Session 2 Objectives

- Students will be able to describe the difference between grounding and centering.

- Students will be able to list and demonstrate at least two ways to ground energy.

- Students will be able to list and demonstrate at least one way to center energy.

Session 3: Sensing and Shielding

Techniques for strengthening the ability to see and feel energy and determine its source. What shielding is, and why you should learn it before you send and receive energy. Basic shielding techniques. Feeling others' shields.

Session 3 Objectives

- Students will practice two techniques for sensing energy.

- Students will be able to explain what shielding is and why it is important.

- Students will choose a form for visualizing their personal shields and practice using that form with a basic shielding technique.

- Students will work with a partner to practice "feeling" each other's shields.

Session 4: Sending and Receiving Energy

Techniques for projecting energy. Techniques for receiving energy. Creating an energy circuit between two people.

Session 4 Objectives

- Students will practice a simple technique for projecting energy.

- Students will practice a technique for receiving energy from another person, then grounding it.

- Students will partner up and practice creating an energy circuit between them, then grounding it.

Session 5: Charging Objects

How to charge and drain objects of energy for magical purposes. Includes a ritual where everyone will charge an object to take home and use on their own.

Session 5 Objectives

- Students will be able to describe three different methods for charging an object.

- Students will be able to describe two different methods for draining or clearing an object.

- Students will practice charging and draining an object.

Syllabus B: Using the Moon in Magic

Session 1: History and Basics

Overview of lore about use of the moon in folk magic. Folkloric names and associations with each moon of the year. Importance of the new and full moons.

Session 1 Objectives

- Students will be able to identify at least one system of naming the full moons and list the names in it.

- Students will be able to demonstrate verbally or in writing a basic understanding of the difference between and magical uses of the full and new moons.

- Students will generate a list of magical tasks that can be done at the full moon and a list of those that can be done at the new moon.

Session 2: Quarters and Phases

Difference between waxing and waning moons and what each is used for. Divisions of the moon's cycle into four quarters and/or eight phases (gibbous, balsamic, etc.), how phases and quarters relate to each other, correspondences for each, and how each is used. Introduction to using an astrological calendar.

Session 2 Objectives

- Students will be able to demonstrate verbally or in writing a basic understanding of the four quarters of the moon and the eight phases of the moon and their magical uses.

- For each phase of the moon, students will list a magical task that would be appropriate to do.

- Students will practice using an astrological calendar to find the full and new moons and determine the quarter or phase of the moon.

Session 3: The Moon's Sign

Importance and significance of the moon's sign in magical timing. Energies and correspondences associated with the moon in each sign.

Session 3 Objectives

- Students will practice using an astrological calendar to determine the sign of the moon.

- Students will choose one sign and list as many magical tasks as they can think of that could be accomplished under that sign.

Session 4: Using Basic Lunar Aspects

Introduction to aspects (angular relationships) between the moon and other planets, their significance, and how they can be used. Significance of the moon void-of-course. Putting it all together to plan timing for a spell or ritual.

Session 4 Objectives

- Students will be able to demonstrate verbally or in writing a basic understanding of the meanings of and differences between the conjunction, square, trine, and opposition aspects.

- Students will be able to explain verbally or in writing the significance of a moon void-of-course.

- Students will practice using an astrological calendar to find the moon's aspects and voids.

Syllabus C: Hands-On Wooden Wand-Making Class
(for a basic wand carved from a branch or root)

Session 1: Planning
Overview of basic wand lore. Folklore and significance associated with various woods. Characteristics of a branch or stick that make it a good candidate for a wand. Ideas on where to find branches for wands locally. How to harvest or collect wood.

Session 1 Objectives
- Students will be able to explain the magical properties of at least three types of wood covered in the class.
- Students will be able to describe characteristics of a branch that make it suitable for a wand.
- (Between classes) students will find at least one branch or stick to make a wand and bring it to the next class.

Session 2: Carving
Safety techniques for using woodcarving tools. How to trim branches and strip bark cleanly. Transferring designs from paper to wood. Carving techniques for shapes and designs.

Session 2 Objectives
- Students will be able to explain the safety techniques for using woodcarving tools.
- Students will practice stripping bark from their branches.
- Students will be able to explain how to transfer a design from paper to a wand.
- Students will begin carving their wands.

Session 3: Finishing and Consecrating

How to sand after carving. Pros and cons of various finishes and how to apply them. How to consecrate the new wand.

Session 3 Objectives

- Students will finish carving their wands.

- Students will be able to explain the pros and cons of using three different wood finishes.

- Students will apply wood finish to their wands.

- Students will consecrate their new wands.

Appendix C

Resources

Below are lists of resources that can be useful to teachers, coven leaders, Pagan clergy, and anyone else in a leadership role in the Pagan community.

Websites

In addition to listing many of the sites that I use or that have been recommended to me by friends, I've listed some sites that I personally have no experience with but that seemed important to include because of their potential value to teachers. As you check out these sites, use your best discretion to determine if the information is completely accurate and/or useful to you. Also, if I've left something out, it doesn't mean it's not great! If I listed every Pagan resource I could find, it would fill another whole book.

Adult Learning and Class Preparation
American Association for Adult and Continuing Education:
www.aaace.org (click on "adult learning")
Publishes *Adult Learning Quarterly*.

American Society for Training and Development: www.astd.org
Meant mostly for corporate trainers but provides books, classes, and other resources that might be useful to Pagan teachers.

Adult and Child Learners: http://online.rit.edu/faculty /teaching_strategies/adult_learners.cfm
An article with succinct descriptions of the differences between adult and child learners.

How Adults Learn: agelesslearner.com/intros/adultlearning.html
Article with links by Marcia L. Conner.

Principles of Adult Learning: www.teachermentors.com /adultLrng.php
A concise rundown of the basics.

What Is Adult Learning? adulted.about.com/od/intro/p /introprofile.htm
About.com article with lots of useful links.

Content
Creative Commons: www.creativecommons.org

Flickr: www.flickr.com

Dealing with People
Isaac Bonewits's Cult Danger Evaluation Frame: www .neopagan.net/ABCDEF.html
This is a frame with a list of criteria to determine if an organization is a cult. Don't do any of this stuff in your class!

Project Pagan Enough: www.incitingariot.com/p/project-pagan -enough.html

Trollspotting: bichaunt.org/Trolls/index.html
Very long but excellent article on dealing with trolls within a spiritual class, group, or coven.

Humor
Why Would You Want to Be a Teacher: www.widdershins.org
/vol10iss3/11.htm
Humor by Sylvana Silverwitch.

Pagan Organizations and Churches
Aquarian Tabernacle Church: www.aquariantabernaclechurch.org
Pagan church founded by Pete "Pathfinder" Davis in Washington
State. Has chapters elsewhere and is the organization behind the
Woolston-Steen Theological Seminary.

Circle Sanctuary: www.circlesanctuary.org

Lady Liberty League: www.circlesanctuary.org/liberty
Advocates for Pagan legal rights.

Mother Earth Ministries: www.motherearthministries.org
Arizona organization that works with incarcerated Pagans.

Our Lady of the Earth and Sky: www.oloteas.org
Interviewee Stephanie Raymond's organization in Washington
State.

Online Learning
eLearn Magazine: http://elearnmag.acm.org/index.cfm

White paper on best practices for teaching online:
http://www.umuc.edu/ctl/upload/bestpractices.pdf

Pagan Podcasts, Blogs, and Other Journalism Outlets
ATC Pagan Information Network: www.atcpin.com

CUUPS (Covenant of Unitarian Universalist Pagans) Podcast:
http://cuups.libsyn.com

Elemental Castings: www.thorncoyle.com/videos-podcasts
/podcasts
T. Thorn Coyle's podcast series.

The Juggler: http://culture.pagannewswirecollective.com
The arts from a Pagan perspective.

Pagan-Centered Podcast: http://imbleedingprofusely.com

Pagan + Politics: http://politics.pagannewswirecollective.com

Pagan Radio Network: www.paganradio.net

Patheos Pagan Portal: www.patheos.com/Religion-Portals
/Pagan.html
Pagan section of multi-religion website Patheos.

Proud Pagan Podcasts: http://paganpodcasting.org
Get Started with Podcasting direct URL: http://paganpodcasting
.org/resources/get-started-with-podcasting

Theologies of Immanence: http://pagantheologies.pbworks
.com/w/page/13621982/Blogs-A-to-F
Huge list of Pagan blogs.

T. Thorn Coyle Musings: www.thorncoyle.com/musings

Warriors and Kin: http://military.pagannewswirecollective.com
Blog for and about Pagans in the military.

The Wild Hunt: http://www.patheos.com/blogs/wildhunt
Pagan news blog by Jason Pitzl-Waters. Recently made a subsection
of the Patheos Pagan portal. Highly recommended.

Witches' Voice Blogs: www.witchvox.com/lx/lx_blogs.html
A list of Pagan blogs.

Witches' Voice Podcast Page: www.witchvox.com/lx/lx_podcasts
.html
A list of Pagan podcasts.

Witchtalk: www.witchtalkshow.com
Witchy radio show.

Pagan or Wiccan Teachers
T. Thorn Coyle: www.thorncoyle.com

Ellen Evert Hopman: http://www.elleneverthopman.com

Patrick McCollum: http://www.patrickmccollum.org

Christopher Penczak: http://christopherpenczak.com/site2009
/contact.html

Oberon Zell-Ravenheart: www.oberonzell.com

Online Training in Paganism and/or Wicca
Grey School of Wizardry: www.greyschool.com

Witch School: www.witchschool.com

Presentation Tips
Icebreakers: http://adulted.about.com/od/icebreakers
/Ice_Breakers.htm
About.com article on icebreakers with links.

Toastmasters: www.toastmasters.org

Seminaries, Clergy and Counseling Training,
Ministerial Credentials
Cherry Hill Seminary: http://cherryhillseminary.org

Covenant of the Goddess: www.cog.org

How to Protect Your Legal Rights: http://paganwiccan.about
.com/od/yourlegalrights/ht/Rights_Intro.htm
About.com article on legalities around religious discrimination.

Ordain Me Please/Celebration Community Church:
www.ordainmeplease.com/Home_Page.php
Ministerial credentials for people of all faiths.

Universal Life Church: www.themonastery.org
Ministerial credentials for people of all faiths.

Woolston-Steen Theological Seminary: http://wiccanseminary
.edu

Software
Adobe Acrobat Reader: http://get.adobe.com/reader

Litmus (LMS): http://www.litmos.com

Moodle (LMS): http://moodle.org

PowerPoint, including free PowerPoint Reader:
http://office.microsoft.com/en-us/powerpoint

Books

Some of these titles might be out of print, but they can often be found online or in used bookstores. As with the website list, I have included a few books here that I haven't read, so I can't vouch for them personally. However, they were recommended to me by trusted others, and they seemed worth including. Use your best judgment, of course.

Burnout and Self-Care

I Should Be Burnt Out By Now ... So How Come I'm Not: How You Can Survive and Thrive in Today's Uncertain World by Peg Neuhauser. This book was designed to keep people from burning out in the workplace, but it contains information that can be very useful to teachers.

The Resilient Practitioner: Burnout Prevention and Self-Care Strategies for Counselors, Therapists, Teachers, and Health Professionals by Thomas Skovholt and Michelle Trotter-Mathison. Information specifically directed to "high-interaction" professionals, such as teachers, counselors, and healthcare professionals. Very useful.

Ethics

Ethics and the Craft: The History, Evolution, and Practice of Wiccan Ethics by John J. Coughlin.

When, Why ... If by Robin Wood. About ethics in Paganism. A simple, straightforward book for teachers discussing ethics with students in a Pagan context.

Group Dynamics / Interpersonal Relationships

Antagonists in the Church: How to Identify and Deal with Destructive Conflict by Kenneth C. Haugk. This book was written for Christians who are dealing with antagonistic personalities in their spiritual groups. Very Christian focus but powerful and helpful information for dealing with interpersonal problems in a spiritual group. Inspiration for the trollspotting article cited in the preceding website section.

Coven Craft: Witchcraft for Three or More by Amber K. Forming and running a coven. Recommended.

Gathering the Magic: Creating 21st Century Esoteric Groups by Nick Farrell. Discusses forming and running esoteric groups.

Truth or Dare: Encounters with Power, Authority, and Mystery by Starhawk. Discusses power and group dynamics.

Wicca Covens: How to Start and Organize Your Own by Judy Harrow.

Ministry/Clergy

Enchantment Encumbered: The Study and Practice of Wicca in Restricted Environments by Ashleen O'Gaea and Carol Garr. Working with incarcerated Pagans.

Joining Hands and Hearts: Interfaith, Intercultural Wedding Celebrations— A Practical Guide for Couples by Susanna Stefanachi Macomb.

The Pagan Book of Living and Dying: Practical Rituals, Prayers, Blessings, and Meditations on Crossing Over by Starhawk and M. Macha Night-Mare. Useful for Pagan clergy or teachers who might be working with people dealing with death or presiding over funerals.

Pagans and Christians: The Personal Spiritual Experience by Gus DiZerega. A discussion of Paganism and Christianity together. Good background for Pagan clergy doing interfaith work.

Pagans and the Law by Dana D. Eilers. Discusses Pagan legal rights.

Promises to Keep: Crafting Your Wedding Ceremony by Ann Keeler Evans. How to write a wedding ceremony. Not Pagan, but useful.

Online Education

Conquering the Content: A Step-by-Step Guide to Online Course Design by
  Robin M. Smith. Content-focused instructional design.

e-Learning by Design by William Horton.

Teaching

101 Ways to Make Training Active by Mel Silberman.

The Adult Learner: A Neglected Species by Malcolm S. Knowles.

Teaching Witchcraft: A Guide for Teachers and Students of the Old Religion
  by Miles Batty. A full curriculum for teaching Witchcraft.

Telling Ain't Training by Harold D. Stolovitch and Erica J. Keeps.
  Designed primarily for corporate trainers but contains lots of
  useful stuff for teachers.

APPENDIX D

About the Interviewees

T. Thorn Coyle

T. Thorn Coyle is an internationally respected mentor and teacher of the magical and esoteric arts. The author of *Kissing the Limitless* and *Evolutionary Witchcraft*, she hosts the *Elemental Castings* podcast and *Fiat LVX!* video series, writes a popular weblog, *Know Thyself*, and has produced several CDs of sacred music. Thorn's spiritual direction, soul reading, and body/spirit coaching practices help people worldwide. Pagan, mystic, and activist, she is founder and head of Solar Cross Temple and Morningstar Mystery School and lives by the San Francisco Bay. For further information, please visit thorncoyle.com.

Sarah Davies

Sarah Davies has been a coven leader in the Gardnerian Tradition of British Traditional Wicca for one year. Sarah has experience in ritual design, writing, and music. She is a web developer for a nonprofit in Seattle and holds a bachelor's degree in physics from the University of Washington, where she is currently a graduate student.

Pete "Pathfinder" Davis

Archpriest Pete "Pathfinder" Davis is the originator of the Aquarian Tabernacle Tradition of English Traditional-based Wicca and the Primate of the Aquarian Tabernacle Church, which he founded in November of 1979 in Washington State. Pete has served two terms as president of the Interfaith Council of Washington State and is a longtime member of the

Washington State Department of Corrections Religious Services Advisory Committee, which advises the department on religious programs in Washington's institutions. He is also active in other interfaith organizations and efforts on behalf of the Wiccan communities in the Pacific Northwest, and he has taught Wicca in several area post-secondary educational facilities. He is a regent of the Woolston-Steen Theological Seminary, a college-level institution that prepares Wiccan students for service as fully competent Wiccan clergy.

Holli Emore

Holli Emore, CFRE, is executive director of Cherry Hill Seminary and president of Emore Development Resources, a consulting firm for nonprofits. A native of North Carolina, Holli is twice a past president of the Central Carolina Chapter of the Association of Fundraising Professionals in Columbia, South Carolina, where she has lived since 1986. An ambassador for the Parliament of the World's Religions and an advisor to the Interfaith Partnership of South Carolina, Holli is committed to building interfaith relationships, both locally and globally. She often teaches public groups about the rapidly growing Neopagan religions and has served as a regional resource for law enforcement, victim services, criminal justice classes, and others since 2004, and is a resource person for the Lady Liberty League. She is the founder of Osireion, as well as the Pagan Round Table, both in South Carolina.

Anne Marie Forrester

Anne Marie Forrester is a third-degree Gardnerian high priestess, a legal minister, an elder in the Gardnerian Church of the Ancient Communion, and a member of one of the longest-running eclectic covens in the Upper Midwest. She is author and illustrator of *Beyond the Veil: 36 Pages of Enchantment Waiting for You to Add Color and Life* and *Gods and Goddesses of the Zodiac*, and co-author (with Estelle Daniels) of *Color-A-Magick-Spell: 13 Mandalas for Personal Empowerment* (available through www.magusbooks.com). Some of her artwork can be viewed online at www.web.me.com/annemarieforrester.

Melanie Henry

Melanie Henry has been a student of Witchcraft for more than thirty years, a Witch in the Sylvan Tradition for sixteen years, and the high priestess of a Sylvan Tradition coven for eight years. She has also read tarot professionally and edited *Widdershins*, the Pagan newspaper that served the Seattle area from 1995 to 2007. She lives outside Seattle, in the foothills of the Cascade Mountains.

Ellen Evert Hopman

Ellen Evert Hopman is a master herbalist, a professional member of the American Herbalists Guild, and lay homeopath with an M.Ed. in mental health counseling. Hopman is a founding member of the Order of the White Oak (Ord Na Darach Gile) and its former co-chief, and was vice president of the Henge of Keltria, an international Druid fellowship, for nine years. She was a professor in the Grey School of Wizardry for four years. Hopman has been a teacher of herbalism since 1983 and of Druidism since 1990 and has presented on Druidism, herbal lore, tree lore, and Paganism at conferences, festivals, and events in Northern Ireland, the Republic of Ireland, Scotland, Canada, and across the United States. She is the author of a trilogy of Celtic novels that take place in Iron Age Ireland: *Priestess of the Forest: A Druid's Story*, *The Druid Isle*, and *Priestess of the Fire Temple: A Druid's Tale*. She has authored a number of nonfiction books on Druidism, Celtic herb lore, and magic, which can be found at www.elleneverthopman.com.

Sylva Markson

Sylva Markson grew up in northern Minnesota, where she developed a deep and abiding love for its lakes and forests. She has a degree in both history and religion, and has always been interested in the roots of spiritual paths and in combining intellectual exploration with mystical or shamanic experiences. She has been practicing the Craft for twenty years and has led a coven (with her husband and magical partner) for about fifteen years, with an emphasis on altered states of consciousness and shamanic techniques. Other interests include nature, animals, equal rights, cultures, and travel. Hobbies include antiquing, camping, and herbalism. She currently lives in northern Minnesota with her husband, three dogs, and three birds.

Patrick McCollum

Reverend Patrick McCollum is an ordained Circle Sanctuary minister, serves as a coordinator for the Lady Liberty League, is a Wiccan chaplain in the California Department of Corrections, and is also development director for Children of the Earth (United Nations, NGO) as well as serving on many other committees. In 2010, Reverend McCollum was honored at the Capitol in Washington, DC, as the 2010 recipient of the Mahatma Gandhi Award for the Advancement of Pluralism. McCollum was also selected as a delegate in 2010 to address leaders of seventy-five counties at Parliament in Astana, Kazakhstan, at the World Forum on Spiritual Culture. In 2011, Reverend McCollum was invited to Thailand by Dhammakaya Buddhists as a World Inner Peace Ambassador. Patrick is dedicated to being a warrior for human rights, social justice, and pluralism. He has recently started the Patrick McCollum Foundation (patrickmccollum.org) to help him with this plight. Through religion and spirituality he is bringing a new message of planetary consciousness on a global level that will alert the world to the sacredness of our connection with divinity and with each other.

Christopher Penczak

Christopher Penczak is a modern Witch, teacher, and healing practitioner. He is an award-winning author who has published over twenty books and recordings on Witchcraft, magick, and spirituality and is the co-founder of the Temple of Witchcraft, a nonprofit religious organization dedicated to community, education, and service. His work draws on the traditions of wisdom from across the world, particularly the ancient Pagan mysteries, synthesized into a harmonious whole for modern practitioners.

Stephanie Raymond

Stephanie Raymond is a third-degree initiate priestess of the Georgian Wiccan Tradition and has been a practicing Pagan for nineteen years. She founded the University of Washington Pagan Culture and Spirit Web student group in 1991, and she cofounded Our Lady of the Earth and Sky, a nondenominational Pagan church, in 1995, serving there as pastor from 1995–1999 and 2011 to the present. She lives with her family in Seattle.

Brian Rowe

Brian Rowe is a British Traditional Wiccan who has just started teaching pre-initiates. Brian believes life must be experienced, not just understood or contemplated, and that the Craft is enhanced by a small group of individuals sharing rites. Brian believes that the Craft is compatible with modern technology and ethics based on human rights. He holds a J.D. and teaches information privacy, ethics, and copyright. When not voraciously reading mythology, Brian enjoys Rodin's sculpture, coffee, ancient Egypt, chess, not watching TV, civil disobedience, and Chado.

Oberon Zell-Ravenheart

Oberon Zell-Ravenheart is a renowned Pagan elder. In 1962, he founded the Church of All Worlds. First to apply the term "Pagan" to the new Nature Religions of the '60s, and through his publication of *Green Egg* magazine, Oberon was instrumental in fostering the modern Pagan movement. He designs altar statuary and jewelry for the Mythic Images Collection and wrote *Grimoire for the Apprentice Wizard*. He is also founder and headmaster of the online Grey School of Wizardry. Oberon and his lifemate Morning Glory live in NorCalifia, where he serves on the Board of the Sonoma County Pagan Network. His website is www.OberonZell .com.

INDEX

GET MORE AT LLEWELLYN.COM

Visit us online to browse hundreds of our books and decks, plus sign up to receive our e-newsletters and exclusive online offers.

- **Free tarot readings • Spell-a-Day • Moon phases**
- **Recipes, spells, and tips • Blogs • Encyclopedia**
- **Author interviews, articles, and upcoming events**

GET SOCIAL WITH LLEWELLYN

 **Find us on**
www.Facebook.com/LlewellynBooks

Follow us on
www.Twitter.com/Llewellynbooks

GET BOOKS AT LLEWELLYN

LLEWELLYN ORDERING INFORMATION

Order online: Visit our website at www.llewellyn.com to select your books and place an order on our secure server.

Order by phone:
- Call toll free within the U.S. at 1-877-NEW-WRLD (1-877-639-9753)
- Call toll free within Canada at 1-866-NEW-WRLD (1-866-639-9753)
- We accept VISA, MasterCard, and American Express

Order by mail:
Send the full price of your order (MN residents add 6.875% sales tax) in U.S. funds, plus postage and handling to: Llewellyn Worldwide, 2143 Wooddale Drive Woodbury, MN 55125-2989

POSTAGE AND HANDLING

STANDARD (U.S. & Canada):
(Please allow 12 business days)
$25.00 and under, add $4.00.
$25.01 and over, FREE SHIPPING.

INTERNATIONAL ORDERS (airmail only):
$16.00 for one book, plus $3.00 for each additional book.

Visit us online for more shipping options. Prices subject to change.

FREE CATALOG!

To order, call
1-877-
NEW-WRLD
ext. 8236
or visit our
website

Wicca for Beginners

Fundamentals of Philosophy & Practice

Thea Sabin

Due to the sheer number of Wicca 101 books on the market, many new-comers to the Craft find themselves piecing together their Wiccan education by reading a chapter from one book, a few pages from another. Rather than depending on snippets of wisdom to build a new faith, *Wicca for Beginners* provides a solid foundation to Wicca without limiting the reader to one tradition or path.

Embracing both the spiritual and the practical, *Wicca for Beginners* is a primer on the philosophies, culture, and beliefs behind the religion, without losing the mystery that draws many students to want to learn. Detailing practices such as grounding, raising energy, visualization, and meditation, this book offers exercises for core techniques before launching into more complicated rituals and spellwork.

978-0-7387-0751-8, 288 pp., 5³⁄₁₆ x 8 $13.95

To Order, Call 1-877-NEW-WRLD

Prices subject to change without notice
order at llewellyn.com 24 hours a day, 7 days a week!